D0111796

Simple
Truths

THE REAL STORY OF THE
OKLAHOMA CITY BOMBING INVESTIGATION

Simple Truths

by **JON HERSLEY,
LARRY TONGATE
and BOB BURKE**

Foreword by Frank Keating, Former Governor of Oklahoma

Series Editor: Gini Moore Campbell
Associate Editor: Eric Dabney

Copyright 2004 by Oklahoma Heritage Association

All rights reserved. No part of this book may be reproduced or
utilized in any form or by any means, electronic or mechanical,
including photocopying and recording, by any information
storage and retrieval system, without permission of the publisher.

Printed in the United States of America.
1-885596-41-3
Library of Congress Catalog Number 2004110526
Book cover and contents designed by
Sandi Welch / www.2WDesignGroup.com

Unless otherwise noted, photographs and illustrations are
courtesy of the Federal Bureau of Investigation, the
United States Department of Justice, and the United States
Attorney for the Western District of Oklahoma.

The authors will not receive any compensation for their efforts
in researching and writing this book.

OKLAHOMA HERITAGE ASSOCIATION
201 NORTHWEST FOURTEENTH STREET
OKLAHOMA CITY, OKLAHOMA 73103

This book is dedicated to the memory of the 168 men, women,and children who lost their lives, and the hundreds who were maimed and injured in the senseless act that destroyed the Alfred P. Murrah Federal Building in Oklahoma City on April 19, 1995.

It was the great sense of loss that inspired hundreds of FBI agents to work countless hours in the months following the bombing to develop evidence to prosecute those responsible for the death and destruction.

Americans should always be proud of the dedicated trial team of Patrick Ryan, Joseph Hartzler, Larry Mackey, Sean Connelly, Beth Wilkinson, Vicki Behenna, Scott Mendeloff, Aitan Goelman, James Orenstein, Geoffrey Mearns, Leslie Yancey, Kathy Skagerberg, and Joyce Webb, who presented the federal government's case in the federal trials of Timothy McVeigh and Terry Nichols.

Table of Contents

Acknowledgments

The solemn revisiting of the events of April 19, 1995, was necessary to tell the real story of the investigation of the bombing of the Alfred P. Murrah Federal Building in Oklahoma City.

Even though two of us lived daily in the aftermath of the tragedy during years of investigation and trial preparation, the detailed explanation of how the FBI gathered evidence brought back vivid memories of the horrible crime perpetrated upon the people of Oklahoma City and indeed, the nation.

We could not have produced a manuscript without the unfailing help of many people. United States District Judges Ralph G. Thompson and David L. Russell gave us the inspiration and encouragement to write the book. Former Oklahoma Governor Frank Keating, Bob Ricks, George and Marcia Davis, Eric Dabney, Stephanie Ayala, Stephanie Hersley, Hank Gibbons, Errol Myers, Brenda Metcalf, Dale McDaniel, and Joe Twardowski proofread the manuscript and added valuable comments.

Thanks to Sandi Welch for a beautiful and intriguing design of both the cover and contents of the book, and to Linda Lynn, Mary Phillips, Melissa Hayer, Robin Davison, and Billie Harry, at the archives of *The Daily Oklahoman*, for photographs.

We appreciate the guidance of managing editor Gini Moore Campbell and the Oklahoma Heritage Association for its consistent commitment to preserve Oklahoma's bold and exciting story.

We are also indebted to the many individuals from the FBI and other law enforcement agencies who tirelessly worked behind the scenes on this massive investigation and trial preparation. Their dedication, patriotism, and professionalism will always represent the finest of what law enforcement exemplifies.

THE AUTHORS
August, 2004

FROM JON HERSLEY:
To my beautiful and lovely wife, Cristy, and my loving children,
Stephanie and Jarrett, thank you for your love, understanding, and
support during the investigation and prosecution of this horrific crime.

FROM LARRY TONGATE:
To my loving wife, Barbara, and my children,
Keely and Adam, I thank you for your understanding, love,
and patience during the long months of this investigation.

FROM BOB BURKE:
To my beautiful wife, Chimene, and my children and stepchildren,
Robert, Amy, Natalie, Lauren, Calli, and Cody; and grandsons,
Nathan and Jonathan—thank you for giving me time in our busy lives
to preserve Oklahoma's incredible history.

T hose of us who were there witnessed a place of unspeakable horror and tragedy. Faces of buildings had been ripped off. Billowing smoke and the detritus of blasted work places stunned the senses and seared life memories of incredulity and anguish. April 19, 1995, and the events that followed, saw the worst and the best from a community and a nation.

Though scores of buildings were damaged, there was no looting. When rescue workers and firefighters asked for something, they got everything. By the box—by the truckload—there was no limit to the love. But there was little comfort from a terrible sight. Flapping canvas, twisted furniture, and smashed office equipment. Papers, blowing and churning in vertical drafts. Unlike the World Trade Center, where only black powder marked where people stood, the Murrah Building was physically and visibly an agonizing photograph of bruised and broken bodies. How could anyone murder 19 babies? What cause, what unbalanced anger could snuff out the lives of 168 of our neighbors and friends?

This monstrous evil demanded justice. Whoever did this should never walk the face of earth again.

Incredible. A rescue and recovery operation involving thousands, for weeks, around the clock, in rain and wind and under the white of lights on cranes, conducted simultaneously with the investigation of the largest criminal case in the history of the United States. Firefighters, police officers, emergency service personnel, construction workers, all feverishly picking the building apart with hearts, hands, and five-gallon buckets. At the same time, the courageous professionals of the law enforcement community, carefully sifting the site with the minutest of detail, locating the key to the Ryder truck, securing the evidence that would tell them the identity of the killers.

Once again, Bob Burke writes for generations of Oklahomans—those who were there and those who must not forget. Jon Hersley and Larry

Tongate tell the story of their's and the FBI's finest hour. It is the closed book on the case. Two evil men did this and two evil men paid. It is a story that needed to be written.

FRANK KEATING
Former Governor of Oklahoma

Oklahoma Governor Frank Keating, right, was a pillar of strength for
Oklahomans during the weeks and months following the Oklahoma City bomb-
ing. In this photograph, the governor takes part in a memorial service on the first
Sunday following the bombing. Left to right, First Lady Hillary Clinton, President
Bill Clinton, Jason Smith and Dan McKinney, son and husband of Secret Service
Agent Laura McKinney who was killed in the blast, Oklahoma First Lady Cathy
Keating, and Governor Keating. *Courtesy Oklahoma Publishing Company.*

Prologue

Helena Garrett grew up in Oklahoma City and attended high school at Star Spencer. She was 28, young, beautiful, full of energy, and had two children. Her daughter, Sharonda, was seven, and her son, Tevin, was 16 months old. Helena worked as a micrographics clerk for the Oklahoma State Regents for Higher Education in the Journal Record Building, located directly north of the Alfred P. Murrah Federal Building on Northwest Fifth Street in downtown Oklahoma City. A medium-size parking lot stood between the Journal Record Building and the Murrah Building.

Each day before arriving for work, Helena took Tevin to the day care center located on the second floor of the Murrah Building. Helena had heard about the day care center from a friend. When she checked it out, she fell in love with it immediately. The workers were nice, the center was clean and open, and large windows faced Northwest Fifth Street. The center was so close, Helena could visit Tevin at breaks or during her lunch hour.

Helena loved Tevin. Her children were her pride and joy. Tevin was a special young boy, beautiful, full of love, energy, and mischief. When Helena dropped Tevin off at the day care center, she would stop to play with the other children. She loved to hug each of them. She knew each by name.

On Wednesday morning, April 19, 1995, Helena awoke just after 6:00 a.m. As usual, she showered and dressed before waking her children. She plugged in her curling iron so she could fix her hair while Sharonda was getting dressed. Helena woke Tevin up first in the morning. He would come into the bathroom while she was getting ready. This morning, Helena motioned toward Sharonda and told Tevin, "Go wake up Sissy." As usual, Tevin woke his sister by gently hitting her on the head

The north door of the Alfred P. Murrah Federal Building faced Northwest Fifth Street. Automobiles and delivery trucks could park within a few feet of the entrance.

with a toy plastic vase—it was gentle, but it was effective. Sharonda never got mad, just awakened, and started getting ready.

As Helena dressed Tevin, she played with him. She gathered him in her arms and swung him into the air, as though he were a make-believe airplane. Sometimes, she ran from one room to the other pretending to fly Tevin through the air before tossing him onto the bed in her room.

Around 7:15 a.m., Helena was finally ready to leave for work. She was running late and took Sharonda straight to kindergarten at St. John Christian Academy before continuing on to Tevin's day care. To save time, she decided to park in the Murrah Building parking lot and return to move her car around 9:00 a.m.

It was now 7:45 a.m. Helena parked, got Tevin out of her car, and headed up the stairs to the day care center. When they were at the door, Helena rang the doorbell. No one answered—so she rang the bell again. Finally, little Aaron Coverdale came to the door. When he saw Helena and Tevin, he ran off, teasing them as though he was not going to let them in.

After a few seconds, Aaron returned and opened the door. When Helena was inside, she realized Aaron answered the door because one of

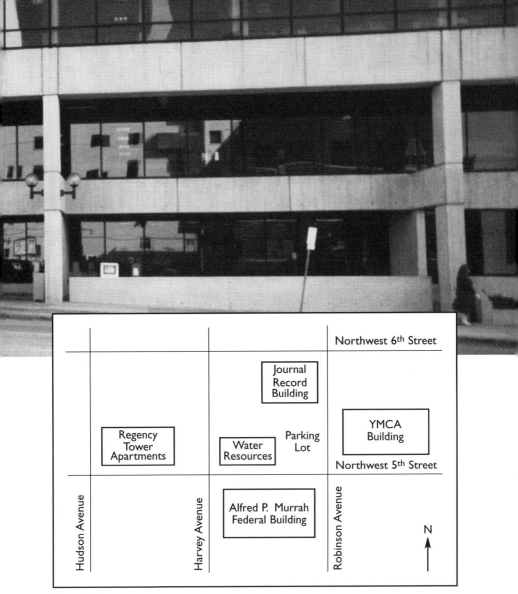

Map of downtown area.

the day care workers was busy changing a baby's diaper. Helena saw Aaron and Elijah Coverdale, chasing playfully after Colton Smith and Zackary Chavez. Aaron and Elijah were brothers, grandsons of Jamie Coverdale who had raised them. Helena also saw Dominique London and Rebecca and Brandon Denny sitting on the floor together.

As Helena started to leave, Tevin began to cry. Aaron and Elijah patted him and tried to make him feel better. The children took care of each other, another reason why Helena liked the day care center. There was much love, warmth, and affection—Helena needed that for her baby.

As she headed out the door of the Murrah Building, Helena ran into an old friend, Anita Hightower, who was working at a table in front of the Social Security Office. After giving her a big hug, Helena told Anita about her new baby and that he attended the day care center on the second floor. Helena motioned for Anita to step outside to the front of the Murrah Building to look up into the windows of the second floor and see the children playing. Within a few seconds, one of the day care workers came to the window with Tevin in her arms so Helena and Anita could see him through the glass.

It was 7:50 a.m. Helena needed to get to work. She told Anita goodbye and headed for the Journal Record Building. Once in her office, she started her camera and began filming files. She worked until just before 9:00 a.m., when she began to think about moving her car. It would be a chance to see Tevin, if just for a minute.

Lou Klaver

Lou Klaver was a hearing officer for the Oklahoma Water Resources Board (OWRB) on Northwest Fifth Street, just east of Harvey Avenue. Her office was located on the third floor of the OWRB building and faced to the north, away from the Murrah Building. The OWRB is responsible for the planning and oversight of Oklahoma's water infrastructure and water use rights. It sets water quality standards and oversees dams and the flood development program in the state.

Klaver, an attorney with degrees from Kansas State University and Washburn University School of Law, had worked for OWRB for 11 years.

April 19 began as a normal morning. Klaver awoke shortly after 6:00 a.m., made coffee, fed her dog, and ate a bowl of cereal. She arrived at work around 7:30 a.m. and began preparing for a 9:00 a.m. hearing. Roy Weikel, a farmer in the Ardmore, Oklahoma, area was seeking approval to use the ground water beneath his land to bottle and sell for public consumption. His neighbors were protesting, concerned that sale of the water for commercial purposes would deplete their water basin. Klaver held many such hearings resolving water use conflicts. It was her job to hear the evidence and make recommendations to the OWRB to grant or deny a permit.

The April 19 hearing was to be held in the OWRB boardroom, located in the middle of the first floor near the center of the building. Weikel and his family, as well as two protestors, were already in the boardroom at 9:00 a.m. They were joined by Klaver and a secretary responsible for recording testimony taken at the meeting.

The recording secretary had just started her tape recorder, and Klaver was beginning to explain the hearing procedure to those present in the boardroom, when a tremendous explosion interrupted the proceedings. It was 9:02 a.m.

Klaver shouted for everyone to get out of the building. She first thought the building was coming down on top of them. It was chaos—debris from the ceiling and walls, lights, and electrical wires were flying everywhere. Klaver knew she needed to get everyone out of the building before it collapsed.

Debris in the hallway blocked their exit to the front door. She decided to try the back door. She and the group encountered more debris, but finally were able to climb over the rubble and make their way from the building through a door facing to the south, directly across from the Murrah Building.

Klaver was the last of her group to exit the building. She headed west from the building, knowing she needed to find out if all her co-workers had escaped the crumbling structure. The ground was littered with glass and twisted metal. The air was filled with smoke and dust. She glanced back toward the east and saw a glimpse of the Murrah Building. The entire face of the building was gone. The area looked like a war zone. Klaver was unable to find all her employees.

Helena Garrett

Just before the explosion, Helena began talking with a co-worker about the filming process she was working with. Helena was still thinking about moving her car and seeing Tevin. As they talked, Helena heard a loud roar. It was like thunder—her body shook. She screamed for her friend, Deborah, who was working in another small room. Deborah and Helena grabbed hands. As they stood together, ceiling tiles and debris fell around them. They heard the screams of others. The lights went out. They made their way through the rubble and darkness to the stairway. They started down, inching their way, finally making it to the first floor.

When they got to the front door of the stairway, rubble prevented them from opening the door. Finally, with the help of someone on the other side of the stairwell, they were able to get the door open. As they moved from the stairway into a small hallway, they realized their path was still blocked. They managed to climb over a marble wall in front of them and finally made it outside. Helena and her friend still did not know what had happened.

As their eyes adjusted to the light outside, Helena and Deborah could see glass strewn all over the sidewalks and street. Windows had been blown out of the surrounding buildings. It was not only the Journal Record Building. Other buildings were damaged, as well. Deborah screamed for her daughter, Kendra. She had dropped Kendra off that morning at the YMCA day care center, located diagonally across North Robinson Avenue east and to the south of the Journal Record Building. Like Tevin, Kendra stayed at the day care center while her mother worked.

An aerial view of the extensive damage to the north side of the Alfred P. Murrah Building. The YMCA Building is in the foreground. Many photographs throughout this book contain the evidence stickers used for identification during the trials of McVeigh and Nichols.

96-CR-68-M
Government Exhibit
745
Date_____

Mangled automobiles on fire outside the Murrah Building after the bombing on the morning of April 19, 1995.

Deborah could see that the YMCA Building had been severely damaged in the explosion. She and Helena were frightened and scared as they ran across Robinson Avenue toward the YMCA. A man standing outside the building assured them everything was okay and that all of the kids were safe and out of the building.

As Helena looked across the street to the southwest, she saw the Murrah Building. The front of the building was gone. As Helena ran toward the building, she was stopped by a policeman, who told her she could not approach the building. She yelled at the policeman, "My baby's in there!" The policeman held his ground.

Helena ran toward the Journal Record Building and found a lady named Margaret, whom she knew. Margaret went back to the corner and talked again with the policeman. Margaret told the policeman, "You have to let her through. Her baby's in there!" Still, the policeman would not let them pass.

As soon as Helena heard the policeman's reply, she began running to the north, back toward the Journal Record Building. There was fire, smoke, and rubble everywhere in the parking lot between the Murrah Building and the Journal Record Building. As cars burned, Helena thought maybe she could get to the Murrah Building from the other side.

She ran around the Journal Record Building to the west and then south on Harvey.

The smoke and debris made it almost impossible to see. Helena was frightened like never before. She was shaking and crying but she had to go on—she had to find Tevin.

As she rounded the corner from Harvey and looked across Northwest Fifth Street, Helena could see the Murrah Building had been almost completely destroyed. The entire face of the building had been blown off. As she ran toward the building, she counted in her mind, "One, two," trying to imagine where the second floor of the day care center would have been. She began climbing the pile of debris—she desperately needed to be where Tevin would have been.

As she pulled at the debris trying to climb, a man grabbed her from behind and pulled her down. Even though Helena told the man her baby was in there, he continued to hold onto her. She saw two women on stretchers outside the building and ran over and asked if they knew where the babies were. They did not.

Helena ran to the south side of the building and began yelling for Tevin and then for Brenda, who worked in the day care center. She saw injured men and women sitting and laying on the ground outside the building. As she moved closer to the plaza area immediately behind the day care center, Helena screamed at two strangers that her baby was inside the building. The men asked what she meant, and Helena screamed, "There's a day care center in there, my baby's in there."

The men went inside the building and immediately began bringing children out. Helena saw one of the men bring out Rebecca Denny. Rebecca's eyes were open and she was conscious. Helena screamed, "Rebecca!" She could see that Rebecca's head, face, and body were covered in blood. Helena told the man, "Her name is Rebecca." When the man did not answer, Helena asked the man, "Did you hear me? Her name is Rebecca." Finally, the stunned man answered, "Okay," and he took Rebecca down the stairway of the plaza.

Helena saw a man bring another baby from the building. She screamed to the man, "That's my baby girl!" But when the man came closer, Helena saw that the child was Nekia McCloud. Nekia's hair was different than Sharonda's. Helena was so frightened that she forgot she had taken Sharonda to kindergarten that morning rather than to the day care center.

Another man yelled out from inside the building, "I need two stretchers. I can put four on two stretchers." And Helena saw another man carry Brandon Denny from the building. Colton Smith was carried out next and laid on the concrete. Helena did not want to leave Colton but she wanted desperately to find Tevin.

She stayed with Colton, watching him, waiting and watching as more and more of the babies were carried out and laid down next to her. She screamed to the men, "Please don't lay our babies on this glass, we don't want our babies on this glass." Pieces of glass were everywhere. A man swept the glass away from the children as they lay on the plaza floor.

Helena had not yet realized the babies were dead. A nurse came and began tagging the tiny bodies, and finally Helena realized they were gone. But still there was no sign of her precious Tevin.

Police officers went to Helena's house to lift fingerprints from Tevin's crib and the mirror that hung over it, fingerprints that could be used to identify the small boy if his body was found. Tevin used to stand up in his crib and look at himself in the mirror, and he would reach out and touch his image. The police took fingerprints from his high chair, too.

On Saturday, three days, and what seemed like years after the bombing, Helena was notified that Tevin had been found. She was at church when the news came. Helena was never able to see Tevin's face again. Tevin had a severe head injury, necessitating a closed casket funeral. She was able to kiss his feet and legs, but the rest of his body remained covered.

Richard Nichols

Just before 9:00 a.m., Bertha Nichols parked her red Ford Festiva on Northwest Fifth Street in front of the Regency Tower Apartments where her husband, Richard, was a maintenance worker. Richard had arrived at work at 7:00 a.m. but was taking a couple of hours off to accompany his wife and nephew, Chad, to a doctor's appointment.

Bertha waited outside for several minutes and then decided to go inside to see if she could find her husband. Just as she entered the front doors and began to ask the security guard to help locate her husband, she heard Richard's keys jingling. Bertha started laughing and said, "Here he comes now."

As Richard and Bertha exited the building, they heard the explosion. It felt like heat and pressure at the same time, and the incredible force spun them around. Richard grabbed his wife and told her that the boilers in the apartment building had blown up. As they lunged for their car, Bertha remembered that Chad was inside the car. He had moved from the front seat to the backseat behind the driver, and Bertha reached in to remove his seat belt.

Glass was flying everywhere. Bertha sat on the door jam of the car and continued to struggle to release Chad's seat belt. Then Richard heard a loud whirling noise and looked up just in time to see a huge object flying end over end through the air. He screamed at Bertha, "Get down!" and pushed her onto the floor of the car. The large object was heading directly at them.

A second later, the object hit the front windshield, hood, and passenger side, knocking the rear of the car into the air, 10 feet up onto the curb. Richard collected himself and ran back to the car to help get Bertha and Chad from the vehicle. The three of them huddled together as they ran across Northwest Fifth Street to get away from the Regency Tower Apartments, as Richard still thought the building had exploded.

As he looked back across the street toward his car, he saw a cloud of smoke over the Water Resources Board Building. Richard also saw that the object which had damaged his car was an axle. He said to his wife, "It was a car bomb. Somebody blew up the Water Resources Building."

As Richard looked at the front of his building, he noticed that almost every window on the south side had been blown out. He told Bertha to take Chad to the hospital—a large bump was forming on the boy's head. Richard had keys to the Regency Tower Apartments and knew he needed to get back inside the building to help people escape. As he looked back to the east toward the Murrah Building, the smoke had separated for a few seconds, and he could see that the whole north face of the building was gone.

Jerry Flowers

At 9:02 a.m., Sergeant Jerry Flowers was at the Oklahoma City Police Department Training Center, about six miles from downtown Oklahoma City.

He heard and felt the blast and knew immediately that he needed to get downtown. Flowers and his friend and partner, Sergeant Steve Carson, drove as fast as they could toward the plume of smoke that covered the area just north of downtown.

They were stopped at Dean A. McGee and North Harvey avenues. They left their squad car and began running toward the Murrah Building.

Flowers first saw a woman sitting on the curb near the southwest corner of the building. She had a head wound—she had rolled up what looked like a shirt and was holding it to her head trying to control the bleeding. She was cuddling a young girl in her arms. The girl was in shock and was shaking and crying.

Flowers and Carson ran to the front of the Murrah Building on the northwest side. There was a hole that had been blown out of the building, and another officer was yelling, "Let's get these people out of here." As they entered the building through the huge hole, a board stretcher was handed out to them. A man's body lay on the stretcher. Flowers leaned over the stretcher to tell the man he was going to be okay, but saw a severe laceration across the man's face. He knew the man was dead.

Flowers and Carson passed the stretcher to other officers and civilians behind them, forming a human chain to remove the body of the dead man from the building. It was impossible to walk around inside the building. There was smoke and debris everywhere, and the officers had to crawl.

Another officer screamed out for everyone to be quiet. As they listened, they heard a faint cry from a female trapped inside. She was crying and asking for help. They crawled toward the voice, moving rocks, sheetrock, ceiling tiles, and cement blocks as they inched forward to where they thought the voice was coming from. As they crawled, the officers had to stop at times to listen again for the crying voice. Unfortunately, they were not able to find the lady and eventually the cries stopped.

Flowers and Carson crawled deeper into the building. It was incredibly dark. The dust was so thick, the officers had trouble breathing. As they crawled deeper into the pit of the building, Sergeant Flowers could feel water rising. It was now over the top of his boots. He could hear voices screaming for help, "Get us out of here!" As they moved toward the screams, Flowers noticed a ray of light coming from the area where the screams could be heard. He continued crawling toward the light until he saw what looked like a cave.

Floors of concrete had fallen and were pancaked on top of where the officers were trying to free a trapped victim. Flowers heard a woman scream and saw her rolled up in a ball, her feet and legs tucked under her chest. She was imprisoned in a mass of cement blocks and steel rebar. He reached up through the concrete and touched the woman, telling her she was going to be okay, although he knew there was no way—it was impossible to move the concrete and steel rebar by hand.

Several Oklahoma City firefighters had dragged a generator into the building pit area. Flowers turned on the switch and the area was illuminated. The officers could see another female victim trapped in an area where more water was accumulating. As the water continued to rise, the woman shouted to the officers, "Don't let me drown. Get me out of here."

Flowers held the light down over the woman as a firefighter tried to free her. The water continued to rise and was almost over the woman's head. She was in a state of panic, screaming, "Please don't let me die in here, just don't let me drown." Something under the water was holding her down. She was pinned in the rubble. But just before the water began to crest over her head, it stopped. She could still breathe.

The firefighters continued their efforts to free the woman. Other officers working on the floor immediately above Sergeant Flowers yelled to him that they were going to hand a stretcher down through a hole in the floor. As they handed the stretcher down, Flowers thought to himself, "Finally, I am going to be able to get somebody out of the building alive." But when he and Sergeant Carson received the stretcher from the floor above, they saw the woman laying on it was already dead. They passed the stretcher to other officers below.

Flowers saw Sergeant Don Hull carrying a small baby wrapped in a blanket. Flowers helped Hull carry the baby to the plaza area. When they unwrapped the blanket, they saw the baby's face was gone. Stunned, the two veteran officers carried the little boy's body to the playground area off the plaza and left him there.

Flowers found another way inside the Murrah Building from the plaza. Once back inside, he noticed he was on the second floor in the nursery. He saw toys, wagons, and baby clothing everywhere. Like everyone else in the area, Flowers began digging through rubble and debris the best he could. As he dug, he uncovered a baby's foot inside a pink sock. He yelled out, "I found another one!" Nearby rescuers rushed to his side and helped to dig the baby from the rubble. Finally, an officer pulled the child from the rubble, held her to his chest and carried her out.

Flowers helped dig five more babies from the rubble, and finally the fire department ordered everyone from the building. It was 2:30 p.m. A more structured search had been ordered. As Flowers exited the building for the last time, he leaned up against a retaining wall, and it all began to hit him. He looked over to where a triage area had been set up and then over to the playground area. There were bodies everywhere.

Flowers had many friends who worked in the Murrah Building but had no way of knowing if they were dead or alive. He somehow managed to get to his car. As he drove home, he heard the news that his friend and neighbor, Oleta Biddy, who worked in the building, was missing. He decided to stop by her home.

As Flowers pulled into the driveway, Henry Biddy and his family met him on the front porch. As they hugged and cried, Flowers apologized to Henry, "I am sorry, I couldn't find Oleta." All Henry could say was, "It's okay." Flowers went home. There was nothing more he could do.

Andy Sullivan

Orthopedic surgeon Andy Sullivan was walking toward his office at Children's Hospital a mile from the Murrah Building when the explosion stopped him in his tracks. He knew something was terribly wrong. Around noon, he received word that a woman was trapped in the basement of the building and would not survive unless her leg was amputated.

From the operating room, Dr. Sullivan grabbed an amputation kit that contained scalpels, knives, and clamps. As he was leaving, he used his pocketknife to cut a piece of nylon rope—it might be useful as a tourniquet.

When he arrived at the Murrah Building, the doctor was led into the dark and smoke-filled basement. He made his way around large pieces of broken concrete and avoided electrical lines strewn throughout the rubble. The smell of gasoline coming from generators providing dim light gagged him. Medical school had not prepared him for this environment—the reality of the moment was overwhelming.

Daina Bradley's leg was caught between the basement floor and a slab of the collapsed floor above. For hours she had laid in six inches of water and was in shock. Dr. Sullivan removed the hard hat he had been given and crawled on his stomach until he reached the patient. A light bulb rigged by rescue workers provided a small glimpse of light.

Dr. Sullivan cleared the rubble from beneath the woman's leg and began to tie a tourniquet. Then the news came—there was a report of a second bomb in the building. He was ordered to leave. As he began sliding back toward a larger opening, Daina screamed, "Please don't leave me! I'm going to die!" It was gut wrenching because Dr. Sullivan had taken an oath to never desert a patient. Her cries echoed in the deepest chambers of his heart and mind as he promised her he would return.

There was no second bomb and rescue workers were allowed back into the building 45 minutes later. Dr. Sullivan again crawled into the crevice where Daina was trapped. He had to make quick decisions. A rescue harness was hooked to her body so she could be pulled immediately from the rubble after he amputated her right leg.

The doctor was afraid to administer Demerol or Morphine in fear that the medicine would kill Daina. Instead, he gave her Versed, an amnesic that would help her forget what was about to happen. He prayed Daina would not bleed to death and die in his arms as he performed the crude surgery.

With the tourniquet tightened, Dr. Sullivan told Daina what he was about to do. At first she said no, but then relented, recognizing that losing a leg was better than losing her life.

Dr. Sullivan began his work. The first, second, and third scalpel blades broke as Daina screamed and thrashed about with her free arms and leg. The doctor used his body to pin her leg against the concrete wall and switched to an amputation knife. Hitting against the concrete dulled the knife, so Dr. Sullivan had to complete his horrible task with his pocketknife.

Because of Dr. Sullivan's heroic effort, Daina survived. There were many other medical personnel, police officers, firefighters, federal agents, and rescue workers with similar experiences that day and in the days to come. Heroes came not only from Oklahoma City and other parts of Oklahoma, but from all over the United States.

Paul Ice

Paul Ice was a handsome special agent for the United States Customs Service. He was a graduate of Oklahoma City University, an Army veteran, and had recently retired with the rank of lieutenant colonel as a United States Marine Corps flight officer. His two decades of Marine Corps active and reserve duty included a tour as radar intercept officer on the A-6 Intruder, a carrier-based precision bomber.

On the morning of the Oklahoma City bombing, Ice was standing next to his secretary, Priscilla Salyers, in their office in the Murrah Building. At the moment of the explosion, the floor shirred. Ice instantly disappeared with the crush of pancaked concrete and steel several floors below. Priscilla was left standing, her feet inches away from the edge of the floor where Ice had stood moments before. As was the case for many victims and survivors, a matter of inches had cost Ice his life and saved Priscilla's.

In the days that followed, rescue workers struggled around the clock to find survivors, and then remains. A temporary morgue was set up across the street in the parking lot of the First Methodist Church. As bodies were found, they were covered on gurneys and rolled to the receiving area of the temporary morgue. Rescuers would pause, remove their hard hats, bow their heads, then return to the rubble to resume their grizzly task. This scene was repeated time and time again.

Immediate
Response

Who could do such a thing? Why would anyone commit such an atrocious, outrageous act? How could anyone be filled with so much hatred and be so evil? There were many questions in the minds of Americans in the hours and days following the bombing—questions that needed answers. The law enforcement community in Oklahoma faced an enormous challenge.

Rescue workers from the Oklahoma City fire and police departments and the Oklahoma County Sheriff's Office were joined by agents from the Federal Bureau of Investigation (FBI), the Bureau of Alcohol, Tobacco and Firearms (ATF), and other federal agencies to formulate an immediate response to the chaos that existed inside and for blocks around the Murrah Building. Police officers, firefighters, and rescue workers from surrounding cities and states began arriving to help in the rescue effort coordinated by Oklahoma City Fire Chief Gary Marrs.

Bob Ricks, Special Agent in Charge (SAC) of the Oklahoma City FBI office, Oklahoma City Chief of Police Sam Gonzales, and Chief Marrs faced what easily was the most difficult challenge of their careers. It was of paramount importance that the three men work together to instill a sense of calm in a city that had come under attack. Fortunately, the three were friends and had worked together previously.

Chief Marrs' primary responsibility was to guide the race to save as many lives as possible. The efforts of locating survivors and removing bodies and body parts of those who had died tried the physical, mental, and emotional abilities of the best of men and women.

Chief Gonzales had been deputy police chief in Dallas, Texas, and had worked terrorism cases. He immediately recognized the bombing in Oklahoma City as an act of terror. United States Presidential Directive Number 2 dictated that primary responsibility for an act of terror fell with the FBI. Chief Gonzalez quickly pledged his support to investigative and rescue efforts.

Ricks, a 25-year veteran of the FBI, had been the SAC in Oklahoma City since 1989 when he left the post of Deputy Assistant Director of the FBI's Criminal Division in Washington, D.C. In that position, Ricks had direct responsibility for the FBI's counter terrorism program, including domestic and international terrorism. He also had worked with British Intelligence on Irish Republican Army terrorism cases in Northern Ireland. Ricks' wealth of experience would now be put to the test.

Because of the magnitude of the bombing, Ricks knew that a joint command post should be established so agents from the FBI and other federal agencies could coordinate their efforts with local law enforcement officers. The area in and around the Murrah Building needed to be secured with inner and outer perimeters to ensure crime scene integrity and to keep unauthorized persons from contaminating potential evidence.

A temporary command post was established by the FBI at Northwest Eighth Street and Harvey Avenue, close enough to the Murrah Building for agents to be dispatched to the scene to develop leads. Because of heavy traffic, cell phones were useless for communication. Messages in the early hours of the investigation were sent by runners.

By Wednesday afternoon, April 19, Southwestern Bell Telephone Company had offered to provide office space in one of their nearby buildings for a more permanent command post. By early evening, the FBI began moving its operation to the building. Within 24 hours Southwestern Bell had installed more than 200 operational phone lines for use by agents and support personnel working the command post. A team of agents was assigned to answer calls from a 24-hour hotline set up by FBI Headquarters in Washington, D.C.

David Weiss of the Oklahoma City FBI office helped install a computer software system, known as Rapid Start, at the command post. The system was used to organize, collate, and track the results of telephone calls and the thousands of leads and interviews being conducted in Oklahoma and across the nation. Cheryl Dunham of the FBI's office in Savannah, Georgia, led a team of Rapid Start employees from across the United States in the days, weeks, and months that followed. Their purpose was to organize the information so that FBI management and case agents could stay on top of the investigation as it was unfolding.

In the face of the disaster, Oklahomans responded in a majestic way. Investigators and support personnel had no time for meals—so local businesses and citizens brought hot meals, drinks, clothing, and other supplies to the command post. The investigative team learned to be cautious in their requests, because when they asked, the community responded. The basic goodness of all Oklahomans was on display for the whole world to see as individuals, law enforcement, and charitable organizations worked together. Their goodwill was a sharp contrast to the cowardly actions of whoever was responsible for the devastation and destruction that had engulfed downtown Oklahoma City.

The FBI and local law enforcement agencies faced an unbelievable challenge.

United States Attorney General Janet Reno visited the FBI command center in Oklahoma City. Left to right, Reno; SAC Weldon Kennedy of Phoenix, Arizona; David Williams from FBI headquarters in Washington, D.C.; and Bob Ricks, Oklahoma City SAC.

FBI agents gather outside the command center in Oklahoma City that was located in space provided by Southwestern Bell Telephone Company.

The Investigation Begins

F **BI Special Agent Jim Elliott was in his office** in McAlester, Oklahoma, on the morning of April 19 when he received a telephone call about the Murrah Building bombing from a friend who was a Drug Enforcement Administration (DEA) agent. Elliott tried to call the FBI office in Oklahoma City, but the lines were busy.

He decided to go home and pack his crime-scene investigation clothing and other equipment that might be needed in Oklahoma City, including field boots, fatigues, utility clothing, cameras, evidence packaging materials, fingerprint supplies, and extra tools that might be necessary to dislodge pieces of trapped evidence. When Elliott returned to his office, a message on his answering machine directed him to report immediately to Oklahoma City.

Elliott was a 32-year veteran of the FBI, the only agent working out of the McAlester Residency Agency. As a one-man operation in southeast

The axle of the Ryder truck, left, beside the Ford Festiva outside the Regency Tower Apartments. The axle was found by Oklahoma County Deputy Sheriff Melvin Sumpter, who together with Agent Jim Norman, identified a partial serial number, PVA26077.

Oklahoma for 18 years, he had worked kidnappings, bank robberies, white-collar crimes, public corruption, stolen cars and trucks, domestic terrorism, and almost every other crime covered under the jurisdiction of the FBI. He had recently attended an eight-week FBI in-service training program regarding the collection and handling of evidence and was a member of the FBI Evidence Response Team.

Elliott arrived in Oklahoma City at approximately 11:30 a.m. He passed through several law enforcement checkpoints set up on North Broadway Avenue and reported directly to the temporary command post at Northwest Eighth Street and Harvey Avenue in downtown Oklahoma City. Elliott was told by Agent Jim Norman that a vehicle axle, which appeared to have come from a large truck, had been found about a block away from the Murrah Building.

Elliott was asked to try to identify the vehicle from which the axle came. He had worked a variety of criminal cases and knew exactly who to call to get the process started. Elliott called the National

Insurance Crime Bureau (NICB) in Dallas, Texas. NICB is a privately financed organization funded by insurance companies to investigate crimes and maintains records of each vehicle manufactured in the United States.

Elliott knew from previous stolen car investigations that the NICB would be able to trace the vehicle's full identification number from the partial number. Elliott recognized that the eight-character number was a Confidential Vehicle Identification Number. All vehicles manufactured in the United States have Vehicle Identification Numbers (VIN) assigned to them. These numbers are unique to each vehicle and can be used to positively identify that specific vehicle. VINs are typically displayed on the dashboard, as well as the driver's-side doorpost of most vehicles. Car thieves and chop shop owners are quick to remove these VINs from stolen cars in order to make it more difficult for law enforcement and insurance recovery investigators to identify the vehicles.

In order to counter the theft problem, vehicle manufacturers stamp a Confidential Vehicle Identification Number on a hidden, metal piece of each vehicle. The confidential number, usually consisting of eight characters, can be used to identify the full, much longer VIN, usually consisting of 17 characters. The Confidential Vehicle Identification Number is usually the last eight characters of the full VIN.

After contacting the NICB in Dallas, Elliott walked to the Regency Tower Apartments, where the vehicle axle in question had been found. Elliott did not yet know the axle was the large object that Richard Nichols had seen whirling through the air before it landed on his Ford Festiva. Elliott read the numbers and letters from the axle, confirming the information he had been provided earlier.

On his way back to the command post, Elliott received a radio message that NICB had returned his call. His pace quickened. He was anxious to receive the information. By phone, he learned that the NICB had been successful in identifying the full VIN from the eight-character number. The full number was 1FDNF72J4PVA26077. The vehicle was a truck registered to Ryder Rental, Incorporated, (Ryder) in Miami, Florida. That information was immediately telephoned to FBI Headquarters in Washington, D.C.

Andy Anderson

Andy Anderson was assigned to Ryder's headquarters office in Miami. He had worked for Ryder for 24 years and was the company's Director of Operations over consumer rentals. In the early afternoon of Wednesday, April 19, 1995, Ryder received a call from the FBI, requesting immediate help in the identification of a Ryder truck whose axle had been found at the scene of the Oklahoma City bombing earlier that day.

Fortunately, Ryder had kept up with computer technology. Each dealer across the country used a computer terminal to input rental information that could be accessed by the home office. The system made it easy to identify any truck, as well as the home destination or last dealer to rent the truck.

Employees working under Anderson's direction quickly located the information the FBI had requested. Vehicle Identification Number 1FDNF72J4PVA26077 was assigned to a 1993 gasoline powered Ford truck with a 20-foot box. The vehicle had a gross weight capacity of 24,000 pounds and a 50-gallon fuel capacity. The box portion of the truck was constructed with fiberglass reinforced plywood, coated with yellow paint and equipped with a rear door that raised overhead, as well as a smaller door on the passenger side where smaller objects could be loaded and unloaded. The vehicle was registered and licensed in the state of Florida and had current Florida license plate number NEE26R. The truck was last assigned to Elliott's Body Shop, a Ryder dealership in Junction City, Kansas. Ryder's records revealed the truck was currently rented.

Scott Crabtree

Special Agent Scott Crabtree was an experienced investigator, a veteran of nearly 15 years with the FBI. He had grown up in Herington, Kansas, approximately 50 miles from Salina, where he was now assigned to the FBI Resident Agency. He was a family man and had grown tired of having to cover such a large territory by himself. The hours were long, there were road trips involved, and family sometimes became secondary, not by design, but from necessity. Many times, he had asked FBI management in Kansas City to send him an additional agent, but his pleas for help went unanswered. Management did not seem to understand the amount of time and effort it took to put a good case together over such a vast area of central Kansas.

Elliott's Body Shop and Ryder rental agency employed about six people and was situated on a hill on Goldenbelt Boulevard, a frontage road that runs parallel with Interstate 70, about one mile west of Junction City, Kansas.

On April 19, at about 3:00 p.m., Crabtree received a telephone call that would turn out to be the most significant call of his FBI career. An agent from the Miami, Florida, FBI office told Crabtree about the axle being found near the Murrah Building and it being traced to a Ryder truck rented in Junction City, Kansas.

Crabtree was instructed to go to Elliott's Body Shop immediately to secure rental documents. The FBI wanted to review the documents for evidentiary value and for additional lead information. They would also be protected for fingerprint analysis that would come later.

In order to offset fixed costs and to maximize profits, Eldon Elliott operated a Ryder truck rental business at the same location as his body shop. Vickie Beemer had worked for Elliott for about six months and was responsible for handling most of the telephone calls and paperwork for truck rentals. Elliott usually performed the walk-around on the trucks before they went out. Both the body shop and Eldon's truck rental business shared common office space.

Crabtree had called ahead to tell Elliott the reason for his visit. By the time the agent arrived, Beemer had already pulled the rental documents for the truck in question. A 20-foot yellow Ryder truck was rented for four days with a final destination of Omaha, Nebraska. The renter, a Robert "Bob" Kling, had provided an address of 428 Maple Drive,

Omaha, Nebraska. Kling used a South Dakota driver's license, in the name of Robert Kling, when he picked the truck up on Monday afternoon. The number on the driver's license was YF962A6, with an expiration date of April 19, 1996. Kling provided his Social Security Number as 962-42-9694. His date of birth on the driver's license read April 19, 1970.

The birth date meant nothing to Beemer or Elliott, but it revealed substantial clues to FBI management and FBI Case Agents Jon Hersley and Larry Tongate. David Koresh's Branch Davidian compound in Waco, Texas, had burned on April 19, 1993, just two years earlier. Eighty-six people died in the Waco tragedy. The date of birth on Kling's South Dakota driver's license was the same month and day as the fiery tragedy that ended the Branch Davidian standoff in Waco. Was there a connection?

The service desk at Elliott's Body Shop. Timothy McVeigh stood only a few feet from clerk Vickie Beemer when she used the Ryder rental computer terminal to complete the rental agreement on the truck that would be used in the Oklahoma City bombing.

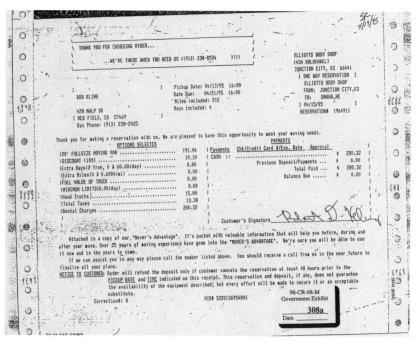

Robert D. Kling's signature on the rental reservation agreement for the Ryder truck rented at Elliott's Body Shop in Junction City, Kansaas, and used in the Oklahoma City bombing.

After securing the rental documents, Crabtree decided to talk first with Elliott before interviewing the other employees. Elliott remembered Kling as a white male, about 5'10 – 5'11', maybe a little taller, medium build, medium complexion, with short, light brown hair, worn about one-half inch long. Elliott said he thought Kling wore a green or camouflage army shirt, but he could not recall the color or type of his trousers.

Crabtree spoke next with Beemer, a middle-aged woman whose children were almost grown. Beemer said a second man was with Kling when he picked up the truck on Monday afternoon, April 17. Beemer admitted she was not very good with faces and could not provide a detailed description of either man. She said she recalled the transaction because she remembered telling Kling, after seeing his driver's license, that she had been married longer than Kling had been alive.

Tom Kessinger worked as a mechanic at the body shop. Tom looked older than his age. He liked his casual friendship with Beemer, and when

A 20-foot Ryder rental truck identical to the truck rented on April 17, 1995, by Timothy McVeigh, using the alias Robert D. Kling, at Elliott's Body Shop in Junction City, Kansas.

it was convenient, he took his morning and afternoon breaks, munching a bag of popcorn and drinking a soda pop in the front office where she worked.

Kessinger remembered that on Monday afternoon, April 17, he was completing a car repair job and was late taking his afternoon break. It was after 4:00 p.m. when he finally made it into the office to grab a snack and take his usual seat. Kessinger was not paying close attention to the customer Beemer was assisting until she asked the customer for his driver's license and noticed the man had a birthday coming up in a couple of days. Kessinger looked up when he heard Beemer joke with Kling that she had been married longer than he had been alive.

Out of curiosity, Kessinger glanced to see what Kling looked like. He studied the customer as Beemer continued the transaction. Kessinger also remembered another man with Kling. The second man had positioned himself behind and to Kling's left near the counter.

As Crabtree talked to Kessinger, he realized that Kessinger had the clearest memory of the two men who picked up the Ryder truck that was now suspected to have been used in the Oklahoma City bombing. As a result, Kessinger was chosen to work with FBI composite artist, Ray Rozycki, who arrived at the nearby Fort Riley army base very early the following morning. Based on the descriptions provided by Kessinger, the FBI artist prepared two sketches depicting the men Kessinger had seen at the body shop on Monday afternoon.

Kessinger described Kling as a white male, 27 - 30 years old, 5'10" – 5'11", 175 – 185 pounds, slender build, with green or brown eyes and light brown hair worn in a crew cut. Kessinger recalled the man was clean-shaven with a rough acne-marked complexion. Kling had a long, narrow head with close-set eyes. His mouth was small and his chin appeared to be creased and pulled forward and upward. His nose was average.

Kessinger described the second man as a white male, 26 – 27 years old, 5'10", 200 pounds, with brown eyes and thick, dark brown hair. This man was clean-shaven, with a smooth complexion and thick, heavy eyebrows. Kessinger said the man was very muscular, had a thick neck, large arms, and a large chest. He was wearing blue jeans, a black tee-shirt, white tennis shoes, and a white ball cap with blue lightning strikes.

When the artist was finished, he showed the drawings to Kessinger who voiced his approval. Kessinger said they were as accurate as his memory would allow—he could neither add nor subtract anything further from the drawings. Kessinger was certain they accurately depicted the two men he had seen inside Elliott's Body Shop on Monday afternoon, April 17. Next, Kessinger worked with the composite artist to prepare a sketch of the cap worn by the second man. Again, Kessinger was satisfied with the artist's drawing.

After working with Kessinger for several hours, artist Rozycki was ready to show the drawings to the other witnesses. Rozycki asked Elliot and Beemer if anything needed to be added or subtracted from the drawings. Both said no.

It was decision time for the FBI.

E rrol Myers had worked in the Oklahoma City FBI Office for more than 20 years at the time of the Murrah Building bombing. He had earned his stripes and an official transfer to Oklahoma City by laboring almost ten years in New York City, the FBI's largest field office.

Myers was a country boy from Sayre, Oklahoma, who was widely respected by both his peers and superiors, including a string of Special Agents in Charge (SAC) of the Oklahoma City office. Myers had supervised the drug and organized crime squad in Oklahoma City for 15 years before April, 1995, mentoring many agents, including Floyd Zimms and Jon Hersley. Oklahoma City was a medium sized office, but it ranked close to the top in statistical accomplishments, the measuring stick applied by FBI Headquarters in Washington, D.C. to determine the effectiveness of an FBI Field Office.

Myers was troubled when he heard that the composite drawings prepared by FBI artist Ray Rozycki were about to be released to the news media. He knew from his experience in New York City and as the drug and organized crime supervisor in Oklahoma City, that once the composite drawings were released, there could be a downside with literally an avalanche of reported sightings. Experience told him that most, if not all, the reported sightings would be inaccurate or bogus, and that they would consume an inordinate number of agent man-hours, regardless of their accuracy—man-hours that might be better spent in other areas of the bombing investigation.

In spite of Myers' concern, FBI management made the decision to release the drawings to the news media on Thursday afternoon, April 20. The drawings, quickly dubbed by the news media as the composite drawings of "John Doe #1" and "John Doe #2," were prominently displayed across the nation as the primary suspects in the Oklahoma City bombing.

The decision to release the sketches was not an easy one. Recognizing that much misinformation would be generated, FBI management believed it was of paramount importance to identify, locate, and apprehend those responsible for the Oklahoma City bombing. This

Above left: **The FBI artist's sketch of John Doe #1.**

Above right: **John Doe #2 was the name assigned to the artist's sketch of a second man allegedly seen with McVeigh at Elliott's Body Shop.**

was necessary not only to bring those responsible to justice but also to ensure that other bombings would not follow.

The death toll in Oklahoma City was mounting and hundreds more had been seriously injured and maimed. The killers had to be found. In retrospect, the decision to release the composite drawings caused mass confusion and exhausted thousands and thousands of FBI investigative man-hours. But at the moment, the FBI's primary concern was that the killers had to be stopped. Would they strike again? Never before had America experienced such an act.

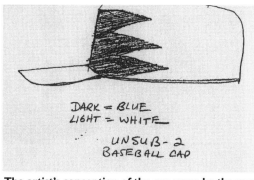

The artist's conception of the cap worn by the man witnesses dubbed John Doe #2.

Hank Gibbons

FBI Agent Henry C. "Hammering Hank" Gibbons was an attorney who grew up in Chicago, Illinois. He had served as the FBI's Special Agent Legal Counsel in the Oklahoma City office for more than 15 years. Legal Advisers in the FBI were looked at by other agents with skepticism—it seemed they were always looking for ways to keep street agents from working their cases. FBI attorneys kept the agency out of lawsuits occasionally, but at the same time it was often hard for street agents to complete their investigations because of a barrage of legal opinions. Agents wanted someone who would help them figure out how to move a case forward, rather than someone who always had a roadblock to throw in the way. Hank Gibbons was that answer.

Gibbons could always find a way that would hold up in federal court under the closest of scrutiny. Street agents such as Jon Hersley and Larry Tongate appreciated Gibbons—he was one of them, a street agent at heart.

Gibbons had worked almost non-stop since the bombing on Wednesday morning. He knew that affidavits and warrants would be needed, and he wanted to get a jump on the application process. He worked feverishly with Vicki Behenna, Kerry Kelly, and Arlene Joplin of the United States Attorneys Office in Oklahoma City in the early days of the bombing investigation.

On April 20, United States Magistrate Judge Ronald L. Howland of the Western District of Oklahoma signed a criminal complaint and arrest warrants authorizing the arrests of John Doe #1 and John Doe #2. Articulated in Agent Gibbons' affidavit for these arrest warrants was the following:

1. On April 19, 1995, a massive explosive device detonated outside the Alfred P. Murrah Federal Building, at Northwest Fifth Street and Robinson Avenue, in Oklahoma City, Oklahoma, at approximately 9:00 a.m.
2. Investigation by federal agents had determined the explosive device was contained in a 1993 Ford truck owned by the Ryder Rental Company.
3. A partial Vehicle Identification Number (VIN) was found at the scene of the explosion and determined to be from a part of the truck that contained the explosive device.
4. Ryder informed the FBI that the truck was assigned to a rental company known as Elliott's Body Shop in Junction City, Kansas.
5. The rental agent at Elliott's Body Shop advised that two men had rented the truck on April 17, 1995. The rental agent provided a description of these two men.
6. On April 20, 1995, the FBI interviewed three witnesses, who were near the scene of the explosion at the Murrah Building prior to the explosion. These three witnesses were shown a copy of the composite drawing of John Doe #1, and they identified him as closely resembling a person they had seen in front of the Murrah Building on April 19, 1995. The witnesses advised the FBI they had observed the man resembling the composite drawing of John Doe #1 in front of the Murrah Building entrance at approximately 8:40 a.m. and again at 8:55 a.m. on the morning of the bombing.
6. The Alfred P. Murrah Federal Building was used by various agencies of the United States, including Agriculture Department, Department of the Army, Department of Defense, Federal Highway Administration, General Accounting Office, General Services Administration, Social Security Administration, Housing and Urban Development, Drug

Enforcement Administration, Transportation Department, United States Secret Service, Bureau of Alcohol, Tobacco and Firearms, and the Veteran's Administration.

6. The detonation of the explosion in front of the Murrah Federal Building constitutes a violation of 18 United States Code, Section 844(f), which makes it a crime to maliciously damage or destroy by means of an explosive any building or real property, in whole or in part owned, possessed or used by the United States, or any department or agency thereof.

Agent Gibbons further articulated in the affidavit that the rental agent at Elliott's Body Shop assisted in the creation of composite drawings of the two men, who allegedly rented the Ryder truck on April 17. The composite drawings were attached to the affidavit.

Jim Elliott

By early Wednesday afternoon, April 19, Agent Jim Elliott had been assigned to coordinate the collection, handling, and recordation of evidence gathered in and around the crime scene, an approximate 16-block area in downtown Oklahoma City. Elliott, who had been instrumental in tracing the truck axle found in front of the Regency Tower Apartments to the Ryder Rental Company, was now being asked to serve as custodian for any and all evidence.

The FBI for years had maintained an evidence storage warehouse on Northwest Fourth Street in downtown Oklahoma City. It had been used to store cars, trucks, boats, and motorcycles seized from drug dealers. Elliott went to the warehouse to help set up computers and prepare the facility to receive evidence from the crime scene.

Late in the afternoon, he decided to walk back to the Murrah Building to determine if more pieces of evidence had been found. At about 6:30 p.m., in front of the Athenia Building, near Northwest Fifth Street and Harvey Avenue, Elliott saw two Oklahoma County Sheriff's Office auxiliary deputies examining a twisted piece of metal that appeared to be a vehicle bumper. Elliott noticed that encased in the piece of metal was a Florida license plate, number NEE26R. Elliott took the piece of metal and license plate to the evidence warehouse and logged them in as evidence.

The mangled and burned Florida license plate found near the rubble of the Murrah Building. The plate matched the license plate registered to the 20-foot Ryder truck last rented at Elliott's Body Shop by Robert "Bob" Kling on April 17.

Dreamland Motel

FBI offices around the nation were on alert as they began to work together in the investigation. Agents from the Kansas City office were arriving in Junction City at a rapid pace and a command post was set up at Fort Riley. Agents were dispatched to businesses and neighborhoods in Junction City to determine if anyone remembered seeing a person or persons in a Ryder truck in the days leading up to the bombing in Oklahoma City.

Special Agent Mark Bouton was a 25-year veteran of the FBI assigned to the Topeka, Kansas, Resident Agency. Bouton, like Scott Crabtree, answered to the Kansas City office. One of the locations to which Bouton was sent was the Dreamland Motel, approximately 4.7 miles east of Elliott's Body Shop on Interstate 70.

Lea McGown, a middle-aged woman of German descent, was the owner and operator of the Dreamland Motel. The motel office was located almost in the center of the building, with rooms on either side. The motel faced to the south on a service road immediately north of Interstate 70.

Lea McGown was a stern woman. She was proud of her German ancestry and proud of the fact that she owned her own business. She had become an American entrepreneur. Running a budget motel and scratching out a meager living was a tough business.

On Thursday afternoon, April 20, Agent Bouton walked into the Dreamland Motel and asked McGown if she recalled anyone coming to the motel in the last week or so with a Ryder truck, the same question he and other agents had been asking other business owners around Junction City.

His assignment seemed fairly mundane when he walked into the Dreamland Motel. Not really expecting much to come from his contact with McGown, Bouton was startled when she answered that she did, in fact, remember having a guest with a Ryder truck. She said a young man had stayed at her motel during the past week, a young man who asked if he could park a Ryder truck at the motel while he was there.

McGown said she remembered the man because he was clean cut, with a nicely pressed shirt and pleasant appearance. He was driving an "old, beat up looking yellow Mercury." That fact bothered her because the young man did not really seem to fit the old yellow Mercury. She decided to put him in room 25 just west of the motel office. There was only one door separating room 25 from the office, and this door led to the laundry room. McGown felt more comfortable having guests who might be a problem

Lea McGown and her teenage children lived in an area of the Dreamland Motel just behind the office. Eric and Kathleen McGown attended high school in Junction City and worked part time at the motel.

The registration card for the Dreamland Motel, Junction City, KS, room 25.

Timothy McVeigh listed his address on the registration card at the Dreamland Motel as 3616 N. Van Dyke Rd., Decker, Michigan. His car was listed as a 1977 Mercury, Arizona license LZC 034.

stay in room 25 so she could keep an eye on them. She remembered there was something about the man in the yellow Mercury that did not seem right. That was just the way she ran the motel. It was a small business, her business, and she liked to keep a close eye on things.

Agent Bouton's heart raced as the motel owner looked for the registration card for the man who had rented room 25. As McGown handed the card to the agent, he was careful to protect it for later fingerprint analysis. McGown had now associated a name with the man in room 25, the man who asked if he could park a Ryder truck at the motel during his stay.

The registration card read "Tim McVeigh." Bouton hoped it might be a break in the case. Sometimes, the most mundane investigative leads produce the biggest results and Bouton hoped this might be one of those times.

The motel owner said McVeigh was alone when he checked into the motel, and he so indicated in completing the registration card. Next to the block specifying the number of occupants was the numeral "1." From years of experience, McGown knew motel guests sometimes lied about the number of people that stayed in the rooms because room rates varied according to the number of guests. When she asked McVeigh how many would be staying in the room, he told her that he was alone.

McGown remembered she quoted McVeigh a rate of $22.00 per night for the room, but he asked for a cheaper rate since he was going to be staying at the motel for four nights. She agreed to charge McVeigh a total of $80.00 for four nights, beginning April 14, 1995, through the evening of April 17, 1995. McVeigh paid in cash. McVeigh's eagerness to get a better price caused McGown to focus even more on him and was one of the reasons she was able to remember him as well as she did.

Agent Bouton showed McGown the composite drawing of John Doe #1 and asked her if the man in room 25 looked anything like it. She answered immediately that the drawing looked just like the man in room 25. She said she had never seen the man depicted in the drawing of John Doe #2 at the motel or anywhere else.

Bouton was excited about what he had learned and was anxious to get back to the command post at Fort Riley to tell his fellow agents. Of course, putting a man named Tim McVeigh in a Ryder truck at the Dreamland Motel did not necessarily mean that McVeigh was involved in the Oklahoma City bombing, but at least it was a place to start.

After receiving Bouton's information, the FBI wanted to know more about Tim McVeigh. Who was he and where could he be found?

Decker, Michigan

The FBI concentrated on the Decker, Michigan, address that McVeigh had listed on the Dreamland Motel registration card. Who lived at this address? Was it McVeigh's residence? Part of the FBI's reputation and mystique was built on its ability to assist local law enforcement agencies, especially in the rural areas of the United States. And in turn, the FBI called on police departments and sheriff's offices in these areas when assistance was needed. It was time to ask for help from local lawmen in Decker.

Agents learned quickly from local law enforcement authorities that 3616 North Van Dyke Road was the family farmhouse of James Nichols. James and his brother, Terry Nichols, had farmed the land, as their father had, for many years. The brothers had married sisters years ago but both had divorced. James continued to live on the family farm, but Terry and his new wife, Marife, had moved.

Agents learned from police officers in Decker that both James and Terry had expressed animosity toward the federal government in past years. Agents learned from James' ex-wife even more detail about the Nichols brothers' hatred for the government and that Lana Padilla, Terry Nichols' first wife, had moved to Las Vegas and could be contacted there.

James Nichols' farmhouse was rapidly becoming a focal point of interest and the FBI wanted to know more about the current whereabouts of Terry Nichols.

Lana Padilla

Leads were immediately sent to the Las Vegas Division of the FBI. Agents were instructed to contact Lana Padilla and interview her as soon as possible. They made contact with her on Friday morning, April 21. She proved to be a wealth of information. Padilla said Terry and Marife Nichols had moved to the Las Vegas area in late 1993, but had since relocated in central Kansas. She believed that Terry was now living at 109 South Second Street in Herington, Kansas. Leads were sent back to the Kansas City Division.

Padilla said she had married Terry Nichols on January 30, 1981. She was five years older than Terry, and they had one child, Josh Nichols, born August 11, 1982, at Cass City, Michigan. Terry, according to Lana, had failed at most jobs he tried, and she had become frustrated with him. Their marriage was failing and Lana could see that changes were necessary. She began encouraging Terry to enlist in the military, hoping that the discipline provided by the army would give him some direction in his life.

Finally, Terry joined the United States Army. While in boot camp at Fort Benning, Georgia, in May, 1988, he met and became best friends with a young soldier named Tim McVeigh.

McVeigh's Arrest

A gent **Walt Lamar was assigned to Squad 5** in the Oklahoma City office of the FBI. Squad 5 agents worked bank robberies, kidnappings, fugitives, gang crimes, and a variety of other reactive crime cases. Lamar had a wealth of experience in tracking fugitives. He had worked bank robberies and fugitive cases for many years in Oklahoma and in the San Francisco Division before returning to Oklahoma City. Lamar, a Native American, was proud of his heritage and took every opportunity to showcase his ancestors' heritage and talents. Through Lamar's efforts, many in the Oklahoma City office became more knowledgeable and aware of Native American accomplishments in Oklahoma and elsewhere.

When Lamar heard the news about Tim McVeigh, the man who brought a Ryder truck to the Dreamland Motel and who looked like the composite drawing of John Doe #1, he went into action. His years of experience tracking down fugitives paid dividends. Walt suggested that contact be made with FBI Headquarters in Washington, D.C., to query the National Crime Information Center (NCIC) to determine if anyone named Tim McVeigh had been arrested anywhere in the United States in the recent past.

By early Friday morning, April 21, two days after the bombing, Lamar learned that a man named Timothy James McVeigh had been arrested by the Oklahoma Highway Patrol (OHP) on Wednesday morning, April 19. Was this Tim McVeigh the same man who had a Ryder truck at the Dreamland Motel just days before the Oklahoma City bombing?

Mark Michalic

Mark Michalic, an agent for the Bureau of Alcohol, Tobacco, and Firearms (ATF) in Oklahoma City, was asked to follow up the results of the NCIC off-line search information that had been relayed from FBI headquarters. He contacted OHP headquarters in Oklahoma City and verified that a Tim McVeigh had been arrested by Trooper Charlie Hanger on Wednesday morning. When he contacted the trooper only minutes later, Hanger said he had arrested a man named Tim McVeigh for carrying a concealed weapon and that he had booked McVeigh into the Noble County jail in Perry, Oklahoma.

Michalic's adrenaline was rushing. He quickly called the Noble County jail and spoke to Sheriff Jerry Cook, who confirmed that McVeigh was in custody and had been taken to a courtroom for a bond hearing. The sheriff did not know if McVeigh was still in the courthouse or had been released on bond. When he was advised by Michalic that McVeigh was wanted for questioning in connection with the Oklahoma City bombing investigation, Cook promised to drop what he was doing and get back with Michalic immediately. Within minutes, Sheriff Cook reported that McVeigh was still in custody and would be held in the Noble County jail pursuant to the FBI request.

There was still no way of knowing whether the man in custody in Perry was the same Tim McVeigh who had stayed at the Dreamland Motel. And if so, did McVeigh have anything to do with the Oklahoma City bombing? SAC Bob Ricks knew he needed to dispatch agents to the Noble County jail as quickly as possible.

The booking card used to log information about Timothy McVeigh when he was booked into the Noble County jail on April 19, 1995.

Ricks sent Danny Coulson and Jim Adams, the SAC and Assistant SAC of the FBI's Dallas Division, and Oklahoma City Agents Floyd Zimms and Jim Norman. Since time was critical, the agents were flown to Perry by helicopter. The helicopter could also be used to transport McVeigh back to Oklahoma City if that became necessary.

As quickly as agents arrived at the jail, arrangements were made for Zimms and Norman to talk with McVeigh. The agents introduced themselves to McVeigh and when Zimms asked McVeigh if he knew why they were there, he responded, "It's probably about that Oklahoma City thing."

The Michigan driver's license carried by Timothy McVeigh and surrendered to authorities at the Noble County jail when he was booked on April 19, 1995.

Agent Norman advised McVeigh of his constitutional rights. McVeigh responded that he wanted to exercise those rights and told the agents that he wanted to speak with an attorney before saying anything further. McVeigh provided only his name, rank, and serial number.

The black jeans worn by Timothy McVeigh when he was arrested alongside Interstate 35 by Trooper Charlie Hanger.

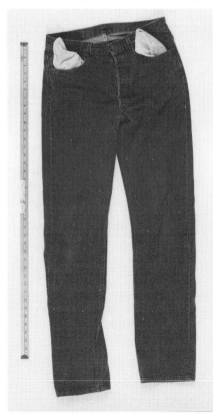

While Zimms and Norman attempted to talk to McVeigh inside the Noble County jail, other agents inspected McVeigh's personal belongings and clothing worn at the time of his arrest, as well as his booking card and personal property sheet. McVeigh had given his address as 3616 North Van Dyke Road, Decker, Michigan, the same address used by the man in room 25 at the Dreamland Motel.

A quick review of McVeigh's driver's license revealed it had been issued in the state of Michigan, using the same Decker address. There was little doubt now that the Tim McVeigh arrested by Trooper Charlie Hanger was the same Tim McVeigh who had stayed at the Dreamland Motel for several days before the bombing—the same man who

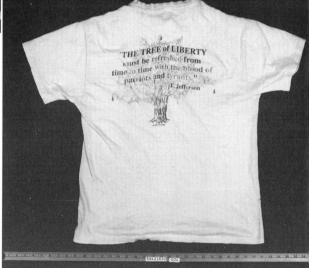

Left: The front of the white tee-shirt worn by McVeigh at the time of his arrest on April 19, 1995. The Latin phrase meant "Death Unto Tyrants," the phrase screamed by John Wilkes Booth when he assassinated President Abraham Lincoln.

Below: The back of Tim McVeigh's tee-shirt worn at the time of his arrest. The words are those of Thomas Jefferson, uttered two centuries ago in describing the tyranny of the British.

brought a Ryder truck to the motel.

In McVeigh's personal belongings were a pair of black jeans, black army boots, a blue windbreaker jacket, and two tee-shirts. One tee-shirt was white with blue, mid-length sleeves. The other was more distinctive. It was a short-sleeve, white shirt with a picture of President Abraham Lincoln on the front. Underneath the picture of Lincoln were the words "Sic Semper Tyrannis," a Latin phrase meaning "Death Unto Tyrants." It was the same phrase screamed by John Wilkes Booth when he fired the fatal shot that killed President Lincoln inside the Ford Theatre in Washington, D.C., in 1865.

On the back of the shirt was a replica of the "Tree of Liberty" complete with red blood droplets. Underneath the Tree of Liberty were the words "The Tree of Liberty must be refreshed from time to time with the blood of Patriots and Tyrants."

The decision was made to take McVeigh into federal custody. Agents took possession of McVeigh's personal property which included a Glock .45 caliber automatic handgun with a fully loaded magazine in the weapon and a black talon round in the chamber. The weapon was contained in a shoulder holster. In law enforcement jargon a black talon round is commonly referred to as a "cop killer bullet" because it expands on impact, forming six razor-sharp claws, intended to cause grave damage to its target. McVeigh also had an extra fully loaded magazine for the Glock, and a knife in a leather scabbard. Strangely, he also had a set of earplugs that he removed from his pockets while being booked.

By 6:00 p.m. on Friday, an angry crowd had gathered outside the Noble County courthouse. Agents Coulson and Adams were concerned about the safety of McVeigh and the welfare of the agents who would be escorting him from the jail to a transport vehicle. A decision was made to back up a van as close as possible to the courthouse door so that McVeigh could be escorted quickly into the van.

Agents and local police officers were assigned to the roof of the courthouse for a better view of the crowd—it was the most advantageous position to relay information if an incident developed while McVeigh was

The Glock .45 caliber automatic handgun that Tim McVeigh carried at the time of his arrest on the morning of the Oklahoma City bombing.

Timothy McVeigh being escorted from the Noble County courthouse in Perry, Oklahoma, on April 21, 1995. FBI Agent Floyd Zimms is to McVeigh's left. McVeigh was flown by helicopter to an initial appearance before United States Magistrate Judge Ronald Howland at Tinker Air Force Base near Oklahoma City.

being transferred from the jail to the van. Other Agents were stationed outside the courthouse. Coulson and Adams did not want another Lee Harvey Oswald incident that occurred in Dallas in 1963 after the assassination of President John F. Kennedy.

Agents Zimms and Norman walked next to McVeigh as he was led outside the courthouse and into the awaiting van. Onlookers booed McVeigh because non-stop media attention to the bombing had already centered its coverage on McVeigh and his possible connection to the horrible crime. The van proceeded immediately to the FBI helicopter for the short flight to Oklahoma City. Sheriff Jerry Cook was relieved to be rid of his most famous prisoner.

Hank Gibbons

Agent Hank Gibbons worked feverishly with Assistant United States Attorneys Vicki Behenna and Arlene Joplin to prepare an affidavit that would be used to file a criminal complaint charging McVeigh with violation of Title 18, United States Code, Section 844(f). The affidavit alleged that McVeigh did "maliciously damage and destroy by means of fire or an explosive, any building, vehicle, and other personal or real property in whole or in part owned, possessed, or used by the United States, any department or agency thereof."

The complaint would be needed soon after McVeigh arrived in Oklahoma City. Federal agents can make arrests based on oral authorization from assistant United States attorneys, but an arrested subject must be taken before a federal magistrate judge at the earliest available opportunity. A complaint and accompanying affidavit must be filed before the initial appearance is made. At this appearance, the person arrested is advised by the magistrate of the pending charges and provided with an affidavit reciting probable cause for his or her arrest.

Gibbons delivered. The affidavit and arrest warrant were ready when McVeigh was brought for his initial appearance before United States Magistrate Judge Ronald Howland at Tinker Air Force Base in Midwest City, a suburb of Oklahoma City. The documents detailed the FBI's investigation as it had begun to unfold.

Gibbons also knew the FBI would need a search warrant for McVeigh's car. Agents learned from Trooper Hanger that McVeigh's yellow Mercury had been left on the east shoulder of Interstate 35 when he was arrested Wednesday morning. Hanger offered to have the car towed, but McVeigh declined, no doubt assuming he would be able to recover the car after he made bond on the weapons charges.

Agents and federal prosecutors assigned to the FBI command post in Oklahoma City were already making arrangements to seize McVeigh's car and have it brought to Oklahoma City. At 3:10 p.m. on Friday, United States District Judge David L. Russell signed the search warrant for McVeigh's car.

McVeigh told the FBI virtually nothing at the Noble County jail before he was taken into federal custody. But the evidence implicating him in the bombing was beginning to mount. The Tree of Liberty tee-shirt worn by McVeigh at the time of his arrest depicted a man with a mentality bent toward vengeance. McVeigh had the FBI's full attention, but the investigation was only beginning.

McVeigh's Car

McVeigh's yellow Mercury was taken to the Oklahoma City FBI warehouse, now fully equipped to receive and store evidence. Agent Bill

Found inside Timothy McVeigh's Mercury was this note that obviously had been placed on the dash of the vehicle to prevent police from moving the car while it was parked near the alleyway behind the YMCA Building. In asking onlookers not to tow the car, McVeigh promised to move the car by April 23, his birthday.

Eppright was assigned the responsibility of searching the car and logging in any evidence that might be retrieved. Eppright was assigned to the Dallas office of the FBI and was one of hundreds of agents responding to the bombing in Oklahoma City.

As he began to search McVeigh's car, the agent noticed a sealed white envelope on the front seat. Next to the white envelope was a single sheet of white paper that contained the words "Not Abandoned - Please do not

The infamous yellow Mercury, without a license plate, that Timothy McVeigh was driving when he was stopped by Trooper Charlie Hanger 78 minutes after the Oklahoma City bombing. The license plate was never found.

> " I have no reason to suppose
> that he who would take away
> my liberty, would not, when he
> had me in his power, take away
> everything else; and therefore,
> it is lawful for me to treat him
> as one who has put himself into
> a 'state of war' against me; and
> kill him if I can, for to that
> hazard does he justly expose
> himself, whoever introduces a
> state of war and is aggressor
> in it." — John Locke
> Second Treatise of Government

Among the documents found in McVeigh's yellow Mercury on April 19, 1995, were handwritten statements by McVeigh such as these excerpts from John Locke's Second Treatise of Government. Such writings were corrupted by McVeigh to support his theory that violence against the federal government was justified.

tow - will move by April 23, (Needs Battery & Cable)." The agent photographed the items before he removed them.

Eppright opened the white envelope and found several folded documents that contained strong anti-government sentiment with various notations highlighted in yellow. The agent was especially careful to photograph the highlighted portions of the documents.

One of the documents in the envelope contained the highlighted quote, "But the real value of all our attacks today lies in the psychological impact, not in the immediate casualties. More important, though, is what

"When The Government Fears The People There Is Liberty When The People Fear The Government There Is Tyranny" S. Adams

McVeigh added the words, "Maybe now, there will be Liberty," under the Samuel Adams quote, "When the Government fears the people, there is Liberty – When the People fear the Government, there is Tyranny." This document was found in McVeigh's car.

we taught the politicians and bureaucrats. They learned this afternoon that not one of them is beyond our reach. They can huddle behind barbed wire and tanks in the city, or they can hide behind the concrete walls and alarm systems of their country estates, but we can still find them and kill them. This is a lesson they will not forget."

Another document contained a quote from one of America's Founding Fathers, Samuel Adams, "When the Government fears the people, there is Liberty - When the people fear the Government, there is Tyranny." Underneath this quote, in what was later determined to be McVeigh's handwriting, were the words, "Maybe now, there will be Liberty."

Still another document contained in the envelope was a quote from John Locke, "I have no reason to suppose that he who would take away my liberty, would not, when he had me in his power, take away everything else; and therefore, it is lawful for me to treat him as one who has put himself into a state of war against me; and kill him if I can, for to that hazard does he justly expose himself, whoever introduces a state of war and is aggressor in it."

Charlie Hanger

After McVeigh's arrest, Trooper Charlie Hanger informed Assistant United States Attorney Scott Mendeloff and FBI Case Agent Jon Hersley that on Wednesday morning, April 19, at 10:20 a.m., he stopped a yellow Mercury driven by Timothy James McVeigh for failure to display a rear license plate and that he arrested McVeigh when he found McVeigh was carrying a loaded Glock .45 caliber automatic handgun in a shoulder holster underneath his left arm.

When Hanger was asked to describe in intimate detail his stop and arrest of McVeigh, he told his story with confidence and without hesitation. Hanger was on his way to Oklahoma City to provide assistance in the aftermath of the bombing. As he drove south on Interstate 35 toward Oklahoma City, he received a call from his dispatcher instructing him to discontinue his travel to Oklahoma City and return to his normal duties. He turned around and began heading back north on Interstate 35, feeling disappointed with the redirection of his assignment. Like most law enforcement officers in Oklahoma, Hanger felt an urgent need to respond to the tragedy and chaos in Oklahoma City.

After he had traveled past Perry, Hanger came upon a yellow Mercury Marquis driving in the right lane. Just as he was about to pass the car, the trooper noticed the Mercury had no rear license plate. He slowed his patrol car and pulled in behind the car and turned on his flashing lights. McVeigh pulled to the right shoulder and Trooper Hanger positioned his patrol car behind and slightly offset to the left of the car, a technique of positioning his car so it could be used as a shield to protect him if the person or persons he was stopping meant to harm him.

As Hanger opened the driver's door to his patrol car, he could see that McVeigh was opening the driver's side door of the Mercury and was beginning to exit his car. Hanger was on high alert because another trooper had been involved in a shooting just two weeks before in the same general area of Oklahoma.

Hanger could see McVeigh's hands as he began walking toward the patrol car. They met at a position just behind and to the left of the Mercury. Hanger told McVeigh the reason he stopped him was for failure to display a rear license plate. McVeigh looked over his shoulder toward the rear of the car as if he was looking where the license plate should have been displayed.

McVeigh said he had purchased the car recently and did not yet have a tag. The trooper asked him for a bill of sale, and McVeigh responded that he did not have one—the person he bought the car from was still filling it out. Hanger asked McVeigh for his driver's license. When McVeigh reached for his wallet, the trooper noticed a bulge under McVeigh's left arm beneath his jacket. As McVeigh handed a Michigan driver's license to him, Hanger instructed McVeigh to use both hands and slowly pull his jacket back so he could see underneath. At that point, McVeigh told Trooper Hanger that he had a gun.

Acting on instinct, Hanger immediately reached for the bulge in McVeigh's jacket and instructed McVeigh to get his hands in the air and turn around. As McVeigh turned around with his hands raised, Hanger drew his own weapon and put it to the back of McVeigh's head. McVeigh told Hanger that his gun was loaded. Hanger responded, "Mine is, too." McVeigh obeyed Hanger's instructions to walk slowly to the back of the Mercury.

When McVeigh reached the back of the car, the trooper told him to spread his legs and put his hands on the trunk. Hanger then removed the .45 caliber Glock from the shoulder holster and threw the gun to the side of the road. Next, the trooper removed a fully loaded ammunition magazine from McVeigh's belt. Hanger continued to search McVeigh and found a knife in a scabbard on McVeigh's belt.

Trooper Hanger tossed both the ammunition magazine and the knife to the side of the road and handcuffed McVeigh's hands behind his back. When Hanger asked McVeigh why he was carrying a loaded firearm, McVeigh answered he believed he had a right to carry the weapon for his own protection. McVeigh was escorted back to the patrol car and placed in the right front passenger seat.

Hanger quickly retrieved the pistol, ammunition magazine, and knife from the roadside. He placed the ammunition magazine and the knife in the trunk of his car. The trooper then checked the chamber of McVeigh's gun and found it to contain a Black Talon round. After unloading the weapon, Hanger took it to his patrol car. Once inside, he contacted the dispatcher and advised her of McVeigh's arrest.

Hanger asked the dispatcher to run a routine criminal record check on McVeigh to see if he had any outstanding warrants. Meanwhile, Hanger searched McVeigh's handgun to identify the serial number. Just as Hanger found the number, McVeigh commented that the serial number on his weapon was VM769. Trooper Hanger told McVeigh that he was close, it was VW769. The trooper told McVeigh that most people do not know their gun serial numbers, but McVeigh responded, "Well, I do."

Hanger recontacted the dispatcher and provided her with the make, model, and serial number of McVeigh's weapon and asked her to run a check to determine if the gun was stolen. A short while later, the dispatcher advised Hanger that McVeigh was not wanted, had no previous criminal history, and his .45 caliber Glock was not stolen.

Hanger told the dispatcher he would get the Vehicle Identification Number (VIN) from McVeigh's car and call her back. Since McVeigh had failed to display a license plate on his car, Hanger wanted to determine if the car was stolen and to whom it was registered.

Prior to exiting his patrol car to retrieve the VIN from McVeigh's Mercury, Hanger asked McVeigh if he wanted to answer some questions. Hanger read McVeigh his Miranda rights and asked if he understood them. McVeigh answered affirmatively and agreed to talk further with the trooper.

McVeigh told the trooper he had a tag from his old car, but he felt it was better to drive the car without a tag than to drive with an improper tag. McVeigh said he purchased the car from a Firestone dealer named Tom in Junction City, Kansas. McVeigh said he paid the Firestone dealer $250.00 cash and traded in his old car, which had broken down on him. Trooper Hanger asked for permission to search the Mercury, and McVeigh consented.

As the trooper exited his car, he placed McVeigh's handgun in the trunk and walked to the front of the Mercury, leaving McVeigh handcuffed and seat-belted in the front passenger seat of the patrol car. Looking through the front windshield of the Mercury, Trooper Hanger read the VIN from a small metal plate located on the dashboard just inside the windshield and recorded the number so he could relay it to his dispatcher.

Hanger entered McVeigh's car through the driver's side door, which was still open. The trooper looked in the glove box, on the front seat and in the rear seat area of the car. Nothing of interest was noticed in the glove box or the rear seat, but Hanger noticed the sheet of white, lined paper lying on the front seat along with a white legal-sized envelope.

After completing his search of the car's interior, Hanger returned to his patrol car and contacted the dispatcher. In a short while, the dispatcher advised Hanger she could find no record of the car in Oklahoma or Kansas. Trooper Hanger then informed the dispatcher the Mercury had a safety sticker on it, possibly from Missouri, and asked her to run the car for Missouri registration, as well. McVeigh said the safety sticker was for Arkansas, not Missouri, leading Hanger to ask the dispatcher to run the VIN for possible registration in Arkansas.

While Hanger waited word from his dispatcher, he again spoke briefly with McVeigh. He asked McVeigh where he had been. McVeigh answered that he was in the process of moving to Arkansas, that he had taken one load and was on his way back to get more of his belongings. McVeigh did not specifically state where he meant he was on his way back to, but the trooper said he understood McVeigh to mean Junction City, since that is where he claimed to have recently purchased the yellow Mercury.

At about this point in the conversation with McVeigh, the OHP dispatcher called and said she had found a registration for the Mercury in Arkansas. The car was registered to Paul or Connie Rescorl, Fayetteville, Arkansas, but the registration had expired in November, 1994.

Trooper Hanger asked McVeigh if he wanted his car towed at McVeigh's expense, but McVeigh declined. Hanger asked McVeigh if he wanted him to obtain any items from the car before they left, but again McVeigh declined. Hanger asked McVeigh specifically about the sealed envelope that lay on the front seat of the Mercury. The trooper was concerned that the envelope contained valuables. However, McVeigh told Hanger to leave the envelope in the car. Before leaving the arrest location, Hanger searched the trunk of the car but found nothing out of the ordinary.

At the Noble County courthouse, Trooper Hanger escorted McVeigh to the county jail on the fourth floor and turned him over to Marsha Moritz, the jailer on duty, for booking.

Noble County Jail

Marsha Moritz was an attractive, personable woman. She and Trooper Hanger were good friends and had known each other for years. Hanger had arrested hundreds of people over the years and Mortiz had booked many of them into the Noble County jail.

Before learning of his possible connection to the Oklahoma City bombing, Moritz considered McVeigh just another arrestee. She asked him to empty his pockets onto the counter. McVeigh was cooperative. As Moritiz began the booking process, a television in the room was tuned into news coverage of the bombing in Oklahoma City earlier that morning.

Moritz noticed that McVeigh had a Michigan driver's license. She asked McVeigh if the information on the driver's license was correct, and he answered that it was. Moritz wrote the name Timothy James McVeigh onto the booking card and noted the arrest date as April 19, 1995, time 10:20 a.m. She took McVeigh's address from his driver's license as 3616 North Van Dyke Rd, Decker, Michigan.

Moritz listed the charges against McVeigh as 1) unlawfully carrying and transporting a loaded weapon in a vehicle; and 2) failure to display a license tag, no insurance. When Moritz asked for his next of kin, McVeigh answered "James Nichols" and gave a telephone number for Nichols as (517) 872-4018.

Moritz pulled out a brown paper grocery sack and wrote McVeigh's name, along with the number 2, on the bag. She told McVeigh to place his articles of clothing in the sack when he changed into jail coveralls. The number 2 was recorded onto the grocery sack because Moritz placed McVeigh's personal belongings in a bank bag, also numbered 2. It was a simple system, but it worked.

Moritz placed the contents of McVeigh's pockets into the bank bag. Included in the contents was a set of earplugs. She had no way of knowing the evidentiary value the earplugs held. On the reverse side of the booking card, Moritz listed McVeigh's articles of clothing.

Moritz was the only jailer on duty when Trooper Hanger brought McVeigh in, so she asked Hanger to go with McVeigh to the back room to change into the orange jail coveralls. Hanger obliged. As McVeigh changed, Hanger instructed him to drop his civilian clothing into the brown paper sack given to him by Moritz.

In later conversations with Agent Hersley and Assistant United States Attorney Mendeloff, Moritz said that what struck her the most about McVeigh on the morning of his arrest was his obvious lack of emotion, compassion, and sympathy toward the victims of the bombing in Oklahoma City. As coverage of the bombing was broadcast on the television, McVeigh seemed unmoved, unattached. It was as if nothing had happened. Everyone else in the jail was heartbroken, but McVeigh remained unaffected.

On Saturday morning, April 22, Trooper Hanger decided to check over the interior of his patrol car, something he routinely did after mak-

(front and back) The Paulsen's Military Supply business card found on the floorboard in Trooper Charlie Hanger's squad car after the arrest of Timothy McVeigh. The "Dave" was David Paulsen, a military surplus dealer McVeigh had met at gun shows.

ing an arrest. He did this to make sure the last person he arrested had not hidden or stashed anything in the patrol car that might be used as a weapon against the trooper by the next person he arrested and transported. Hanger had been off duty since Wednesday, the day he arrested McVeigh.

When he checked his car, Hanger found a business card on the floorboard directly behind the passenger seat of the car. The card was crumpled. Hanger was sure the card was not in the car before he arrested McVeigh on Wednesday, and no one had been in the car since that day.

The front of the business card was simple enough. It read, "Paulsen's Military Supply, Antigo, Wisconsin." The back of the card is what interested Agent Hersley and Prosecutor Mendeloff. Hand printed on the back of the card were the words, "TNT @ $5/stick, Need More, Call after 01May, see if I can get some more." McVeigh's sister, Jennifer, and FBI handwriting experts later identified this hand printing as that of McVeigh.

In hand printing, noticeably different than the TNT statement, was the wording, "Dave, 708-288-0128." Agents wanted to know who Dave was and what, if anything, he had to do with Tim McVeigh. Agents wanted to know everything about McVeigh. Who he was, where he was from, and who were his friends?

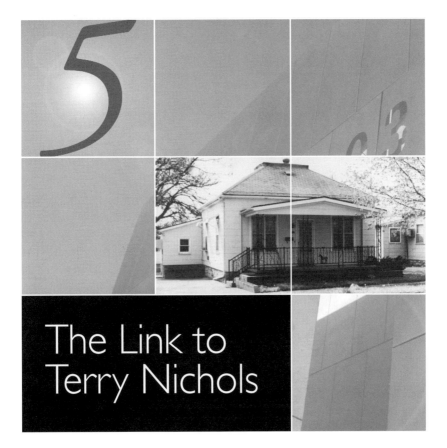

The Link to
Terry Nichols

A*gents Steve Smith and Jack Foley* were dispatched to Herington, Kansas, shortly after the FBI learned that Terry Nichols lived in this small town in central Kansas, 25 miles south of Junction City where the Ryder bomb truck had been rented. Lana Padilla had provided information linking Terry Nichols as "best friends" with Tim McVeigh. Was it coincidence or evidence that Nichols lived so close to where the Ryder bomb truck was rented? Smith and Foley set up surveillance of Nichols' house at 109 South Second Street in Herington.

Nichols was growing restless in his house. By Friday afternoon, April 21, he had spotted surveillance cars outside his residence. He was in a near state of panic. Who was watching his house? What did they want? Nichols decided to leave the residence. He took his wife, Marife, and his young daughter, Nicole, and drove his blue 1984 GMC pickup to the Surplus City store located on the edge of town.

Terry and Marife Nichols' home at 109 South Second Street in Herington, Kansas.

He knew he was being followed so Nichols decided to turn around and head for the Herington Department of Public Safety. He pulled into the police station parking lot.

Nichols was in a tough spot and he knew it. He had people following him. His name and his brother's name were being mentioned on the radio in connection with the bombing. He knew McVeigh had been arrested. Should he run? Should he confront the people following him? He had few options—so he decided to talk. It would be a reasonable response for a man who had nothing to hide—but a huge risk for someone with dark secrets. Nichols decided to talk his way out of the problem.

Before entering the police station, Nichols admitted to his wife that he had not gone to Omaha to pick up McVeigh on Easter Sunday—that instead he had picked up McVeigh in Oklahoma City. What else had he failed to tell Marife?

Once inside the building, Nichols demanded to know who was following him and why his name was being mentioned on news reports. Agents Smith and Foley, who had been following Nichols from the time he left his residence, were surprised when he turned in at the police station.

Right: Marife Nichols, the second wife of Terry Nichols, was a native of the Philippines. *Courtesy Oklahoma Publishing Company.*

Far Right: Lana Padilla was Terry Nichols' first wife and mother of his son, Josh Nichols. *Courtesy Oklahoma Publishing Company.*

By now, the agents knew Nichols was a close friend of McVeigh. The two had attended United States Army basic training together during the summer of 1988 and had stayed together in the Army until Nichols received his discharge in 1989. Smith and Foley wanted to know what was going on inside the police station. Was Nichols holding anyone hostage? The agents placed a call to Public Safety Director Dale Kuhn, who effectively served as the Herington police chief. Once the agents determined everything was alright inside, they were able to brief Chief Kuhn about Nichols and his association with McVeigh.

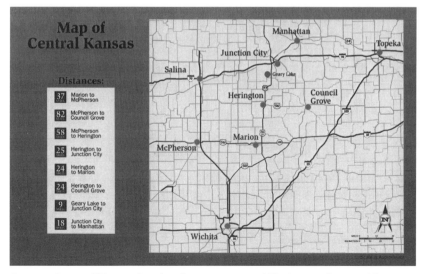

A map of central Kansas showing the towns around Herington that would become important in the Oklahoma City bombing investigation.

Chief Kuhn took the necessary precautions. He moved Nichols and his family further inside the offices of the police department. The Chief told Nichols he wanted to search him for weapons. Nichols complied by raising his coat, allowing the Chief to see he had no weapons. Marife and Nicole were also searched. Agents Smith and Foley entered the police station minutes later. They wanted to talk with Nichols.

The Herington police station housed a small law enforcement department, consisting of Chief Kuhn, a deputy chief, and only a few officers. The small building had an entryway, where citizens could enter unescorted. There were several small offices inside the inner sanctum. Several jail cells were located on the backside of the first floor.

Agents Smith and Foley introduced themselves to Nichols and told him they would like to search him for weapons. Nichols again consented. The agents told Nichols they had some questions for him, and Nichols replied, "Good, because I have some questions for you." Chief Kuhn escorted the agents, along with Nichols, down to the basement, the largest single room in the police station, and the quietest place to conduct an interview without interruption.

During the initial stages of the conversation, Nichols told the agents that he had grown up on the family farm in Decker, Michigan, with his brother, James. He married Lana Padilla in January, 1981. They had one son together, Joshua "Josh" Nichols. Nichols and Lana divorced after he entered the army at Lana's urging in 1988. Nichols later married Marife Torres, a young girl from the Philippines he met by answering an advertisement for young brides in that country.

Nichols made his living selling military surplus items, such as hand shovels, axes, and sandbags at gun shows. He said he first heard of his possible involvement in the Oklahoma City bombing on Friday afternoon, April 21, while he was driving to the local lumber yard in Herington. A radio station in Manhattan, Kansas, had broadcast that Terry Nichols and his brother, James, of Michigan, were possible suspects in the bombing.

Nichols told agents that after hearing the broadcast, he returned home. He was anxious. Finally, he told Marife what he had heard on the radio broadcast. She did not believe him. He turned the television to a news station and heard that Tim McVeigh had been arrested in connection with

Terry Nichols' 1984 GMC pickup truck parked outside the police station in Herington, Kansas.

the bombing. The cable television in his house had been hooked up earlier that same morning.

Nichols said he saw the composite drawing of John Doe #1, but convinced himself that it did not look like McVeigh. He began considering whether to go to the police station to find out if he was wanted. He was concerned federal officers might storm his house. He did not want another Waco—Nichols had often talked with disgust about the tragic fire in Waco, Texas, that killed 86 residents of David Koresh's Branch Davidian Compound on April 19, 1993, two years to the day before the Oklahoma City bombing. Becoming more anxious, he decided to leave his house, ending up at the Herington police station.

Nichols said McVeigh had stayed with him for awhile at the farmhouse located on Van Dyke Road in Decker, Michigan. Smith and Foley recognized the address. It was the same address McVeigh had used when he registered at the Dreamland Motel on Friday, April 14.

Based upon the early conversations and Nichols' involvement with McVeigh, Smith and Foley decided to advise Nichols of his constitutional rights. It was 3:26 p.m. The agents asked Nichols to read the list of rights contained on what is known in the FBI as an "Interrogation, Advice of Rights Form." Nichols read his rights aloud from this form.

When the agents asked Nichols to sign the form indicating that he had read and understood his rights, he declined, saying he did not like the word "Interrogation" on the form because it reminded him of the Nazis. Nichols told the agents he understood his rights, but he did not want to sign the form. There was no legal requirement that a suspect sign the Advice of Rights form. Smith and Foley were satisfied that Nichols understood his rights and continued the interview.

Nichols was asked when he had last seen McVeigh. He said he saw McVeigh on Easter Sunday, April 16, 1995, the first time he had seen his friend since November, 1994. Nichols then blurted out, "In my eyes, I did not do anything wrong, but I see how lawyers can turn things around." He said he did not know anything about the bombing before it happened, and he was hesitant to talk because of the way lawyers can manipulate information.

The agents asked Nichols if he had seen McVeigh at any motel in Junction City or if he knew where McVeigh was staying before the bombing. Nichols responded that he did not know where McVeigh was staying, and he had not seen McVeigh at any motel in Junction City. Nichols was then asked if he knew anything about McVeigh having a Ryder truck. By now, the agents already knew McVeigh had stayed at the Dreamland Motel and that the Ryder truck, used in the Oklahoma City bombing, was last rented at Elliott's Body Shop, only a few miles from the Dreamland Motel on Interstate 70. Nichols answered that he had not seen McVeigh with a Ryder truck.

About 30 minutes after Agents Smith and Foley advised Nichols of his constitutional rights, Agents Scott Crabtree and Dan Jablonski joined them in the interview. The agents asked Nichols if he would be willing to allow them to search his house and his pickup. He said yes and signed the consent to search form at 4:34 p.m., adding the words, "Without prejudice U.C.C. 1-207," spuriously referring to a portion of the Uniform Commercial Code and basically indicating he was not giving up his rights even though he agreed to the search.

The agents asked Nichols if they could expect to find any materials for making bombs in his house. He responded they would not, but he told the agents he wanted to make sure they could tell the difference between cleaning solvents and bomb building materials. Smith and Crabtree continued the interview with Nichols and Agents Foley and Jablonski left the room.

Nichols was asked about his most recent contact with McVeigh before Easter Sunday. He said that about two months earlier, in February, 1995, he sent a letter to McVeigh at his residence near Kingman, Arizona. In the letter, Nichols said he told McVeigh that if he happened to be in Las Vegas, to go by Lana's, Nichols' ex-wife's, house to pick up a television for him. Nichols said he had given the television to his son, Josh, in November, 1994, so that he and Lana could watch it, but now he wanted it back.

Nichols said the next time he heard from McVeigh after this letter was on Easter Sunday, April 16, 1995. His wife, Marife, had prepared Easter dinner and the family had completed their meal around 3:00 p.m., when Nichols received a call from McVeigh. Nichols said McVeigh told him during this call that he was in Oklahoma City and was having car trouble. Nichols said McVeigh told him he was pressed for time trying to get back east to visit relatives, and that if Nichols wanted his television, he would have to come to Oklahoma City to get it.

Nichols said McVeigh instructed him not to tell Marife he was picking up McVeigh in Oklahoma City, but rather to tell her that he was picking him up in Omaha, Nebraska. Nichols said McVeigh told him, "Just keep this between the two of us." Nichols said he left his house about ten minutes after receiving the call from McVeigh. He said he respected McVeigh's request not to tell Marife that he was going to Oklahoma City. In fact, Nichols said he did not tell Marife the truth about picking up McVeigh in Oklahoma City until they were driving to the police station on Friday afternoon, April 21, two days after the Oklahoma City bombing.

Nichols said he thought it would take about five hours to drive to Oklahoma City to get McVeigh. McVeigh had given him precise directions, including specific exits and streets. Nichols told the agents he could no longer recall many of the directions given to him by McVeigh, but that McVeigh told him to drive around city blocks and "Make sure you come down Eighth Street."

Nichols said he drove to Oklahoma City. As he approached the downtown area, he exited the freeway and drove around for about 30 minutes looking for McVeigh. Nichols told the agents he "went past that building a couple of times," referring to the Murrah Building. Nichols said he drove as far as a car dealership in one direction and past a post office in another. The post office was located on the northwest corner of Northwest Fifth Street and Harvey Avenue, diagonally across the street from the Murrah Building. Nichols said he continued to drive around until he finally spotted McVeigh at the other end of an alley. He turned north and then back west before picking up McVeigh.

Nichols recalled that it had been raining lightly while he was trying to find McVeigh who was wearing a tee-shirt, jeans, and tennis shoes and was clean-shaven. Nichols said McVeigh had Nichols' television with him. He also had a green military-issue rucksack. He said McVeigh placed the television and the rucksack in the cab of Nichols' pickup and climbed inside.

Nichols said that in spite of the rain, neither McVeigh nor his personal belongings seemed to be wet. Nichols said he did not see McVeigh's car, but the way McVeigh described the car, it was a large model. McVeigh told Nichols he was leaving the car in Oklahoma City. McVeigh directed Nichols as they drove out of the downtown area. As they left, it began to rain harder. It continued to rain until they were in Kansas. They arrived in Junction City, according to Nichols, at about 1:30 a.m. on Monday morning, April 17.

Nichols said that McVeigh sometimes spoke in code as they drove from Oklahoma City to Junction City. Nichols said he did not understand what McVeigh was telling him until later. Nichols described McVeigh as being hyper and nervous on the trip back. He said they discussed articles about Waco, which had appeared in the *Spotlight* Newsletter.

While discussing each other's future, McVeigh told Nichols, "You will see something big in the future." Nichols said he asked McVeigh, "What are you going to do, rob a bank?" McVeigh responded, "Oh no, I got something in the works." Nichols said they were distracted by something and McVeigh never explained what he meant by "something in the works."

McVeigh told Nichols about a rally or gathering in Washington, D.C. scheduled for the following week on the anniversary of the Waco incident. But McVeigh did not say he was going to be a part of the rally. He reminded Nichols that it had been two years since the Waco fire.

Nichols said as they neared Junction City, he thought to himself that McVeigh must know someone in town he was going to stay with and from whom he might be able to borrow a car, but he did not ask McVeigh about it.

As they arrived in Junction City, Nichols pulled into the McDonald's restaurant on South Washington near Interstate 70. The restaurant was closed. McVeigh directed Nichols to drop him off there anyway, saying he would call someone. Agents Smith and Crabtree already knew McVeigh had stayed at the Dreamland Motel, only 3.5 miles from the McDonald's where Nichols said he left him.

Nichols said McVeigh took his green military-issue rucksack and exited the pickup and said, "I'll catch you on the way back." McVeigh began walking toward a nearby convenience store and Nichols drove to his home in Herington, arriving around 2:00 a.m.

Terry Nichols' House

A continuous stream of FBI agents from the Kansas City office began arriving in central Kansas. A fully functional field office was set up in a World War II vintage barracks at Fort Riley. The office was surrounded by concertina wire, army trailer barricades, and armed sentries.

Supervisory Special Agents Tom Moore and Mike Shanahan, both with more than 25 years FBI experience, took charge of two full squads of Kansas agents focusing on McVeigh and Terry Nichols. While Agents Smith and Crabtree continued their interview of Nichols at the Herington police station, other agents had been posted at Nichols' residence on South Second Street. The FBI wanted to make certain the property was secure until a court ordered search warrant could be obtained. Agents also began talking to Terry Nichols' neighbors.

On April 22-23, FBI agents led by Mary Jasnowski conducted a thorough search of Nichols' Herington residence. The search yielded a volume of evidence that pointed toward Nichols' possible involvement in the Oklahoma City bombing. As the investigation continued, additional searches were conducted at the residence during the next several weeks. Among the items found:

1. A receipt for the purchase of 2,000 pounds of ammonium nitrate fertilizer, 34-0-0. The receipt was found inside a kitchen cabinet drawer by Joanne Thomas, an FBI analyst from the Omaha Division. The receipt documented the purchase of 2,000 pounds of ammonium

The kitchen cabinet inside Terry Nichols' home in Herington, Kansas. The September 30, 1994 receipt for 2,000 pounds of ammonium nitrate was found in a drawer of the cabinet.

nitrate fertilizer from Mid-Kansas Co-op in McPherson, Kansas, on September 30, 1994. The customer's name on the receipt—Mike Havens. FBI chemist Steve Burmeister would later identify small white prills found on the front porch and sidewalk of Nichols' residence as the same type of ammonium nitrate fertilizer purchased by customer Mike Havens on September 30, 1994.

2. Five rolls of orange Primadet non-electric blasting caps were found by Agent Larry Tongate in the basement of Nichols' residence. Each roll of Primadet consisted of a blasting cap connected to shock tube that was 60 feet in length and number 8-delay. The blasting caps were found in a cardboard box filled with empty plastic bottles.

3. *Hunter,* a book by Andrew Macdonald, was found in the house by Agent Leslie Earl. Macdonald had also written *The Turner Diaries,* a book that later investigation would reveal was one of McVeigh's favorites. *Hunter* was of paramount interest to Case Agents Jon Hersley and Larry Tongate. The book provided a graphic, detailed description

of the ingredients of an ammonium nitrate bomb. The book contained 14 fingerprints belonging to Nichols that were spread throughout the book's pages. Three key excerpts from the book were noted, as follows:

> *a. Then he bought himself a used Chevrolet pickup. With the pickup he drove to a large feed and fertilizer store on the edge of town and bought 15 bags of fertilizer-grade ammonium nitrate. He would have bought more, but 1,500 pounds was about as much as he estimated he could manage in one load without damaging his truck. After unloading that in the garage, he stopped at a hardware and farm-supply store and bought two 50-pound*

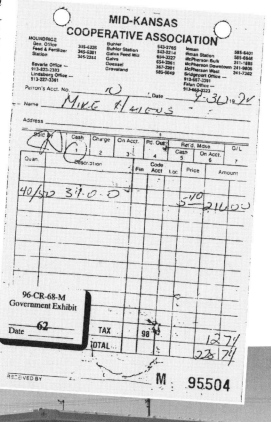

Right: A customer using the name Mike Havens purchased 2,000 pounds of ammonium nitrate on September 30, 1994 from the Mid-Kansas Co-op. This receipt was found in a drawer of Terry Nichols' kitchen cabinet.

Below: Mid-Kansas Co-op in McPherson, Kansas, was where the ammonium nitrate was purchased to build the bomb that destroyed the Murrah Building.

cases of Tovex cartridges and a box of electric detonators. Tovex was an aluminized water-gel dynamite commonly used by farmers and contractors for blasting stumps and boulders.

b. In his rented garage he removed several five-gallon cans of wallpaper adhesive and dozens of rolls of wallpaper from the back of the van, replaced them with four 40-gallon plastic trash barrels he had purchased earlier in the day, and spent the next three hours emptying sacks of ammonium nitrate into the barrels and stirring a fuel-oil sensitizer into the white pellets. The barrels were closely grouped around one of his 50-pound cases of Tovex. It was after four o'clock in the morning when he finally was ready to place a time-delay detonator in the Tovex.

c. At 9:50 AM he turned into the alley which ran behind George's Stationery. He pulled up as close to the bricks as he could, directly outside two of the tightly curtained windows in George's rear wall. He leaned back into the cargo area just long enough to set the detonator for five minutes and start it counting down. Then he stepped out into the alley, locked the door of the van, and made his way back to the busy sidewalk.

4. A debit calling card coupon booklet in the name of Daryl Bridges, 3616 North Van Dyke Rd., Decker, Michigan. The Decker address was the same address used by McVeigh when he registered at the Dreamland Motel in Junction City, Kansas. It was also the same address McVeigh gave when he was booked into the Noble County jail in Perry, Oklahoma. The Bridges calling card had been purchased from the Spotlight Company in Washington, D.C. The coupon booklet contained notations indicating several payments had been made against the calling card. Written notations in the booklet identified $30, $50, and $100 payments, in the form of money orders, made against the calling card on February 17, 1994; August 22, 1994; September 29, 1994; November 7, 1994; January 21, 1995; and February 14, 1995.

5. Thirty two handguns and shoulder weapons were found scattered throughout Nichols' house. Nichols was not a registered, licensed firearms dealer. Where had he obtained such a large cache of weapons?

6. Four 55-gallon barrels were found in the garage of Nichols' residence. Inside one of the barrels were two safe deposit box keys. What did they

Right: A 50-pound bag of ammonium nitrate similar to the 80 bags purchased to build the bomb used in the Oklahoma City bombing.

Below: The receipt for the second purchase of ammonium nitrate made at the Mid-Kansas Co-op on October 18, 1994.

mean? Where had they come from?

7. McVeigh's rifle and green military-issue rucksack were found in the garage of Nichols' home.

8. A liquid fuel meter was found in the garage. What use did Nichols have for such a fuel meter?

9. A Makita cordless drill and two cases of drill bits were also found in Nichols' house.

The FBI machine was beginning to churn, beginning to piece together evidence, one step at a time. The search of Nichols' residence had yielded much evidence. FBI management and Case Agents Hersley and Tongate wanted to know more about Nichols—much more.

As the searches of Nichols' residence continued, agents were dispatched to Mid-Kansas Co-op to obtain records regarding the purchase of ammonium nitrate fertilizer. A second large purchase of 2,000 pounds of ammonium nitrate by Mike Havens was discovered. The second purchase was on October 18, 1994.

Employees of the Co-op knew most of their customers. McPherson was a small, friendly community in central Kansas. Everyone knew each other and each other's business. The Mike Havens' purchases were different. No one at the Co-op knew Mike Havens. They were two very unusual purchases.

Who was Mike Havens? Why did he need 4,000 pounds of ammonium nitrate? In years past, farmers had used ammonium nitrate prill to accelerate the growth of wheat. But, farmers had stopped using ammonium nitrate in this form years before.

The FBI wanted to know where Nichols had obtained the Primadet blasting caps, an explosive, often used to detonate a much larger, more potent blast. Agents were directed to identify any large purchase or theft of explosives in the recent past.

Agents were also sent to the Spotlight Company in Washington, D.C. to find out who Daryl Bridges was. What was his connection to Nichols and the Nichols' family farm in Decker, Michigan?

Terry Nichols Continues to Talk

The goal of Agents Smith and Crabtree was to keep Terry Nichols talking as long as they could. The agents asked Nichols if he had seen McVeigh again after dropping him off near the closed McDonald's restaurant in Junction City, Kansas, in the early morning hours of April 17. Nichols said the next time he heard from McVeigh was Tuesday morning, April 18, when McVeigh called him at his residence around 6:00 a.m.

Nichols said McVeigh told him he would like to use Nichols' pickup for a little while to pick up a few things and look at a few vehicles. Nichols told McVeigh he was planning to attend a sealed bid auction at Fort Riley that same day, but that if McVeigh was not going to need the truck for too long, he could drop Nichols at the auction and then pick him up later. They agreed to meet at 7:30 a.m., according to Nichols, at the same McDonald's where Nichols said he had dropped McVeigh off the previous morning. Nichols said he picked McVeigh up at McDonald's, and they drove to Fort Riley.

Nichols told agents that he asked McVeigh to return for him around noon. When McVeigh was not back by the appointed hour, Nichols continued to look at items for sale. When McVeigh finally arrived, the two drove back to McDonald's.

Nichols said McVeigh then told him he had a room in Junction City, and that he knew someone in town he could possibly get a car from and continue on his way to New York to see his relatives. Nichols said McVeigh told him he had bought the car that he had left in Oklahoma City for a cheap price and he did not know if it was worth fixing.

Nichols told the agents that McVeigh had some personal belongings in a storage shed in Herington and that McVeigh had instructed him to pick them up if McVeigh did not return from his trip back east in time to do so himself. Nichols said this was the last time he saw McVeigh.

Nichols said that on Thursday, April 20, two days after he dropped McVeigh off at the McDonald's in Junction City and one day after the Oklahoma City bombing, he went to the storage shed in Herington and removed McVeigh's belongings. The belongings consisted of a sleeping bag, rucksack, and rifle. Nichols removed the items from the storage shed and put them in the garage at his residence in Herington.

Agents Smith and Crabtree asked Nichols if he had any storage lockers under his control. Nichols said he had maintained a storage locker in Council Grove, Kansas, from October, 1994, until March, 1995, to store his personal belongings.

Herington Storage Units

While the interview of Terry Nichols continued, agents were dispatched in Herington to locate the storage locker that Nichols had earlier told them about. The Herington storage facility, located on the east side of US-77, was owned by Verlin Mueller and his son. The Mueller family also owned Clark Lumber, the only lumber company in Herington. Verlin's sister, Helen Mitchell, served as the bookkeeper for Clark Lumber Company and also for the Herington Storage Units.

Mitchell remembered the day, September 22, 1994, when she rented storage shed #2 to a man who identified himself as Shawn Rivers and provided her with an address of Route 3, Box 83, Marion, Kansas. When asked by Mitchell for a telephone number, the man told her that he did not have a telephone.

Mitchell could not remember anything about the man's description, but did remember thinking it was unusual for a man with a rural post office box address to be in need of a storage shed. She completed and signed the lease agreement and asked Rivers to also sign the

Above: **A man using the name Shawn Rivers rented storage shed #2 at the Herington Storage Units. FBI experts later identified eight of McVeigh's fingerprints on the rental agreement.**

Below: **An aerial view of the Herington Storage Units in Herington, Kansas.**

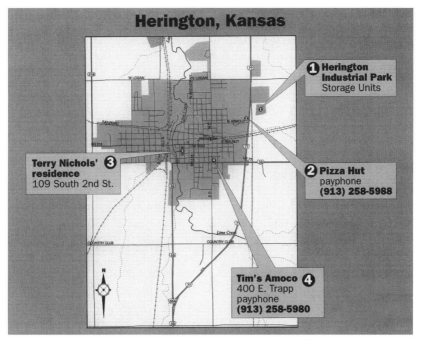

Herington, Kansas

1 Herington Industrial Park
Storage Units

3 Terry Nichols' residence
109 South 2nd St.

2 Pizza Hut payphone
(913) 258-5988

4 Tim's Amoco
400 E. Trapp payphone
(913) 258-5980

A map of Herington, Kansas, showing the close proximity of Terry Nichols' residence to the storage units at the Herington Industrial Park and the payphone at Tim's Amoco, which was later identified as the telephone McVeigh used to call Nichols on Easter Sunday afternoon.

agreement. The man gave Mitchell $80.00 cash, covering four months rental, and left.

Mitchell said she was somewhat surprised when Rivers came back into the lumber company only a month later, on October 23, 1994, and made another $80.00 cash payment on storage shed #2, covering the storage rental until May 22, 1995.

One of the benefits in Nichols deciding to talk to agents was the real-time lead information being developed. The ability to immediately check out Nichol's statements, even though much of his information turned out to be lies or half-truths, was an enormous benefit to investigators. Much of the information would have eventually been uncovered, but Nichols' information saved the FBI time and allowed witnesses to be interviewed within days while their memories were fresh.

An example was the Herington storage shed. When agents arrived, they noticed large tire tracks near storage shed #2. A perimeter was immediately established and agents were posted until a search could be conducted the following day and personnel from the FBI Laboratory could determine the likely source of the impressions before spring rains hit central Kansas.

Agents Hersley and Tongate pondered several questions. Why had Nichols removed McVeigh's belongings from the Herington storage shed on April 20, only two days after McVeigh allegedly told Nichols he was going back east to visit relatives? After all, McVeigh had paid the rent on the Herington storage shed up to May 22, 1995. How did Nichols already know on April 20 that McVeigh was not coming back? Nichols had removed McVeigh's belongings from the storage shed before any public announcement that McVeigh had been arrested.

Eyewitness Sightings

A s the FBI case agents continued to piece together more information about McVeigh and Nichols, other agents in Oklahoma City, such as John Hippard and Lou Ann Sandstrom, were following up on leads that resulted from alleged eyewitness sightings in the vicinity of the Murrah Building on the morning of the bombing.

One such witness, identified here with the initials M.A., told FBI Agent Martin Maag that he was in downtown Oklahoma City on the morning of the bombing looking for temporary work. The man said he saw two white males, Middle Eastern in appearance, running north across Northwest Fifth Street, away from the Murrah Building, about five minutes before the explosion. M.A. said the two white males entered a dark brown Chevrolet pickup. He described the two men as wearing blue jeans, white shirts, black vests, and dark colored boots. He also told agents the pickup had smoked windows and a smoke colored bug guard. M.A. said the pickup sped away on Northwest Fifth and turned north onto Hudson Avenue, which is a one-way, southbound street.

Shortly after Agent Maag reported the results of his conversation with M.A. to FBI managers, a decision was made to put out an all points bulletin, or BOLO, be on the lookout, for a dark brown Chevrolet pickup, possibly carrying two white males of Middle Eastern appearance. The news media jumped on the announcement and began broadcasting the description of the brown pickup and its possible occupants. Literally hundreds of telephone calls were received on an FBI telephone hot line.

Witnesses reported seeing a brown pickup at various locations all over Oklahoma City, the state of Oklahoma, and in neighboring states. Agents were assigned these leads as they came in. Brown pickup sightings were reported in parking lots, at stores, on city streets, almost anywhere one could imagine. The problem that agents faced was that callers were not able to provide license plate numbers and by the time agents were able to follow up on the alleged sightings, the vehicles were no longer at the reported locations. However, in many other instances, the vehicle owners were identified and eliminated one by one as suspect vehicles in the Oklahoma City bombing.

One such caller, G.S., reported that he was driving in the southbound lanes of Interstate 35, at approximately 10:35 a.m., on Wednesday morning, April 19, when he saw Timothy McVeigh, handcuffed with his hands behind his back, being led to a squad car. G.S. said he noticed a brown and white truck 20 yards ahead of the squad car and on the same shoulder of the road. The witness reported that the man driving the pickup was turned around with his arm outside the window and was backing up toward the squad car.

Another caller, K.B., said he was driving north on Interstate 35 at about 10:30 a.m. on the morning of the bombing when he saw McVeigh being arrested. K.B. reported he saw a 1974 or 1975 Chevrolet pickup stopped on the exit ramp immediately to the north of the arrest location. He described the pickup as having been primed with rust brown primer paint.

However, in pretrial interviews, Trooper Charlie Hanger told Agent Hersley and Prosecutor Mendeloff that he was absolutely certain there was no brown pickup or any other vehicle parked along Interstate 35 when he made the stop and arrest of McVeigh. Hanger said he was certain he would have noticed such a vehicle parked on the shoulder or exit ramp of the highway to the north of the arrest location. Traffic stops are one of the most dangerous contacts law enforcement officers have with civilians, and troopers are trained to be aware of their surroundings. Trooper Hanger reminded Hersley and Mendeloff he was on high alert when he made the stop of McVeigh because of the shooting involving a trooper two weeks before in the same area.

In the days following the bombing, agents conducted follow up interviews of M.A., the witness who initially gave the information about the brown pickup with Middle Eastern occupants. M.A. had difficulty remembering what he had previously told Agent Maag. His subsequent statements were inconsistent with his initial statement in that he now told agents that the brown pickup had turned south on Hudson.

M.A. also gave new information—now saying he remembered the pickup had a red license plate with white lettering. He said he did not get a good enough look at the license plate to see the number or state of origin. In assessing the accuracy and reliability of the man's alleged sighting, Agent Hersley and other agents assigned to the Oklahoma City Command Post had to consider that M.A. had provided an unusually detailed description of not only the brown pickup, but also the two alleged Middle Eastern males who reportedly had sped away in the vehicle.

The detailed description of M.A.'s reported sighting, coupled with the fact that his observations were made before the bombing when there was really no reason for him to focus on the brown pickup or its occupants, caused Hersley and other agents to question the accuracy and reliability of the alleged sighting. Nevertheless, agents continued to cover all leads regarding brown pickup sightings until it became no longer practical to do so. Hundreds of man-hours were exhausted in the process.

Following are additional examples of reported sightings of brown pickup trucks reported to the FBI:

1. D.C. reported seeing a brown pickup with a bug catcher on the front of it double parked outside the Murrah Building on April 18, 1995 at approximately noon. She said the driver of the brown pickup, a white male in his approximate 50s and wearing a ball cap, drove slowly away

from the building. She said that shortly after the pickup drove away, she saw a Ryder truck drive by the building very slowly. This sighting was reported on May 11, 1995.

2. E.C. reported seeing a Ryder truck, a brown pickup, and an old Mercury with Arizona tags at the EconoLodge in Oklahoma City on April 18, 1995, at approximately 1:30 p.m. E.C. reported that McVeigh was standing by the Ryder truck and was wearing a military uniform. She said that John Doe #2 was also present and was talking to McVeigh. This sighting was reported on June 24, 1995.

3. I.W. reported seeing McVeigh and John Doe #2 buying gasoline at the Star Mart Conoco in Guthrie on April 18, 1995, at approximately 1:30 p.m. She said there was a Ryder truck, an old yellow car, and a brown Chevrolet pickup at the Star Mart at the same time McVeigh and John Doe #2 were there. This sighting was reported on April 24, 1995.

4. D.S. reported seeing the driver of an old yellow car and the driver of a brown pickup with Arkansas tags talking in the parking lot of the Murrah Building on April 18, 1995, at approximately 4:15 p.m. The driver of the brown pickup was Native American, and the driver of the yellow car looked like John Doe #2. D.S. described this man as a white male with brown hair pulled back in a ponytail. He said the men sped away when he beeped his horn at them. This sighting was reported on April 22, 1995.

5. L.M. reported seeing a white man, about 40 years old with a gray beard, run out of the Murrah Building on April 19, 1995, at approximately 8:40 a.m. She said the man entered a blue pickup with a red bug shield. This sighting was reported on December 7, 1995.

6. M.S. reported seeing two men with dark complexions, wearing blue trench coats, walk out of the Murrah Building and across Northwest Fifth Street on April 19, 1995, at approximately 8:55 a.m. She said the two men entered a brown pickup, where a third person wearing a mask was waiting. The pickup screeched its tires and sped away. This sighting was reported on April 24, 1995.

7. D.J. reported seeing two white males run across Northwest Fifth Street away from the Murrah Building toward a newer model brown Ford pickup with dark tinted windows on April 19, 1995, at approximately

9:01 a.m. D.J. said one of the men, whom he later identified as Timothy McVeigh, was wearing jogging pants, possibly blue with a white 6-inch angled stripe on one leg. D.J. said the second man was about 5'8", stocky build, with black hair and a dark complexion. This sighting was reported on April 21, 1995.

As with the hundreds of other brown pickup sightings, none of the above reported eyewitnesses were able to provide license plate numbers of the vehicles they allegedly observed. What bothered Case Agents Hersley and Tongate about the veracity of these sightings was that most of them were not reported until weeks or months after the bombing and after vehicle descriptions had been reported by television and newspapers.

Another caller, R.C., the owner of a motel in the Oklahoma City metropolitan area, said he was certain McVeigh, accompanied by three Middle Eastern males, had stayed at his motel the night before the Oklahoma City bombing. Agents Hersley and Zimms were dispatched to interview R.C. in person.

Initially, it was difficult for the agents to assess the accuracy and reliability of R.C.'s statements. Hersley and Zimms had conducted thousands of witness interviews in the more than ten years they worked together on the FBI Organized Crime/Drug Squad in Oklahoma City. They had learned not to rush, to let the witness talk, and to provide detail about what they had seen.

As R.C. continued, he became inconsistent in his reported observations. Not only did he state that McVeigh and the three alleged Middle Eastern men had been guests at his motel on the night before the bombing, but also that the men had parked the yellow Mercury and the yellow Ryder truck at the motel.

R.C. told agents that in February, 1995, he had another guest at his motel who strongly resembled James Nichols in appearance. R.C. said this motel guest had stored up to 80 bags of fertilizer in his motel room on the second floor. He also said that during this same time period, one of the guests at the motel had brought a large Ryder truck to the motel, and that he had observed a large number of barrels in the back of this truck.

R.C. said that when the truck departed, he noticed a large diesel spill in the motel parking lot where the truck had been parked. Agents

Hersley and Zimms asked for, and received, a copy of a guest registration card for the man who stayed at the motel in February. The FBI interviewed the man, a resident of a rural Oklahoma town, who had stayed at R.C.'s motel, as was reported. However, he was in Oklahoma City on legitimate business in February, 1995. The man was certainly not James Nichols, and he had neither a Ryder truck nor 80 bags of fertilizer at the motel.

As Agents Hersley and Zimms continued the interview, R.C. was asked if he had any conversations with any television reporters regarding his reported sightings. R.C. informed the agents that he had several conversations with Jayna Davis, a reporter from KFOR-TV in Oklahoma City, and that he had discussed his alleged sighting of McVeigh and the Middle Eastern men at his motel on the evening before the Oklahoma City bombing in great detail with this reporter on more than one occasion.

In subsequent telephone conversations, R.C. informed Agents Hersley and Jimmy Judd that he was no longer certain of the observations he had made at his motel and that he believed the truck he had seen at his motel that evening was white rather than yellow.

R.C. was another example of thousands of such alleged sightings reported to the FBI in the weeks and months after the bombing.

Truck Parts

As FBI agents continued to interview witnesses in Oklahoma and Kansas, other agents were methodically searching the area around the Murrah Building. The Ryder truck rear axle assembly had been found in front of the Regency Tower Apartments. The rear bumper and Florida license plate of the truck had been found near the Athenia Building on the north side of Northwest Fifth Street east of the Regency Tower Apartments.

By Thursday morning, April 20, agents had divided the search area into quadrants so that grid searches could be conducted. The search was conducted systematically, block by block, building by building, and rooftop by rooftop. Parking lots, sidewalks, alleys, and building interiors were searched. The search yielded many additional Ryder truck parts:

1. Front axle of the truck - found near Northwest Fifth Street and Broadway Avenue.

2. Rear axle gear part - found in the parking lot of the Fred Jones automobile dealership on Northwest Fifth Street about two blocks west of the Murrah Building.
3. Front wheel tire rim - found in front of the Murrah Building.
4. Front wheel tire rim - found in front of the Journal Record Building.
5. Rear wheel tire rim - found in front of the Murrah Building.
6. Rear wheel tire rim - found in front of the Murrah Building, east of Harvey Avenue.
7. Rear wheel tire rim - found on the south side of Northwest Fifth Street, west of Harvey Avenue, across from the Regency Tower Apartments.
8. Piece of Ryder box embedded with ammonium nitrate crystalline - found in parking lot between the Murrah Building and the Journal Record Building.
9. Frame rail piece - found in the parking lot between the Murrah Building and the Journal Record Building.
10. Ford logo emblem - found in front of the YMCA building.
11. Rear leaf spring - found near Northwest Sixth Street and Harvey Avenue.
12. Rear door-latch assembly - found on the eighth floor of the Regency Tower Apartments.
13. Frame rail piece - found on the roof of a building on Northwest Sixth Street east of Robinson Avenue.
14. Spindle rod connector - found in Bentley's Carpet Company at Northwest Fifth Street and Broadway Avenue.
15. Ryder truck key - found in the alley behind the YMCA Building.

The Ford Motor Company, in an effort to assist the investigation, voluntarily repurchased a 1993 Ford truck that was identical in all respects to the truck used in the bombing. The repurchased vehicle was the very next truck in the assembly line process at the Ford Motor Production Plant when the actual truck used in the bombing was manufactured. Ford disassembled and labeled the repurchased truck parts for comparison with the actual bomb truck parts found in the search of the multi-block crime scene. This process was extremely beneficial to investigators in corroborating the theory that only one truck was used in the bombing. This repurchased truck was later reassembled in the courtroom of both federal trials and Ford Motor Company engineer Ed Paddock testified to the comparisons.

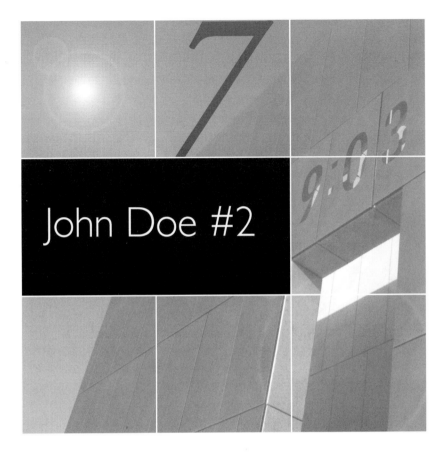

John Doe #2

Following the arrest of Timothy McVeigh and the release of the composite drawings of John Doe #1 and John Doe #2 to the news media on Thursday afternoon, April 20, the FBI received thousands of telephone calls of reported sightings of McVeigh, Nichols, and the two individuals depicted in the composite drawings.

Caller M.M. advised the FBI that at approximately 8:30 a.m. on the morning of the bombing, a white male driving a Ryder truck pulled into his business near Northwest Tenth Street and Hudson Avenue in downtown Oklahoma City. M.M. said he was certain the driver of the truck was McVeigh and that McVeigh was accompanied by another person seated in the passenger seat of the Ryder truck. M.M. reported that the second person had a cap pulled down over his head, which prevented him from getting a look at this person.

M.M. said McVeigh asked him for directions to the Murrah Building during a 5 to 10-minute conversation. McVeigh and the other person in the Ryder truck, according to M.M., then waited in the parking lot of his business for another 8-10 minutes before leaving.

In assessing the accuracy and reliability of M.M.'s alleged sighting, Agent Hersley and other agents assigned to the Oklahoma City Command Post had to consider whether or not it was reasonable that McVeigh would need to stop and ask for directions to the Murrah Building on the morning of the bombing. McVeigh had trained extensively in the military in reconnaissance missions. Was it possible that someone with this kind of training would not know the exact location of his target, if in fact, McVeigh was involved in the bombing, as it now appeared? Also, agents had to consider whether or not McVeigh or anyone else responsible for the bombing would have risked a lengthy conversation with a witness who could later provide a detailed description of the man to authorities.

Agent Hersley was becoming intimately acquainted with the character and actions of McVeigh. He was certain McVeigh would never have waited until the morning of the bombing to identify the exact location of his target.

The following are examples of the thousands of sightings of John Doe #2 and others allegedly connected to the Oklahoma City bombing.

1. J.A. reported seeing McVeigh and Terry Nichols standing on the corner of Northwest Fifth Street and Robinson Avenue near the YMCA on April 13 or 14 at approximately 12:15 p.m. She said a Ryder truck and McVeigh's car were also parked at the YMCA at that time. This sighting was reported on June 20, 1995.

2. M.B. reported seeing McVeigh driving a yellow Mercury north on Interstate 35 near the intersection of Interstate 40 in Oklahoma City on April 16, 1995, at approximately 11:00 a.m. He said McVeigh had a passenger in the Mercury with him, and the passenger appeared to be nervous. This sighting was reported on June 25, 1995.

3. D.C. reported seeing McVeigh and John Doe #2 buying gas at a Quick Trip Store at 46th Street and Peoria in Tulsa, Oklahoma, on April 16, 1995, at approximately 4:00 p.m. She said McVeigh and John Doe #2 were driving a 20-foot Ryder truck and were towing a late 1970s model Mercury. This sighting was reported on September 9, 1995.

4. R.C. reported seeing two men who resembled McVeigh and John Doe #2 at the EconoFoods Store on East Chestnut in Junction City, Kansas, on April 13, 1995, at approximately 9:00 p.m. She described the man she believed was John Doe #2 as being a white male, 25 years old, 6' tall, 180 pounds, muscular build and possibly a little taller than the first man, thick dark hair worn in a GI-type cut, olive complexion, very handsome, no glasses or moustache. She said this man had a tattoo on one of his arms and wore a short sleeve light colored shirt, dark blue jeans, and light colored shoes. This sighting was reported on May 6, 1995.

5. M.C. reported seeing McVeigh and John Doe #2 near the corner of Northwest Sixth and Harvey in Oklahoma City on April 19, 1995, at approximately 9:10 a.m. She said she heard McVeigh and John Doe #2 laughing at the blood-covered victims. She described John Doe #2 as an Indian male, 5'6" - 5'7", stocky muscular build, dark hair, wearing sunglasses and denim shorts. This sighting was reported on April 26, 1995.

6. L.D. reported he saw McVeigh and John Doe #2 with a large Ryder truck and a yellow Mercury Marquis in the parking lot of the AA Club on North Western Avenue in Oklahoma City on April 18, 1995, at approximately 6:30 a.m. This sighting was reported on May 2, 1995.

7. G.J. reported seeing McVeigh and another man standing by an old yellow Mercury in the alley behind Betty K's Sub Shop, located south of Northwest Fifth Street and west of Broadway in Oklahoma City on April 19, 1995, at approximately 9:25 a.m. G.J. was in the Murrah Building when it exploded. She said McVeigh asked her what had happened and how many people had been killed. She initially reported this sighting on April 24, 1995, but did not state that she recognized one of the men as McVeigh until she was again interviewed on August 14, 1995, and September 11, 1995.

8. M.K. reported seeing McVeigh and John Doe #2 having breakfast at the Braum's store on Northwest 23rd Street in Oklahoma City on April 18, 1995, at approximately 10:40 a.m. This sighting was reported on May 14, 1995.

9. A.L. reported seeing a Ryder truck parked in front of her house on April 18, 1995, at approximately 7:45 p.m. The next day, at approximately

8:45 a.m, she saw two males resembling McVeigh and John Doe #2 in the Ryder truck, which was now blocking her driveway. McVeigh and John Doe #2 later moved the truck out of her way. This sighting was reported on April 24, 1995.

The sightings of John Doe #2 were not limited to the Oklahoma City area. After McVeigh and Terry Nichols were arrested, alleged sightings of various groupings of McVeigh, Nichols, and John Doe #2 intensified, not only in Oklahoma but also in Kansas, Arizona, New York, and many other states.

In Herington, Kansas, the owner of a restaurant told agents that Nichols, McVeigh, and John Doe #2 were in the diner the morning of the bombing. The woman said that when she asked them where they were headed, John Doe #2 said, "Oklahoma." The restaurant owner said McVeigh then gave John Doe #2 a look that ended the conversation.

Two clerks at the Great Western Motel in Junction City, Kansas, told the FBI they saw John Doe #2 driving a Ryder truck at the motel on April 17. One clerk said the person paid for a room in cash, but the other clerk said he paid with a $50 traveler's check. A thorough investigation of individuals staying at the motel failed to produce any evidence of a person with a Ryder truck on April 17. Bank records revealed that no guests paid for a room with traveler's checks until April 21, two days after the bombing.

These examples of John Doe #2 sightings are only a few of the thousands of reported sightings received by the FBI in the months after the bombing. They are set forth to provide a glimpse of the number and types of sightings being reported to the FBI hotline and followed up by agents across the nation.

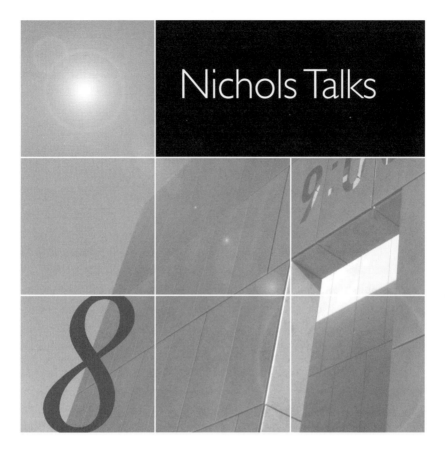

Nichols Talks

During the afternoon and evening of Friday, April 21, Agents Smith and Crabtree continued to elicit information from Terry Nichols at the Herington police station. Nichols said he first heard about the bombing on Thursday when he was at the cable television store in Herington to get service hooked up at his house. He said that after seeing a news report about the bombing at the cable television store, he bought three different newspapers. He said he had not heard anything about the bombing until Thursday because the television at his house had little reception until after he had the cable service hooked up Friday morning at 9:00 a.m.

Nichols said he received a telephone call Friday morning from his ex-wife, Lana Padilla, who was upset that Nichols had told their son, Josh, about $3,000 cash that Nichols had given to Lana for Josh in January,

1995. Lana was supposed to open an account for Josh with the money and send the bank statement to Nichols as proof she had done as Nichols instructed with the money. Nichols said that despite Lana's promise, he never received the bank statement.

When he got off the phone with Lana, Nichols' current wife, Marife, began complaining to him that she wanted to go home to the Philippines because she had friends there and none in Kansas. Marife told Nichols, "You got friends like Tim." Marife complained to Nichols that McVeigh lived his life on the edge, using McVeigh's fast driving as an example. Marife's comments came before she and her husband heard that McVeigh had been arrested.

Later on Friday morning while Nichols was away from his house, he heard his name mentioned on a radio broadcast regarding the Oklahoma City bombing. As he re-entered the house, he noticed Marife was getting off the phone with one of her friends, a man named Raymond in California. Marife and Raymond, who had met in the Philippines, had heard about the Oklahoma City bombing and were "joking about McVeigh possibly having been involved."

Nichols said it was at about this same time that Marife told Nichols she did not believe him when he said his name had been mentioned on the radio. Nichols said he turned the television to a news station for about 15 minutes and he and Marife heard Janet Reno giving what appeared to be a press conference. Nichols said, "I then heard Tim's name on the television for the first time."

Nichols said he thought and swore that he could not believe it was McVeigh, because McVeigh had said he was headed back to see his family in New York, and now he was in Oklahoma. Nichols said when he heard McVeigh's name on television, he figured out that his own name was being mentioned by newsmen because he and McVeigh were friends. Nichols said he asked himself, "How am I involved? How am I connected to it?" He said he thought about McVeigh, "I must not have known him that well for him to do that."

Nichols said that he and McVeigh had gone their separate ways recently because McVeigh did not like Nichols' practical jokes. McVeigh had even told Marife that he did not like "all the joking around." Regarding his possible involvement in the bombing, Nichols told agents, "I feel upset that I am involved, in a sense, because of him, and knowing that I am not. I feel I cannot trust anyone any more than Tim. I would be shocked if he implicated me. Tim takes responsibility for his actions and lives up to his arrangements." In discussing McVeigh's possible involvement in the bombing, Nichols said he could not see why McVeigh would do it. He said McVeigh was going to receive an inheritance shortly from his grandfather's estate and would be able to do whatever he wanted. "So why would he do a bombing?" Nichols thought.

Marife Nichols

Agents Gene Thomeczek and Sheila Dobson spoke with Marife Nichols while her husband was being interviewed by Agents Smith and Crabtree at the Herington police station. Marife talked freely with the agents and began to look upon them as her new found friends. Agent Thomeczek was a veteran investigator and knew how to conduct an interview. Marife befriended the agent and looked at him as a father figure. Agent Dobson was a young, attractive professional, the perfect compliment to Thomeczek. Marife related to Dobson almost immediately. During the next several days, Marife told the agents that McVeigh was Nichols' best friend. She had grown jealous of the time and attention Nichols gave to McVeigh.

Marife said that McVeigh had visited them at their home in Michigan while traveling from New York to Arizona. Terry and Marife helped McVeigh move from an apartment on Dysinger Road in Pendleton, New York, to the Nichols' farmhouse in Decker, Michigan, in early 1993, about a year after McVeigh had completed his military service.

Marife said the last time she had seen McVeigh before his arrest on April 19, was in September, 1994, when McVeigh came to live with her and her husband in Marion, Kansas. Nichols had begun working for an area rancher, Tim Donahue, in March, 1994.

Marife said McVeigh and her husband frequently discussed the Waco tragedy. Both of them believed the government had set fire to the Waco compound. They spoke openly about their opinions. Marife stopped short of telling the agents that McVeigh and her husband spoke of retaliation against the government.

During the 1994 visit, Terry announced plans to go on the road with McVeigh to gun shows, and Marife knew this meant her husband would not be home very much. She said Terry gave her one week to decide whether she wanted to travel with him. She was upset and wanted to return to the Philippines, which she did on September 18, 1994. Marife did not return until March 17, 1995, after Nichols went to the Philippines to persuade her to come back to the United States.

Marife said that after she returned to Kansas, Terry was involved in selling army surplus items at gun shows. Marife confirmed what Nichols' former wife, Lana Padilla, had earlier told the FBI in Las Vegas. Her husband had never been able to keep a steady job. She said Nichols bought surplus items at Fort Riley, stored them in a shed behind their house, and resold the items through personal contacts with individuals and companies and at gun shows.

Marife said she knew of no storage facilities that were rented by her husband for the purpose of storing the army surplus items or for any other reason. Marife said her husband also sold fertilizer in small containers at gun shows. Nichols told Marife that he had purchased an unspecified amount of fertilizer in prill form. She said Terry crushed the prills into powder and sold it at the gun shows as house-plant fertilizer. Marife said she knew of no inheritance received by her husband. She said he had sold his house and 80-acre farm in Michigan. She did not know the sale price, but believed it was a large sum of money, maybe as much as $100,000, that Terry used to purchase stocks and coins. She said Terry paid all of his bills in cash or with postal money orders.

Marife told Agents Thomeczek and Dobson that as she and her husband were leaving their house through the garage on Friday afternoon, April 21, to go to the surplus store, Terry commented to her that he needed to sell the fuel meter which she noticed was still in the garage.

Terry Nichols

Meanwhile, Agents Smith and Crabtree continued to interview Terry Nichols. Nichols told the agents that about a month before, he bought two 50-pound bags of ammonium nitrate fertilizer from the Manhattan Elevator. He claimed to still have the receipt for this purchase. Nichols said he had purchased the fertilizer because he was going to sell it as plant food in one-pound bags for $5 to $10 at gun shows.

Nichols said he had sold some of the fertilizer but that he had put what remained of the ammonium nitrate on his lawn earlier Friday morning.

He said he did not mention this ammonium nitrate earlier in the interview because, "It would make me look guilty to a jury." He added that he believed people found in possession of ammonium nitrate would be potential suspects in the bombing in Oklahoma City. The agents asked Nichols if he really thought every farmer and homeowner would be a potential suspect based solely on the fact they had ammonium nitrate, and he said he did.

Nichols spent a great deal of time talking about his army service and his marriages to Lana Padilla and Marife, and the places they had lived. He confirmed Marife's statement that McVeigh wanted him to sell guns with McVeigh at gun shows and that Marife despised the idea. Nichols said that after Marife went to the Philippines, he and McVeigh traveled together to gun shows. They usually pooled their money, deducting their expenses, and split any resulting profits. Nichols said he always paid his expenses in cash and did not have a checking or savings account or credit cards. He said he did not pay taxes and did not believe in the federal income tax system.

Nichols said when he returned from the Philippines after persuading Marife to come back to Kansas, he began looking for a house in central Kansas, ultimately buying the house on Second Street in Herington.

Nichols said he had heard people remark at gun shows that the FBI and the ATF went to Waco and murdered the people there and that something should be done about it. Nichols said he would respond to these people's comments with the word, "possibly." He said those people believed the government was getting out of hand, and that he, too, felt that way on occasion. Nichols said some of these people get hyped up and want to do something about it.

Nichols was asked if McVeigh had said anything on the trip from Oklahoma City to Junction City, on Sunday night and Monday morning, that caused him to believe McVeigh was involved in the Oklahoma City bombing. Nichols answered, "Yes, McVeigh was much more hyped about Waco than I was."

Nichols said he had noticed a change in McVeigh after McVeigh returned from Desert Storm. He knew McVeigh tried out for the Army Special Forces, but decided to quit while on a training run. McVeigh left the Army a short time later, and Nichols presumed he received an honorable discharge. He said McVeigh was "pissed off" at his sergeant before he was discharged.

Nichols described McVeigh as a "loner," whom he believed "has the knowledge to build a bomb, and could be capable of doing it." When asked directly if Nichols believed McVeigh was involved in the Oklahoma City bombing, Nichols answered, "I suspect it now."

Nichols said he recently had attended a gun show in Tulsa, Oklahoma, where he talked to a man about explosives. He said he learned there are a lot of chemicals involved in making an explosive, including ammonium nitrate and potassium. Nichols said that nitrogen, potassium, and phosphorous from fertilizers can be used for bombs.

Nichols said he also had read bomb-making articles that come across the table at gun shows. Nichols would review the articles and talk to McVeigh about the different types of bombs and whether or not they would work. The pair discussed whether or not one bomb was better than another. Nichols told the agents that McVeigh knew as much about making bombs as he did. He said McVeigh had a lot of free time and liked to busy himself reading about guns and bombs.

Nichols then gave agents specific details of how to build a bomb. He admitted he knew how to make a bomb from fertilizer. He also demonstrated great knowledge of the use of blasting caps and diesel fuel in the making of a bomb. Nichols said he had talked with different people at gun shows and admitted he had heard that certain types of fertilizer are needed to make a bomb, specifically nitrogen-based fertilizer.

He said a farmer had stopped by his booth at one of the gun shows and talked to him about mixing ammonium nitrate and diesel fuel to blow tree stumps from the ground. He heard from another individual at a gun show that a mixture of ammonium nitrate and diesel fuel is also used to cause explosions at rock quarries. When asked by the agents of his own first hand knowledge about bomb making, Nichols said he had not made any bombs himself.

Nichols said he was aware of books that explained the ratios for mixing bombs using fertilizer and said he assumed electricity could be used to detonate an ammonium nitrate bomb. He volunteered that he knew electric blasting caps could be used to detonate a bomb. He also said he was aware that ammonium nitrate could be purchased at the farm elevator in Junction City, Kansas.

Nichols admitted having previously rented storage units in Herington and Council Grove, Kansas. When asked about several large barrels in his garage, Nichols said he bought them from the dump in Marion, Kansas. Nichols said the fuel meter in his garage was purchased at Fort Riley at a fraction of its worth, and he intended to resell it.

At approximately 11:15 p.m. on Friday night, Nichols was allowed to listen to a tape recorded message from his son, Josh, and his ex-wife Lana Padilla, both of whom urged him to cooperate with authorities.

At approximately 12:03 a.m. on Saturday morning, Nichols was handed a four-page letter that had been turned over to the FBI in Las Vegas by Lana Padilla. The letter consisted of Nichols' handwritten notes found by Padilla behind the kitchen drawer in her Las Vegas home after Nichols had departed for the Philippines in mid-November, 1994.

One page was a letter that Nichols wrote to McVeigh. Another page was entitled, "Pick up storage." Another was entitled, "Read and do immediately," and the last page was the reverse side of the Read and do immediately letter. Nichols read the letters, and then remarked, "I wrote it because I did not have a will." Nichols said he sent these letters to Padilla, with the instructions to send the letters to McVeigh in the event of his death in the Philippines before January, 1995.

Nichols was asked if he would be willing to take a polygraph examination that could be used by agents to determine if he was telling the truth. He declined the polygraph, saying he believed they were unreliable. At the conclusion of the interview early Saturday morning, Nichols was placed under arrest as a material witness to the bombing in Oklahoma City.

As in the arrest of McVeigh in Perry, Oklahoma, an angry crowd had gathered outside the Herington police station. As a precaution, a convoy of police and FBI vehicles escorted Nichols to the Dickinson County jail in Abilene, Kansas, for an appearance before a federal judge.

At 1:58 p.m. on Saturday, April 22, Nichols was picked up in Abilene by FBI Agents Smith and Crabtree to take him for an appearance in federal court in Wichita, Kansas.

During the ride from Abilene to Wichita, Nichols told the agents that the only things present in his residence in Herington that could harm anyone were guns that he kept loaded for his protection and the protection of his family. Nichols denied the presence of any booby traps or similar devices that might harm someone.

After the agents arrived with Nichols at the federal courthouse in Wichita, he was asked if he wanted to speak further with them while waiting for his court appearance. Nichols agreed and told the agents he had used an alias, Ken Parker, in Council Grove, Kansas, and that he had also used the alias, Jim Kyle. Nichols said he believed McVeigh had used the aliases, Tim Tuttle and Shawn Rivers. He said he first started using alias names at the insistence of McVeigh, and that McVeigh had tried to get him to do so for quite some time.

Nichols said he had "parted ways" with McVeigh the previous fall because,"The ways we both live did not jive." When asked if either he or his brother, James Nichols, belonged to the Michigan Militia or any similar group, Nichols answered that it would surprise him to learn that James was involved with the Michigan Militia. When asked why someone would want to be a member of such a group, Nichols responded, "I believe in the Constitution." Nichols was afforded his appearance before the federal judge in Wichita and was transferred to the custody of the United States Marshal.

Among Nichols' personal belongings at the time of his arrest early Saturday morning was a receipt from a Wal-Mart store in Arkansas City, Kansas. The receipt was dated April 13, 1995, and was time stamped 5:42 p.m. It referenced the purchase of four quarts of oil and an oil filter. The receipt would later prove valuable in the investigation.

Adding to
the Evidence

The investigation at the Dreamland Motel had confirmed that
McVeigh was registered at the motel from April 14-18, 1995.
Agents learned from the motel's owner, Lea McGown, that telephone calls made from the individual rooms were recorded onto a paper
printout. A check of the motel's phone records regarding room 25 during
the time McVeigh was registered determined that four separate calls were
made from the room between April 14 and April 18:

1. On Saturday, April 15, 1995, a call was made from room 25 at 9:36
   a.m., using the Bridges calling card, to the home of Terry Nichols.
   Phone records indicated this call was not answered.

2. On Saturday, April 15, 1995, two calls were made from room 25 to the
   Hunam Palace Restaurant in Junction City, Kansas. The first call was

made at 4:58 p.m. and lasted 1 minute and 42 seconds and the second call was made at 5:46 p.m. and lasted only 30 seconds.

3. On Monday, April 17, 1995, a call was made from room 25 at 9:25 a.m., using the Bridges calling card, to the home of Terry Nichols. The call lasted 57 seconds.

Yuhua Bai

Yuhua Bai was the owner of the Hunam Palace Restaurant in Junction City, Kansas. She was a remarkable, middle-aged woman of Chinese descent. Bai held several advanced college degrees, but it was a struggle for her to speak the English language. Her restaurant was located a short distance from Fort Riley where federal agents were quick to learn Tim McVeigh, Terry Nichols, and a third friend, Michael Fortier, were stationed after completion of basic training.

Bai explained to agents that her restaurant received a large number of telephone delivery orders. She had a simple record keeping system. When a customer called, the order was written on a telephone order log. This log contained the time of the call, a description and price of the food that was ordered, as well as the name of the customer and the delivery location.

Next to the time of the call entry, the delivery person placed his initials. A delivery receipt was also prepared for each order. These receipts and the telephone order log were placed into a brown

The delivery receipt from the Hunam Palace Chinese restaurant in Junction City, Kansas, showing a customer named Kling ordered food for delivery to Room 25 at the Dreamland Motel.

paper sack at the end of the day and were maintained for a month, at which time they were thrown out one day at a time and replaced with records for the same day of the following month.

Bai's records revealed that on Saturday, April 15, at approximately 5:00 p.m., a customer called the restaurant requesting an order of Moo Goo Gai Pan. The caller requested the order be delivered to room 25 at the Dreamland Motel. When Bai asked for a name, the caller responded "Kling." Bai entered the request onto the telephone order log and delivery receipt, "One order of Moo Goo Gai Pan - Mr. Kling, Room 25 at the Dreamland Motel." The total price was $9.65. The order request was now a part of Ms. Bai's records at Hunam's, at least for the next month.

Unfortunately for Kling, the receipts were still on hand when the FBI arrived and were now part of the FBI's mounting evidence against Tim McVeigh. Agents knew that Kling was the same name used by the man who had rented the suspected bomb truck from Elliott's Body Shop on April 17. Bai's order form indicated that employee Jeff Davis had made the delivery to the Dreamland Motel.

When contacted by the FBI, Davis confirmed he had made the delivery to a man named Kling in room 25 of the Dreamland Motel. He described Kling as a white male, about 28-29 years old, approximately 6'0", 180 pounds, with a light complexion. He said the man was clean cut with short, sandy color hair about 1-2 inches long and no facial hair. He was dressed in casual clothes. Davis said he could not remember the man's face because he made too many deliveries. However, the description he provided fit McVeigh almost perfectly.

Firestone Store

When Tim McVeigh was arrested on the morning of the bombing, he told Trooper Charlie Hanger he had purchased the yellow Mercury he was driving from Tom at the Firestone Store in Junction City, Kansas. Within hours of learning the information, FBI agents were dispatched to the Firestone Store in Junction City to learn what they could from Tom Manning.

Manning remembered McVeigh. He had worked on McVeigh's car in past years while McVeigh was stationed at Fort Riley. Manning said that when McVeigh first came into the store on Friday morning, April 14, he

The bill of sale on the 1977 yellow Mercury Marquis purchased by Timothy McVeigh on April 14, 1995, from Tom Manning at the Firestone Store in Junction City, Kansas.

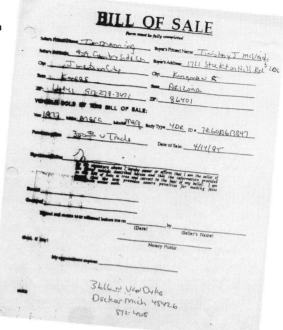

did not recognize him because he had not seen McVeigh in several years. However, as they talked, Manning remembered him.

Manning told agents that McVeigh was having problems with his car, a blue 1984 Pontiac J-2000 station wagon, when he arrived at the Firestone Store on Friday morning. Manning asked one of his mechanics to take a look at McVeigh's car. The mechanic discovered the car had a blown head gasket and white smoke was coming from the tailpipe. McVeigh asked how much it would cost to repair the car, but Manning told him it was not worth fixing.

McVeigh asked if Manning knew where he could get a good car cheap. Manning said he had a 1977 Mercury Marquis "out back." It was an older car, but it had a good engine in it. Manning told McVeigh he wanted $300 for the Mercury. After paying Manning the $300, McVeigh told him he did not have enough money left to get back to Michigan. Manning gave $50 back to McVeigh. McVeigh instructed Manning to mail the bill of sale to him in Michigan and gave Manning the 3616 North Van Dyke Rd. address in Decker, Michigan. McVeigh left in the Mercury and also left the broken down Pontiac station wagon in Manning's parking lot.

Jon Hersley

Agent Jon Hersley had been with the FBI since 1969. He had worked for the FBI in Dallas and spent almost 10 years in Los Angeles. Agents of Hersley's vintage had been required to work in one of the FBI's Top 10 offices. Los Angeles, Chicago, and New York City were all considered Top 10 offices—highly populated, financial centers in the United States where complicated criminal cases of all types were plentiful.

Agents in Top 10 offices worked a wide variety of criminal cases. In Los Angeles, Agent Hersley worked primarily white-collar crime cases—financial crimes, bank fraud, insurance fraud, con-artists, advance fee schemes, and fraud in the medical and financial communities. In addition, he occasionally worked bank robbery, kidnapping, extortion, and fugitive cases. In 1984, Agent Hersley was transferred to Oklahoma City. He had grown up and attended college in West Texas and later in the Dallas area, so the re-assignment to Oklahoma City was a chance for him and his wife to return to a part of the country where they had grown up, where they wanted to raise their children.

In Oklahoma City, Agent Hersley continued to widen his investigative experience. Working the streets was his love. His first assignment in Oklahoma City was a heavy equipment undercover project, along with Agent Floyd Zimms. Other assignments included public corruption and white-collar crime, and finally the Organized Crime and Drug Squad headed by Errol Myers. On this squad, Hersley investigated and assisted in the successful prosecution of numerous Colombian/South American drug trafficking organizations with operations in the United States and foreign countries. Agents Hersley and Zimms became partners in 1984 and continued to work together for the next 11 years.

In the days after the Oklahoma City bombing, Special Agent in Charge Bob Ricks knew the challenge that lay ahead for the agent he chose to lead the McVeigh investigation and work with federal prosecutors to prepare the case for the court system. He needed an agent with a great deal of experience in putting together sophisticated and complex criminal cases and one who had managed trials and testified repeatedly in federal court. The investigation and prosecution of those responsible for the bombing in Oklahoma City would test the skills of the very best of agents.

Hersley, like most federal agents in Oklahoma City, had worked virtually non-stop in the days following the bombing. Most agents had acquaintances in the building and desperately wanted to find those who were responsible. Ricks summoned Agent Hersley to the command post and told him of his decision to assign Hersley as the FBI case agent responsible for the investigation and potential prosecution of McVeigh. To Hersley, it was an honor and privilege, and he knew it would be an enormous challenge.

Larry Tongate

Tongate was a 24-year veteran FBI agent. Like Hersley, he grew up in Texas. Tongate had a wide array of investigative experience in FBI offices in Minneapolis, Minnesota, Dallas, Texas, and Miami, Florida, before being assigned to the Kansas City office. During his years in Miami, he worked on a drug squad that investigated some of the most significant drug cases in FBI history.

Arriving in Kansas City in 1990, Tongate was assigned to the squad of Supervisory Agent Mike Shanahan and worked on complex drug and organized crime investigations. Occasionally, Tongate worked undercover in South America and Europe. On one occasion, posing as an undercover drug dealer in Bolivia, he purchased a bathtub made of 10 kilograms of cocaine base.

Because of his extensive experience in preparing cases for trial, Tongate was initially named the Kansas City office case agent for the Oklahoma City bombing investigation. In April, 1996, he was named co-case agent, with Agent Hersley, of the entire investigation and joined other members of the trial team for the McVeigh and Nichols trials in Denver, Colorado.

McVeigh's Preliminary Hearing

McVeigh had been in federal custody since April 21, 1995. He had been held at the federal penitentiary at El Reno, Oklahoma, after his initial appearance before United States Magistrate Judge Ronald Howland at Tinker Air Force Base.

Howland was assigned to preside over a preliminary hearing scheduled for April 27. In the federal system, a defendant is entitled to a preliminary hearing within ten days of his arrest unless an indictment has been returned against him. Defense Attorney John Coyle and Susan Otto, the Federal Public Defender for the Western District of Oklahoma, were assigned to defend McVeigh at the preliminary hearing. Merrick Garland, now a United States Court of Appeals judge in Washington, D.C., served as the federal prosecutor at the preliminary hearing.

Trooper Charlie Hanger and Agent Hersley were the only witnesses scheduled to testify for the government. Hanger testified about his arrest of McVeigh on the morning of the bombing. Hersley testified for several hours, detailing the government's case against McVeigh.

Hersley told the judge that McVeigh had been arrested at 10:20 a.m. on the morning of the bombing 78 miles from the bomb site, a time and distance consistent with McVeigh having been in Oklahoma City at the time of the blast.

Hersley testified that clothing worn by McVeigh at the time of his arrest tested positive for traces of penta erythratol tetral nitrate (PETN), an explosive commonly used in detonation cord. Hersley also testified that the FBI had traced truck parts recovered at the bomb site, including a rear axle, rear bumper, and Florida license plate to a 20-foot Ford Ryder Truck, last rented by Robert "Bob" Kling at Elliott's Body Shop in Junction City, Kansas.

Hersley laid out in detail the FBI's investigation linking McVeigh to the motel near the body shop where the Ryder truck was rented, to the delivery of Chinese food ordered by Kling to McVeigh's room, and told of witnesses identifying an FBI artist's drawing of Kling as being defendant McVeigh.

Cross-examination by defense attorney John Coyle centered on the inaccuracy of eyewitness sightings of those who claimed to have seen McVeigh around the Murrah Building on the morning of the bombing. After several hours of direct and cross-examination testimony by Trooper Hanger and Agent Hersley, Magistrate Howland ruled the government had presented enough probable cause to bind McVeigh over for trial. The government had won the first round.

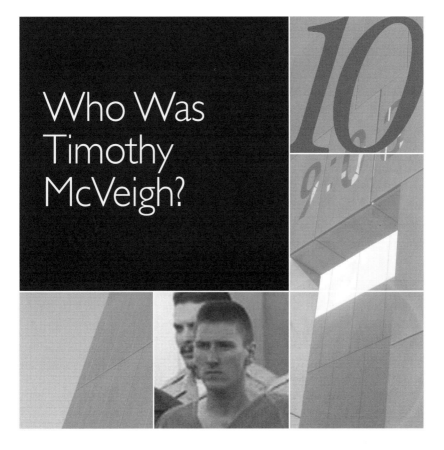

Who Was Timothy McVeigh?

H *ersley, Tongate, and other federal agents* assisting in the bombing investigation wanted to know everything about Tim McVeigh. Who was he? Where had he been? What was his life all about?

In the days and weeks that followed, the FBI determined that McVeigh was born April 23, 1968, in upstate New York to Bill and Mildred "Mickey" Frazer McVeigh. McVeigh's parents divorced while he was attending StarPoint High School in Lockport, New York. McVeigh was the middle child. His older sister, Patricia, who was 32 at the time of McVeigh's arrest, had married and was living in Florida with her husband, Bill Davis. His younger sister, Jennifer McVeigh, was 21 years old. Both were in shock at what had happened to their brother, Patricia more so than Jennifer.

McVeigh was upset about his mother and father's divorce. Bill McVeigh was a quiet man who had worked his entire career at the

Harrison Radiator Shop. He was the epitome of a blue-collar worker. When not at work, he liked to tend his garden. He enjoyed sharing tomatoes and other vegetables with his neighbors and family. He was a simple man. Bill's wife, Mickey, on the other hand was not content to sit at home. Friends said she liked to party, and the fact that Bill was not a party man at heart, did not slow her down. She reportedly frequented nightspots without her husband. Eventually, it led to their divorce. Tim McVeigh was devastated. He would later tell his military associates of his disgust for his mother and refer to her in the most derogatory terms.

McVeigh graduated from StarPoint High School in 1986. School records indicated he had an IQ of 119. He did not have many friends in high school and did not excel in athletics. He was skinny, causing students to refer to him as "Chicken McVeigh." His teachers spoke kindly of him, those who remembered him. He did not cause problems in school even after his grades began to drop following the divorce of his parents.

After high school, McVeigh attended one year of college at the Bryant and Stratton Business College. He worked for a time at two different Burger King restaurants and as a security guard at Burke Security. His life was less than remarkable. High school and family friends could remember no significant relationships that McVeigh had with anyone of the opposite sex. They said he might have dated a girl once or twice, but never had a meaningful relationship with a girl. He was awkward and just not comfortable around them.

Rural, upstate New York is the polar opposite of New York City. The countryside is beautiful. Deer roam the fields and meadows. Hunters are plentiful and gun rights are a major political issue. McVeigh was given a rifle by his grandfather when he was a young boy. The rural setting afforded a young boy the opportunity to own a rifle, as well as a place to target practice and hunt. McVeigh liked to shoot and he was good at it.

While working as a security guard and living with his father, McVeigh decided to join the army. The decision was his alone—he did not discuss it with his father until he was adamant about going.

McVeigh attended boot camp at Fort Benning, Georgia, beginning in May of 1988. That is where he met and befriended Terry Nichols and

Michael Joseph Fortier. McVeigh and his new friends were transferred together to Fort Riley, Kansas, in September, 1988, where he was assigned to the infantry.

McVeigh excelled during his early months in the military. He was a good soldier, quick to volunteer for field and night training exercises and reconnaissance trips. Rather than accompany other members of his unit hitting nightspots, McVeigh preferred to stay in the barracks and read. He loved to read about guns and was extremely fond of a book, *The Turner Diaries.*

The author, William Pierce, using the pseudonym Andrew Macdonald, wrote about a group of people who were fed up with the government and decided to take things into their own hands and move forward in an effort to start a civil war. The group wanted to strike first against the government for passing stringent gun laws, which they felt infringed upon their rights. Actions taken by the group included building a truck bomb and murdering and assassinating people.

McVeigh's best friend in the army, Terry Nichols, was 13 years his senior. Nichols left the army after only a year of service. McVeigh's other friend, Michael Fortier, also left the army early, although he lasted slightly longer than Nichols.

McVeigh continued to do well in the military. He was a gunner on the Bradley Fighting Vehicle and was an expert shot. In January, 1991, he was sent to the Middle East as part of America's buildup leading to Desert Storm. Privately, he confided to a close family friend of Bill and Mickey McVeigh that he was afraid of war. He was afraid he would not come back, not an uncommon feeling for a young man dispatched to fight a war against a foreign enemy.

McVeigh did his part. He fought in Desert Storm and was awarded the Bronze Star. Other members of his Bradley crew reported that McVeigh had fatally shot an Iraqi soldier in the head from a distance of several hundred yards.

McVeigh returned from Desert Storm in April, 1991, and was given an opportunity to try out for the Army's Special Forces. Being in Special Forces required a soldier to be a contributing member of a small unit of men. It required a sense of camaraderie, a closeness to other members in the unit, perhaps even a willingness to die for one's fellow soldier.

McVeigh's dream was short lived. He dropped out of Special Forces training after only a couple of days. He complained that a five-mile walk with a rucksack was too hard.

In reviewing McVeigh's military record after he was arrested and charged with the Oklahoma City bombing, FBI agents were first told that McVeigh had flunked out of Special Forces training because he could not pass the required psychological testing. However, Agents Hersley and Zimms later learned that McVeigh's psychological tests were not graded until after he had been arrested. The psychological tests would have resulted in McVeigh's dismissal from Special Forces training had he not dropped out voluntarily.

McVeigh was deeply disappointed. He had dreamed of being a member of Special Forces. He was subsequently reassigned to Fort Riley to serve out the remainder of his active-duty assignment. In December, 1991, McVeigh returned to Pendleton, New York, and completed his military service in the National Guard in June, 1992.

McVeigh moved in with his father at the family house on Campbell Road. On December 18, 1991, he returned to his work as a security guard, this time for Burns Security. In October, 1992, he moved into an apartment on Dysinger Road. He lived alone and continued to work as a security guard until January, 1993.

McVeigh's anger and disenchantment with the federal government continued to grow. He expressed his disgust for the government to others, including fellow worker, Carl Lebron. He told Lebron that something should be done to keep the federal government from usurping the rights and freedoms of its citizens. McVeigh inundated Lebron with rhetoric. Finally, he became upset with Lebron telling him, "You stomp your feet but you don't do anything about it." LeBron was happy when McVeigh left the security company.

During 1992, McVeigh renewed contact with an old friend, Steve Hodge. The two were childhood friends and had remained close acquaintances while they were growing up and attending school in Pendleton and Lockport and even after McVeigh joined the army. Just as he had done with others, McVeigh continued to spew anti-government rhetoric to Hodge. He told his old friend about *The Turner Diaries*. It was important to McVeigh, and he pressed Hodge to read the book. He left a copy of the book, along with a letter, for Hodge to read.

The letter stated in part, "Steve, Read the book when you have time to sit down and think. When I read it, I would have to stop at the end of every paragraph and examine the deeper meaning of what I had just read…..It is like you have written a diary during now and (when) a "revolution" took place in about 3 years; you keeping a diary the whole time. Then, in 10 years or so, or even a thousand, an "archeologist" discovers your diary…..I am not giving you this book to convert you. I do, however, want you to understand the "other side" and view the pure literal genious of this piece. Again this is accomplished by not just simply reading this, but in analyzing every sentence you've read. Think "what made the author write that paragraph", or "what deeper meaning is he trying to convey", or "How, by wording it like that, is he trying to subliminally influence someone's thinking". If you look at it like that, it is a masterpiece."

The following are excerpts from *The Turner Diaries*:

Today it finally began! After all these years of talking—and nothing but talking—we have finally taken our first action. We are at war with the System, and it is no longer a war of words.

The plan, roughly, is this: Unit 8 will acquire a large quantity of explosives—between five and ten tons. Our unit will hijack a truck making a legitimate delivery to the FBI headquarters, rendezvous at a location where Unit 8 will be waiting with the explosives, and switch loads. We will then drive into the FBI's freight-receiving area, set the fuse, and leave the truck.

Sensitized with oil and tightly confined, it (ammonium nitrate) makes an effective blasting agent, where the aim is simply to move a quantity of dirt or rock. But our original plan for the bomb called for it to be essentially unconfined and to be able to punch through two levels of reinforced concrete- flooring while producing an open-air blast wave powerful enough to blow the façade off a massive and strongly constructed building.

The plate glass windows in the store beside us and dozens of others we could see along the street were blown to splinters. A glittering and deadly rain of glass shards continued to fall into the street from the upper stories of nearby buildings for a few seconds, as a jet-black column of smoke shot straight up into the sky ahead of us.

The scene in the courtyard was one of utter devastation…Overturned trucks and automobiles, smashed office furniture, and building rubble were strewn wildly about—and so were the bodies of a shockingly large number of victims.

But the real value of all our attacks today lies in the psychological impact, not in the immediate casualties. For one thing, our efforts against the System gained immeasurably in credibility. More important, though, is what we taught the politicians and bureaucrats. They learned this afternoon that not one of them is beyond our reach. They can huddle behind barbed wire and tanks in the city, or they can hide behind the concrete walls and alarm systems of their country estates, but we can still find them and kill them.

To Agent Hersley, it was clear. *The Turner Diaries* had deeply influenced McVeigh. He had allowed the perverse beliefs in the book to become part of him.

McVeigh continued to press Hodge about his growing hatred for the government. Later in 1992, he again wrote to his friend. In this letter, McVeigh said goodbye to Hodge, accusing him of becoming too indifferent to the grievances around him. McVeigh wrote, "Every site I travel to, from Williamsville to Niagara Falls, young and old tell me alike, they are fed up. Part of my job [as a Security Guard] is public relations with the workers. They all strike up the same conversations. Men, women, retired, young - fed up with blacks, with welfare and Medicaid, and with the government. And these people come from all over - the middle of Buffalo to Clarence; The happily-retired extra-income workers to the struggling young ones, they all say the same thing. Is this a biased opinion; I don't think so. Steve, if you're happy, fine. Let's see what happens some day when someone finally takes something away from your secure world. Steve, this letter is hard to write, hard to send, because we've known each other for so long, but it has to be said. So until you wake up, see ya. Tim."

David Darlak was another of McVeigh's high school friends. After they graduated from high school in 1986, and before both went into the military, they jointly purchased a nine-acre tract of land near Humphrey, New York, for approximately $7,000.00. The land was located about 50 miles to the south of Wheatfield, where Darlak had grown up. After a short time, McVeigh told Darlak that he wanted to construct a bomb shelter on the property. Darlak thought this was a little far out, but later told Agent Hersley and Prosecutor Scott Mendeloff that he thought McVeigh was afraid of a nuclear war.

After McVeigh and Darlak completed military service, they renewed their friendship in New York. During 1992, they saw each other about once a month. McVeigh continued his work as a security guard for Burns. During the late spring or summer of 1992, McVeigh gave Darlak a copy of *The Turner Diaries* and later asked him several times if he had read the book. Darlak said he never did read the book, prompting McVeigh to request he return the book so he could give it to someone else. Darlak said McVeigh left up-state New York in late 1992, without telling Darlak where he was going and without saying goodbye.

Kyle Kraus, McVeigh's second cousin, lived in Amherst, New York. McVeigh was several years older that Kraus. However, despite their age difference, McVeigh spent time with Kraus at family gatherings while they were growing up. After McVeigh joined the army, they exchanged letters a couple of times, and Kraus would see McVeigh when he came home on leave.

Kraus told Agent Hersley and Prosecutor Beth Wilkinson that during the fall of 1991, when Kraus was just 18 years old, McVeigh sent *The Turner Diaries* to him. Kraus said he read the book and found it very powerful and that it contained some information that was of interest to him. For example, the book talked about the Brady bill, gun control, and the government's movement to take people's guns away from them. Gun control was of interest to Kraus, who worked at Johnson's Country Store and sold hunting and fishing equipment.

Kraus said that in December of 1991, probably around Christmas after McVeigh had returned from the army, he and McVeigh talked about *The Turner Diaries*. McVeigh told Kraus that someday it would take a civil war or revolution against the government if the government continued to take guns away from the people.

In 1992, McVeigh sent Kraus another book, *Hunter*, also by William Pierce. Kraus described this book as providing details of how to build an ammonium nitrate/fuel oil bomb. He said that after hearing about the bombing in Oklahoma City, it seemed to mirror what he had read in *The*

Turner Diaries. After Kraus learned of the bombing, he turned the two books McVeigh had given to him over to the FBI.

The Turner Diaries and *Hunter* were not the only books about explosives with which McVeigh had become infatuated. In May, 1993, he ordered and received a book called *Homemade C-4*, by Ragnar Benson, from the Paladin Press Company in Boulder, Colorado. Both the order form and the money order, sent to pay for the book, were completed in McVeigh's handwriting. Paladin Press confirmed the book was sent to McVeigh's delivery box in Flint, Michigan.

Agent Hersley reviewed *Homemade C-4* and identified the following relevant excerpts:

1. *Try mixing ammonium nitrate with nitromethane, one especially knowledgeable former marine demolitions expert suggested. The stuff is a real pisser, he wrote, as fast as TNT, with just as high a brisance. It is useful for cutting steel and other paramilitary survival applications.*

2. *Although fertilizer-grade ammonium nitrate can usually be purchased from nurseries and garden-supply stores, a better source for explosives manufacture is farm-supply stores.*

3. *Nitromethane is the second of three chemical components needed to put C-4 together in one's home chemistry lab...the best place to look for nitromethane is at drag strips and stock-car races. Often a local petroleum dealer will bring a 55-gallon barrel of the fuel to the track and sell it by the gallon to the drivers and mechanics.*

4. *Another likely place to look for nitromethane is in hobby shops...If all else fails, nitromethane can be ordered at extremely high prices from chemical supply houses.*

5. *Although the combined material seems safe to handle, it is definitely exciting when detonated with a number six or eight cap....I estimate the velocity of detonation to be about 21,000 feet per second or slightly less than TNT, which detonates at about 22,600 feet per second. C-4, the explosive benchmark, roars out an incredible 26,600 feet per second. The additional speed between commercial dynamite at 19,000 feet per second and C-4 is what cuts steel and shatters concrete.*

6. *Other materials exist that can be combined with ammonium nitrate to produce high-grade explosives. Some quite powerful ones aren't as deliquescent as nitromethane, giving the impression that they might be more desirable*

than nitromethane. One formula that is currently making the rounds among survivors involves mixing two parts of NH4NO3 with one part hydrazine. The resulting liquids are reportedly the most powerful chemical explosive known to man - short of an actual atomic reaction.

It was no small coincidence that the book, *Homemade C-4*, ordered and shipped to McVeigh in May, 1993, detailed the mixture of ammonium nitrate fertilizer with nitromethane and/or anhydrous hydrazine to complete a powerful explosive material. FBI explosives experts were certain the bomb that was exploded in front of the Murrah Building on April 19, 1995, was an ammonium nitrate based bomb.

Who was Mike Havens? How did the customer receipt for the purchase of 2,000 pounds of ammonium nitrate fertilizer, in the name of Mike Havens, on September 30, 1994, get into the kitchen cabinet drawer in Terry Nichols' house in Herington, Kansas? And what about the second purchase of another 2,000 pounds of ammonium nitrate from Mid-Kansas Co-op, on October 18, 1994, again in the name of customer Mike Havens?

Agent Hersley and other Agents assigned to the investigation took full note of the fact that *Homemade C-4* was ordered and delivered to McVeigh approximately one month after the fire on April 19, 1993, at David Koresh's compound in Waco, Texas.

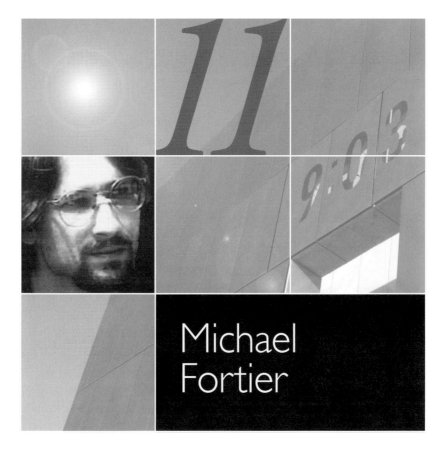

Michael
Fortier

Michael Fortier attended boot camp with Tim McVeigh and Terry Nichols at Fort Benning, Georgia, in 1988. All three were subsequently transferred to Fort Riley, Kansas. Because of back problems, Fortier exited the army early in May, 1989.

Fortier was born in Maine but had moved with his parents to Kingman, Arizona, at the age of seven. He graduated from Kingman High School in 1987. After dropping out of the army in 1989, Fortier returned to Kingman and attended classes at Mojave Community College in 1991 and 1992. He later began working at the Kingman TruValue Hardware store and married his sweetheart, Lori. They had a daughter named Kayla.

When Fortier was first approached by the FBI on April 21, 1995, regarding McVeigh and the Oklahoma City bombing, he refused to cooperate, saying he believed McVeigh was innocent and not capable of the bombing. Fortier was deeply concerned that if the FBI was able to link McVeigh to the bombing, they might also believe that Fortier, as one of McVeigh's best friends, was also involved.

He felt trapped. Who could he trust? Only Lori. He could not tell anyone else what he knew. He lied to his friends when they asked. He lied to his parents and to the news media. Fortier had grown accustomed to lying. By early 1995, he was using crystal meth (methamphetamine) and marijuana on a regular basis.

By Monday, April 24, Fortier had seen news coverage about the arrest of Tim McVeigh and also the search of the Nichols' farmhouse in Decker, Michigan. He was afraid and concerned that the FBI would raid and search his home in the same manner they had raided the Nichols' farmhouse. He asked agents if they would notify him if they wanted to conduct a search of his home. He said he did not want the FBI to come into

Above left: Michael Fortier. *Courtesy Oklahoma Publishing Company.*

Above right: Lori Fortier coming out of the federal courthouse in Oklahoma City on the day her husband, Michael, was sentenced to prison for not alerting authorities about the bombing plan. In the background is Michael Fortier's father, Paul. *Courtesy Oklahoma Publishing Company.*

his home with automatic weapons and dressed in black raid gear. He was afraid for not only himself, but also his wife and daughter.

Fortier did receive such a call from the FBI informing him that agents were going to search his house and that he might consider leaving while the search was being conducted. Initially, Fortier complained, telling agents he wanted to be there when the search warrant was served so he could see what they were doing. Later, Fortier relented and took Lori and his daughter to meet agents at a local community college.

Not knowing what the agents would find, or what they considered important, clearly concerned Fortier. He was not thinking clearly and had developed tunnel vision. He knew there were stolen weapons and evidence of drug use inside his house, but he was much more concerned that the FBI might link him in some way to the Oklahoma City bombing. Fortier knew the FBI was watching his every move. If he left his house to destroy evidence of his crimes, he believed he would be caught. Was he going to be implicated in the bombing? He was afraid, almost desperate.

Additionally, pursuant to a court order, agents placed a wiretap on the telephone at the Fortier residence to monitor his conversations. Numerous conversations were overheard and recorded, but yielded little evidence against Fortier, who had become cautious. His statements were guarded and sometimes exculpatory in nature. His conversations with friends, family, and the news media were purposely calculated in an attempt to exonerate not only himself but also his old friend McVeigh. The pressure on Fortier increased. Within days, Michael and his wife, Lori, were served with subpoenas to appear before the federal grand jury in Oklahoma City. Fortier knew much more about McVeigh and the Oklahoma City bombing than he had told the FBI thus far. So did his wife, Lori. Fortier was becoming more nervous by the day.

When the day neared for him and Lori to be in Oklahoma City, Fortier knew they had to do something. When the Fortiers arrived in Oklahoma City, they contacted the United States Attorney's office and left word where they were staying.

Agents Floyd Zimms and Jim Volz contacted Fortier and asked to interview him and his wife. They agreed. On that day and over the course of the next several weeks, Fortier and his wife met with Agents Zimms,

Volz, and Hersley, as well as, federal prosecutors Joe Hartzler and Arlene Joplin. The Fortiers gave agents incredible details of the circumstances surrounding the Oklahoma City bombing, and in the process, deeply implicated their old friend McVeigh.

Fortier described his army experience with McVeigh, including the fact that early in the friendship McVeigh gave him a copy of *The Turner Diaries*. After Fortier left the army in 1989, he did not see McVeigh again until McVeigh visited him in Kingman in April, 1993, shortly after the Waco fire.

McVeigh told Fortier on this visit that he had been living with James and Terry Nichols at their farmhouse in Decker, Michigan. McVeigh and Terry Nichols were planning to travel to Waco to demonstrate and protest the government's actions and involvement at Waco. McVeigh said he and Nichols were packing McVeigh's car to leave for Waco when the fire occurred. After they heard news coverage of the fire, Nichols stayed in Michigan, but McVeigh traveled to Kingman. McVeigh told Fortier that he had already been to Waco the previous month by himself to protest the government's involvement there.

Michelle Rauch, a college journalism student at Southern Methodist University, verified the story that McVeigh related to Fortier about his trip to Waco before the fire on April 19, 1993. Rauch had traveled to Waco to complete research for a story she was writing for the campus newspaper. While there, she encountered McVeigh selling anti-government bumper stickers laid out on the hood of his car. Rauch remembered that McVeigh was extremely upset with the government and its actions at the Koresh compound.

Fortier said after arriving in Arizona, McVeigh stayed at his home for a week before moving into a trailer home and going to work as a security guard. Fortier and McVeigh talked about Waco on many occasions. They both concluded the federal government had intentionally attacked the people living at Koresh's compound, and that even though the government might not have intentionally started the fire, it certainly was the cause of it. Fortier said they both believed the government had murdered the compound's residents.

During his stay in Kingman, McVeigh and Fortier watched a video titled *Waco, The Big Lie* in which the federal government was accused of murdering the people in the Branch Davidian compound and covering it up in subsequent investigations. McVeigh and Fortier believed someone should be held accountable. Fortier said McVeigh became incensed as he watched the video.

McVeigh lived in Kingman until September 14, 1993, after which he moved back to the Nichols' farmhouse in Decker, Michigan. A few months later, Fortier received a phone call from McVeigh who said he was unhappy living in Michigan and wanted to move. Fortier offered to help him find work in Kingman, so McVeigh returned to Arizona.

Fortier helped McVeigh get a job at the Kingman TruValue Hardware Store, where Fortier worked. McVeigh again stayed for a few days at Fortier's home until he moved into a rent house in Golden Valley, Arizona, about five miles from Kingman. During their workday at the hardware store, McVeigh and Fortier continued their increased anti-government rhetoric.

Some of the conversations focused on Waco while others centered around their discontent with the United Nations (UN). Fortier said that both he and McVeigh believed the UN was actively trying to form a one-world government. They believed that an elite group in the UN was trying to form a single government to control the world—they called it a New World Order. They believed it could be accomplished only if the government first prohibited citizens from having weapons. One night, McVeigh and Fortier jumped the fence at the local National Guard armory to see if they could detect any evidence of UN activity at the Armory.

Fortier said that on another occasion during the spring or summer of 1994, he and Lori accompanied McVeigh into the desert outside Kingman. McVeigh had constructed a pipe bomb he wanted to explode. McVeigh ignited the bomb which he had placed under a rock.

A hot topic of conversation between McVeigh and Fortier was conspiracy theories involving the federal government. Fortier subscribed to anti-government literature published by *The Spotlight* and also the *Patriot Report*, a monthly newsletter that talked about the United Nations takeover. Fortier said that McVeigh suggested he subscribe to these flyers, and that McVeigh was becoming more angry at the government because he believed it was usurping the rights of its citizens. Fortier said that

McVeigh told him he believed the United States government had declared war on the American people and was actively taking away their rights.

Just before July 4, 1994, McVeigh prepared a flyer containing his thoughts and ideas and a collection of quotes from our Founding Fathers. McVeigh and Fortier planned to photocopy the flyer and distribute it on July 4th, but for no particular reason they never followed through.

McVeigh moved out of the rent house in Golden Valley in early June, 1994, and moved into Fortier's house. McVeigh continued to live with Fortier for nearly the full month of July. Fortier's memory was sharp on the subject because it was the month of his marriage to Lori. McVeigh was the best man at their wedding in Las Vegas on July 25, 1994.

After the Fortiers returned from their honeymoon, McVeigh moved from their house and left Kingman. During the next month, Fortier received a letter from McVeigh in which McVeigh told Fortier that he and Terry Nichols had decided to take action against the federal government and they wanted to know if Fortier would like to join them. Fortier said he wrote back to McVeigh and asked what he was talking about, what action were they planning to take?

About a week after the exchange of letters, McVeigh unexpectedly showed up at Fortier's trailer house in Kingman. During this visit, McVeigh told Fortier that he and Nichols were thinking of blowing up a federal building. McVeigh asked Fortier if he would help them. Fortier declined, telling McVeigh that he would never do anything like that unless there was a United Nations tank in his front yard. Neither he nor Lori were interested in McVeigh and Nichols' plan to blow up a building. McVeigh left Kingman after his conversation with Fortier and headed back to Kansas again to meet up with Terry Nichols.

Frankly, FBI agents did not like working with the Fortiers, but information they provided was checking out. In criminal investigations, the use of cooperative individuals, especially insiders, is highly effective. The FBI did not simply take the Fortiers at their word but made painstaking efforts to corroborate or disprove their information independent of their statements. Hundreds of FBI agents across the nation checked out information given by the Fortiers.

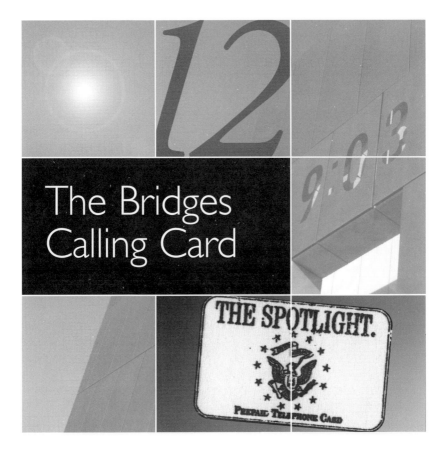

The Bridges
Calling Card

THE SPOTLIGHT.

PREPAID TELEPHONE CARD

Agent *Lou Michalko was a vital part* of the FBI Task Force assembled in Oklahoma City. His job was to learn everything he could about the Daryl Bridges calling card, evidence of which had been found in Terry Nichols' house when it was searched by the FBI.

Michalko had majored in accounting and was assigned to work white-collar crime cases in Oklahoma City. He worked cases involving con artists and the most complicated theft and embezzlement schemes. He was the perfect agent to be assigned to the Bridges calling card investigation.

The FBI wanted to know who had initially obtained the card. Who was Daryl Bridges? What was his connection to the Nichols family in Decker, Michigan? How was the calling card paid for? What was it used for? Michalko and Unit Chief Fred Dexter, from FBI headquarters in Washington, D.C., provided answers to these questions and more.

Left: The application card for the Daryl Bridges calling card received by The Spotlight in Washington, D.C., on November 12, 1993. The handwriting on the application was identified as that of Terry Nichols.

Right: The payment book for the Bridges calling card was found in Terry Nichols' residence in Herington, Kansas, during the initial search by the FBI.

The FBI had already discovered that the Daryl Bridges calling card was obtained from the Spotlight Company, 300 Independence Avenue SE, Washington, D.C., in November, 1993, by a person or persons using the address of 3616 North Van Dyke Rd., Decker, Michigan, the address of the Nichols family farm. It was the same address that McVeigh had used in registering at the Dreamland Motel in Junction City, Kansas, on April 14, 1995, and when he was arrested by Trooper Charlie Hanger on April 19, 1995, shortly after the Oklahoma City bombing.

The Bridges calling card was a debit card, which meant that payment had to be made in advance of calls being placed against it. Bill Sweet of the Spotlight Company provided records of payments that had been made against the card. Included among the records was the application card received by Spotlight on November 12, 1993. FBI handwriting experts and Terry Nichols' former wife, Lana Padilla, confirmed that the handwriting on the application was that of Terry Nichols. Sweet confirmed that the application was received by the Spotlight Company, along with a United States Postal Money Order, in the amount of $50.00, dated November 7, 1993, as a first payment against the card. FBI experts and

Jennifer McVeigh identified the handwriting on the money order as that of Tim McVeigh.

Additional investigation by Agent Michalko determined that the money order had been purchased by McVeigh in Deford, Michigan. Not only did this information tie McVeigh and Terry Nichols to the calling card, but it also confirmed they were, in all likelihood, together in Deford, Michigan, on or about the date of its purchase. The money order and application, completed by McVeigh and Nichols, respectively, were received together by the Spotlight Company on the same day.

The FBI learned from authorities in Michigan that McVeigh had obtained a Michigan drivers license, using the Decker, Michigan, farm address. It was the same drivers license McVeigh provided to Trooper Hanger and Jailer Moritz when he was arrested and booked into the Noble County jail in Perry, Oklahoma, on the morning of April 19.

Sweet produced records that identified six additional payments that had been made against the Bridges calling card. All payments were made with United States Postal Money Orders purchased in the name of Daryl Bridges and using the Decker, Michigan, address.

United States Postal Money Order, dated February 15, 1994, in the amount of $50.00: FBI handwriting experts and Lana Padilla identified the handwriting on this money order as Terry Nichols' handwriting. Further investigation by Agent Michalko determined the money order was purchased by Nichols in Las Vegas, Nevada. Nichols and his new wife, Marife, had moved to Las Vegas in November, 1993, after the suffocation death of Marife's son, Jason.

United States Postal Money Order, dated August 21, 1994, in the amount of $50.00: FBI handwriting experts and Lana Padilla identified the handwriting on this money order as Terry Nichols' handwriting. Investigation by Agent Michalko determined the money order had been purchased by Nichols in El Dorado, Kansas. Nichols had re-located to Marion, Kansas, in March, 1994, and worked at the Donahue Ranch from March, 1994 until September 30, 1994.

United States Postal Money Order, dated September 29, 1994, in the amount of $30.00: FBI handwriting experts and Jennifer McVeigh identified the handwriting on this money order as Tim McVeigh's handwriting. Investigation by Agent Michalko determined the money order had

A copy of the United States
Postal Money Order, dated September 29, 1994, to make payment on
the Bridges calling card. The FBI determined Timothy McVeigh bought the
money order in Marion, Kansas.

been purchased by McVeigh in Marion, Kansas. Marife Nichols had
already told the FBI that McVeigh had come to stay with Terry Nichols at
the Donahue Ranch in early to mid-September, 1994.

United States Postal Money Order, dated November 7, 1994, in the
amount of $100.00: FBI handwriting experts and Lana Padilla confirmed
the handwriting on this money order was that of Terry Nichols.
Investigation by Agent Michalko determined this money order was purchased by Nichols in Manhattan, Kansas. Further investigation by agents
assigned to the FBI Command Post at Fort Riley eventually placed Terry
Nichols in Manhattan, Kansas, on November 7, 1994, the same day the
money order was purchased.

United States Postal Money Order, dated January 21, 1995, in the
amount of $100.00: FBI handwriting experts and Lana Padilla identified
the handwriting on this money order as that of Terry Nichols.
Investigation by Agent Michalko determined this money order was purchased by Nichols in Junction City, Kansas. Additional investigation by
the FBI eventually placed Nichols in Junction City, Kansas, on January
21, 1995, the same day the money order was purchased.

United States Postal Money Order, dated February 14, 1995, in
the amount of $100.00: FBI handwriting experts and Lana Padilla
identified the handwriting on this money order as that of Terry
Nichols. Investigation by Agent Michalko determined this money
order was purchased by Nichols in Junction City, Kansas, on

February 14, 1995. Additional investigation by the FBI placed Nichols in Junction City, Kansas, on February 14, 1995, the same day the money order was purchased.

The Bridges calling card was becoming an important part of the FBI's investigation. Hersley, Tongate, Michalko, and other agents assigned to the Oklahoma City Task Force recognized that the calling card was beginning to give them more insight into the travels and activities of McVeigh and Terry Nichols. The fact that the application for the calling card, as well as all seven payments made against the card, had been purchased and completed by McVeigh and Nichols, led the agents to believe the name Daryl Bridges was just an alias used for the purpose of obtaining the calling card.

The investigation was already well underway to identify the total number of telephone calls made with the card, as well as the origination, destination, and length of each of the calls. Agent Michalko and Fred Dexter spent months tracking the calls, which FBI case agents saw as vital to the prosecution of the case. Eventually, Michalko and Dexter identified a total of 685 telephone calls made against the Bridges calling card between November, 1993, when it was obtained, and April 17, 1995, when the last call was made.

Had McVeigh and Nichols obtained the Bridges calling card to hide their identity? Could the calling card now be used by the FBI to trace the activities and whereabouts of these two men, and possibly others that might have used the calling card in the days, weeks, and months, leading up to the Oklahoma City bombing?

Tim Donahue

Tim Donahue was a farmer and rancher following in the footsteps of his father. The elder Donahue started what is now known as the Donahue Hayhook Ranch with 160 acres of land in the early 1960s. Tim and his brother, Dudley, had continued to operate the Donahue Ranch, located near Marion, Kansas, in partnership with their father. By 1994, the ranch had grown to approximately 15,000 acres and a cattle operation of more than 2,000 head. The Donahues were honorable people, hard workers, who lived on the land they farmed and ranched. They grew hay, wheat, and milo to feed their livestock.

Tim Donahue told FBI Agent Tongate and Prosecutor Larry Mackey that Terry Nichols came to work for him on the ranch around the first of

Internal Revenue Service
DISTRICT OFFICE
271 W. 3RD
WITCHITA, KANSAS 67202/TDC

TERRY L. NICHOLS
RT.3 Box38
MARION, KANSAS 66861/TDC

Internal Revenue Service
Regional Office
1100 COMMERCE ST.
DALLAS, TEXAS 75242/TDC

NOTICE OF REVOCATION

TAKE NOTICE that I, TERRY L. NICHOLS , hereby revoke the U.S.
individual income tax returns, forms 1040 and attachments, which I filed
with the Internal Revenue Service for the years 19 73 through 19 90 ; and

TAKE NOTICE that I, TERRY L. NICHOLS , hereby cancel my
signature on the U.S. individual income tax returns, forms 1040 and
attachments, which I filed with the Internal Revenue Service for the years
19 73 through 19 90 .

Respectfully,

/TDC

State of KANSAS

ss.

County of MARION

BEFORE ME, a Notary Public, on this day personally appeared the above
named individual, proved to me on the basis of satisfactory evidence to be the
person whose name is subscribed to this instrument and who acknowledged
personally executing it for the express purpose of revoking his/her U.S.
individual income tax returns filed with the Internal Revenue Service for the
years 19 73 through 19 90 , and for cancelling his/her signatures thereon,
and for those purposes only.

Subscribed and sworn before me on this 16 day of march 199 4 .

Kansas   Marion
Notary in & for said State & County

Seal:

August 8, 1995
My commission expires

Charles Kennedy

Charles Kennedy
Notary Public
State of Kansas
My Appt. Exp.

A copy of the 1994
affidavit in which Terry Nichols attempted to revoke his income tax
returns from 1973 to 1990. Nichols sent a copy of the document to many public
officials, from the President of the United States to the local county attorney.

March, 1994. Mr. Donahue paid Nichols a salary and allowed him to live
free in a rent house, a small three-bedroom dwelling located near the ranch.

Donahue knew from conversations with Nichols about his anti-government sentiments. On one occasion, Donahue was concerned enough
about documents he saw in Nichols' pickup truck that he took them

home and copied them. Among the documents was what appeared to be an attempt by Nichols to cancel all federal tax returns he had ever filed with the Internal Revenue Service.

Nichols sent copies of an affidavit declaring that he was not subject to United States law to many public officials, including Kansas Governor Joan Finney, United States Attorney General Janet Reno, President Bill Clinton, FBI Director Louis Freeh, and United States Supreme Court Chief Justice William Rehnquist. When Keith Collet, the county attorney of Marion County, Kansas, received a copy of the affidavit, he wrote Nichols, "While you are in the business of undoing your relationship with the U.S. government, may I suggest you cease to use the roads and the postal services, both of which are creatures of the government."

Nichols terminated his employment with Donahue on September 30, 1994, saying he had been offered a job with a friend traveling to gun shows and that he would make twice as much money as Donahue was paying him. Donahue said the mailing address of the rent house he provided for Nichols was Route 3, Box 83, Marion, Kansas.

Agents Hersley and Tongate recognized that address as the same address the man using the name Shawn Rivers had given to Helen Mitchell on September 22, 1994, when he rented Herington Storage Unit #2. Marion, Kansas, was located 24 miles south of Herington. FBI fingerprint experts had identified eight of McVeigh's fingerprints on the rental agreement for this storage shed. McVeigh's sister, Jennifer, confirmed that the handwriting on the Shawn Rivers rental agreement was that of her brother.

Why had McVeigh used a false name to obtain the storage shed? Why had he used the name Shawn Rivers? Why had he paid cash in advance for four months rent, only to return one month later to pay cash for an additional four months, paying the rental to May 22, 1995?

Nichols asked to leave work early on his last day on the job at the ranch. Donahue went to Nichols' house that same night to look at a waterbed he had for sale. When he arrived around 7:00 p.m., Donahue was met on the front porch by Nichols. The two men went inside the residence and looked at the waterbed. Donahue agreed to purchase the waterbed and gave Nichols a check for $125.00. The check was dated September 30, 1994. Donahue said he also provided Nichols with his last paycheck in the amount of $592.59. The paycheck was also dated September 30, 1994.

Donahue said that Terry Nichols was not alone at his residence when Donahue went there on Friday evening. Donahue had noticed a small silver car at the residence, and there was another man present. Donahue said he did not know the man's name at the time but, after seeing news coverage of the Oklahoma City bombing, he was absolutely certain the man at Nichols' house was Tim McVeigh. McVeigh was working on the back of Nichols' blue 1984 GMC pickup.

Donahue told agents he had seen McVeigh at the ranch on another occasion. Toward the end of Nichols' employment, Donahue was working on a piece of farm equipment when he saw the same small silver car driving toward him. When the car came to a stop, Marife Nichols got out and asked Donahue where her husband was working.

Marife was hard for Donahue to understand because of her broken English. Rather than try to explain to her where Terry was, Donahue offered to take Marife and the driver to where Terry was driving a tractor. Donahue saw the driver, whom he later identified as McVeigh, get out of the car and approach Nichols.

Case Agents Hersley and Tongate remembered Marife had told Agents Thomeczek and Dobson about an occasion when she and McVeigh visited Terry Nichols in the field at the Donahue Ranch shortly before she left for the Philippines in the fall of 1994. Marife said that after visiting with her husband on this occasion, McVeigh drove her to a coin shop in Wichita, Kansas. The coin dealer had given them a check in exchange for several coins. The check was made payable to Marife. It was dated September 14, 1994, in the amount of $2,330.00.

Information from Marife Nichols, Michael Fortier, and Donahue proved that McVeigh was in central Kansas in the fall of 1994. Of more significance to Agents Hersley and Tongate, Donahue placed McVeigh in central Kansas on the day the first 2,000-pounds of ammonium nitrate was purchased at Mid-Kansas Co-op by a customer who used the name Mike Havens, and eight days after McVeigh had rented the storage unit in Herington.

From many sources, agents learned that McVeigh traveled light with hardly any personal belongings. Why did he need a storage unit? Was it mere coincidence that Nichols needed off early the day the first ammonium nitrate purchase was made and that the customer copy of the receipt for this purchase was found in Nichols' house?

Gathering Bomb Components

FBI explosives experts knew that an ammonium nitrate bomb required not only ammonium nitrate, but also fuel oil and a high explosive such as dynamite. A blasting cap and timing device were necessary to ignite the blast. It appeared that the ammonium nitrate used in the Oklahoma City bombing had been purchased by a customer or customers, using the name Mike Havens, at the Mid-Kansas Co-op in McPherson, Kansas. If so, where had the high explosives and fuel oil been acquired? The FBI found the answer in the burglary of a Kansas rock quarry.

Ed Davies was sheriff of Marion County, Kansas, when he investigated a burglary at the Martin Marietta rock quarry a mile north of Marion during the fall of 1994. On October 3, 1994, a caller reported that someone had broken into the explosives sheds, called magazines, at the quarry before

One of the explosive magazines burglarized at the Martin Marietta rock quarry near Marion, Kansas, during the first weekend of October, 1994.

employees reported for work that morning. The burglar(s) had taken 229 sticks or sausages of Tovex, an aluminized water-gel dynamite, 93 rolls of Primadet non-electric blasting caps, and 544 electric blasting caps. Sheriff Davies advised that a trailer containing hundreds of bags of ammonium nitrate had also been broken into, but no ammonium nitrate was missing.

According to Sheriff Davies, the burglar(s) used a cordless drill to drill through the locks on the explosives magazines and also the lock on the ammonium nitrate trailer. The sheriff had collected metal shavings from the ground underneath where the locks were drilled. The locks from the magazines were missing, but the burglars failed to take the lock from the ammonium nitrate trailer.

Sheriff Davies carefully preserved the lock and metal shavings and later gave them to FBI Agent Cullen Scott for possible use in the Oklahoma City bombing investigation.

Bud Radtke, an employee of the company operating the rock quarry, gave specific details of the explosives taken in the burglary. The Tovex came in 16-inch sticks that were 2-3 inches in diameter. He described the non-electric blasting caps as Primadet, consisting of a blasting cap and an orange cord, 60 feet in length and number 8 delay. Agent Tongate noted this was the same color, length, and delay of the Primadet blasting caps he had found during the search of Terry Nichols house on April 22-23, 1995.

Radtke said he was certain the burglar(s) had stolen the explosive materials sometime during the weekend of September 28 and October 3, 1994. When FBI agents searched Terry Nichols' home on April 22-23, they first noticed, but did not seize, a Makita cordless drill in a blue case. After learning that the padlocks on the explosive magazines and the ammonium nitrate trailer at the Martin Marietta rock quarry were drilled, agents returned to Nichols' home and seized the Makita cordless drill and two cases of drill bits.

James Cadigan, an FBI tool mark expert, was asked to make a comparison of the tool markings left on the padlock that the burglars had inadvertently left behind with sample markings from each of the drill bits found in Nichols' home. The markings on the padlock perfectly matched sample markings made by one

Above: **Burglars left one of the drilled locks behind when they burglarized the rock quarry. The evidence proved valuable in linking Terry Nichols to the crime.**

Right: **The FBI Laboratory compared the markings on the drilled lock at the Martin Marietta rock quarry with sample markings made by a drill bit found at Terry Nichols' residence. It was an identical match.**

of Nichols' drill bits. Cadigan's comparison proved that one of the drill bits seized from Nichols' home had been used to drill the ammonium nitrate trailer lock at the rock quarry.

Witnesses at the rock quarry placed the time of the explosives burglary during the first weekend of October. The rock quarry was within ten miles of the rent house on the Donahue ranch.

The investigation revealed that McVeigh was in Kansas on September 30, Nichols' last day of employment at the Donahue ranch. Donahue said he last saw Nichols on October 2, when he saw a pickup hauling away Nichols' furniture and personal belongings from the rent house.

Agents continued to trace the travels of McVeigh and Nichols. Records at Northern Storage, a Kingman, Arizona, storage facility, showed that McVeigh rented a storage unit there in his own name in early October, 1994. Payments were made on the storage unit on three separate dates in October. Officials at the storage facility confirmed that by mid-February, 1995, McVeigh's storage unit had been cleaned out. Such independent evidence confirmed the statements of witnesses about McVeigh's travels between Arizona and Kansas.

Kingman, Arizona, was nearly 1,100 miles from Marion, Kansas. Agents worked to piece together information provided by Michael and Lori Fortier with other evidence that was beginning to surface. The Fortiers told agents that McVeigh called Michael Fortier sometime during the fall of 1994. During this phone conversation, McVeigh told Fortier he wanted him to rent a storage shed somewhere outside Kingman. McVeigh instructed Fortier to use a false name and to pay cash for the storage shed.

Fortier was unable to recall the exact date he received this phone call from McVeigh, but did recall it was on a Saturday. McVeigh told Fortier during this call that he was going to be in Kingman in a few days. Fortier said after receiving the call from McVeigh, he and Lori drove to Golden Valley, Arizona. However, when Fortier tried to rent a storage unit there, he was told the facility had no vacancy. Fortier said he and Lori drove around awhile longer that day but could not locate another facility and finally stopped looking.

Fortier said that several days after McVeigh called him, he showed up in Kingman. When Fortier informed McVeigh that he had not been able

Right: Tovex Blastrite dynamite stored in boxes such as this were stolen from the Martin Marietta rock quarry in early October, 1994.

Below: These rolls of Primadet blasting caps were found in the residence of Terry Nichols by Agent Larry Tongate. They were identical to the Primadet stolen from the rock quarry near Marion, Kansas.

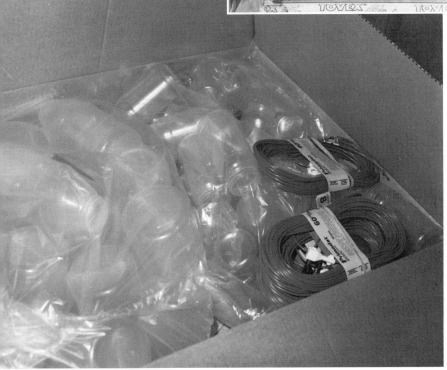

to find a storage unit, McVeigh said it was okay because he and Nichols had already rented one.

Within a night or two, McVeigh returned to Fortier's house and told Fortier he had something to show him. Nichols was with McVeigh. Fortier rode with McVeigh in McVeigh's car, and the pair followed Nichols, who was driving the blue GMC pickup with the white camper shell on the back.

The Makita cordless drill and drill bits found by Agent Tom Brown in Terry Nichols' house in Herington, Kansas, provided the FBI with absolute proof that one of the drill bits was used to drill a lock on the ammonium nitrate trailer and the burglarized explosives magazines at the rock quarry near Marion, Kansas.

McVeigh and Fortier followed Nichols to the Northern Storage facility a short distance from Fortier's house. McVeigh showed Fortier explosives that were inside the storage unit McVeigh had rented. The explosives were in a box that had an orange or yellow triangle on it. Fortier recalled seeing about 12 boxes of explosives, which McVeigh had covered with a blanket. Fortier said that as McVeigh was showing him the explosives, Nichols was taking a spare tire from the shed and putting it into his pickup.

Fortier told agents that after seeing the explosives, he invited McVeigh and Nichols to spend the night at his house in Kingman. Nichols declined the offer, but McVeigh accepted. That night, McVeigh confided to Fortier that he and Nichols had burglarized a rock quarry near where Nichols worked in Kansas and had stolen the explosives. McVeigh told Fortier that he and Nichols used a Makita, battery-operated, cordless drill to drill the locks on the magazines where the explosives were kept.

McVeigh told Fortier that he and Nichols traveled to Kingman after the theft, in McVeigh's car and Nichols' pickup, and that Nichols carried the explosives in the back of his pickup. McVeigh said he was upset with Nichols because Nichols had almost wrecked the vehicle and was almost stopped by the police for speeding while they were enroute. McVeigh stayed at Fortier's house for several days while he was in Kingman, but Nichols stayed elsewhere.

Council Grove Storage Units

While agents from the Kansas City Division uncovered details of McVeigh renting the storage unit in Herington, FBI Agent Kim West determined that Nichols had rented a storage unit at Boots-U-Store-It in Council Grove, Kansas. The storage units in Council Grove were owned and operated by Vernon "Boots" Hager, who also owned the Conoco Deli and Service Station. Sharri Furman had worked for Mr. Hager for about eight years. She primarily kept the books and records for his business, and from time to time rented out the storage units when he was not available.

Agents provided known aliases of McVeigh and Nichols to Furman, who then searched the rental records at the Council Grove storage facility. She produced records for two storage units. One had been rented in the name of Joe Kyle and the second in the name of Ted Parker, both

The middle storage unit is #37 at the Boots-U-Store-It facility in Council Grove, Kansas. The FBI investigation determined that Terry Nichols rented the unit using the name Ted Parker.

names similar to previous aliases used by Nichols. Furman said that storage unit #40 was rented on October 17, 1994, to a customer using the name Joe Kyle. She said no rental agreement was completed because the owner, Hager, had rented the unit, and he often did not take the time to have a rental agreement completed and signed.

However, she was able to locate a Conoco cash receipt in the amount of $30.00, dated October 17, 1994, in the name of Joe Kyle regarding Unit #40. The receipt was signed by Joe Kyle in the lower left corner. Furman said it was likely that Hager or one of his employees had given this receipt to Kyle on the date the storage unit was rented. She said that sometimes storage unit customers leave their payments at the Conoco

Right: A copy of the receipt provided to the man using the name Joe Kyle for storage unit #40 at the storage facility in Council Grove, Kansas. The FBI determined that Terry Nichols was Joe Kyle.

Below: Unit 40 at the Boots-U-Store-It facility is the center unit. Terry Nichols, using the name Joe Kyle, rented the unit.

Station and are given receipts in return. Furman said that her records showed that rental of storage unit #40, in the name of Joe Kyle, had been paid for through the month of April, 1995.

To the FBI, the timeline was growing clearer. Nichols had rented this storage unit on October 17, just one day before customer Mike Havens purchased the second 2,000 pounds of ammonium nitrate at Mid-Kansas Co-op in McPherson. Was the timing a coincidence? Council Grove is 24 miles east of Herington. Why had Nichols gone to Council Grove to rent the Joe Kyle storage unit? Why had he used a false name? Why had he not rented a storage unit in Herington as his friend, McVeigh, had?

The second rental agreement at the Council Grove storage facility was for storage unit #37, in the name of Ted Parker. This agreement was dated November 7, 1994, and was signed by Parker in the lower left corner. Parker's address was listed as 3616 North Van Dyke, Decker, Michigan. His telephone number was listed as (517) 872-4108, James Nichols' home telephone number in Michigan.

Furman later told Agent Hersley and Prosecutor Mendeloff she was certain Terry Nichols was the man she rented unit #37 to on November 7, 1994. She also remembered that Nichols was driving a blue pickup with a white camper shell. Furman's records showed that the rental of Ted Parker's storage unit had been paid through April, 1995.

FBI handwriting experts and Lana Padilla identified the signatures of Joe Kyle and Ted Parker on the rental documents as that of Terry Nichols. What need did McVeigh and Nichols have for a third and fourth storage unit?

Tracking the Calling Card

T he tireless efforts of Agent Lou Michalko and other FBI employees assigned to coordinate the FBI's efforts to track calls made using the Daryl Bridges calling card began to produce results.

There was a series of calls made using the card during late September, 1994. Some of the calls were made from Terry Nichols' home telephone in the rent house provided by Tim Donahue. Other calls were made from various payphones located just outside Marion, Kansas, and close to Nichols' rent house. The calls were made during the same time McVeigh was staying with Nichols.

Greg Pfaff

On September 24, 1994, four calls were made using the calling card to a man named Greg Pfaff in Harrisonburg, Virginia. The first three calls were very short in duration, but the fourth call lasted 6 minutes and 28 seconds. When Pfaff was interviewed by Agent Hersley and Prosecutor Mendeloff, he said that he first met Tim McVeigh at a gun show in Monroeville, Pennsylvania, in early 1992. Pfaff sold McVeigh some armor piercing ammunition and spoke with McVeigh for about 30 minutes at the gun show.

Pfaff did not see McVeigh again until they ran into each other at another gun show in Buffalo, New York. Again, the two spoke for awhile, and Pfaff bought some blast simulators and military smoke grenades from McVeigh. Pfaff said he saw McVeigh again at gun shows in Monroeville in late 1992, and early to mid 1993. He remembered the 1993 gun show in Monroeville was after the Branch Davidian standoff had begun in Waco, because McVeigh talked to him about it. He said McVeigh told him he had been to Waco and that federal agents had raised a perimeter fence around the Branch Davidian compound, and he had crawled up to the fence and back without being noticed.

McVeigh was upset and angry about the standoff and told Pfaff the federal government had no right to do what they were doing to the Davidians. McVeigh told Pfaff that he was selling bumper stickers with anti-government slogans from the hood of his car to protest the government's actions. As McVeigh spoke to Pfaff, he became more agitated. McVeigh told Pfaff he believed the government's actions could be the start of the government coming house to house to seize weapons from its citizens.

Pfaff did not see McVeigh again after the Monroeville gun show in 1993, but McVeigh called him during September or October, 1994. McVeigh told Pfaff he needed to buy some "det cord," and wondered if Pfaff could obtain it for him. Det, or detonation cord, is a high explosive used to set off multiple explosive charges simultaneously. Pfaff told McVeigh that det cord could not be shipped in the United States because of its high explosive nature. However, McVeigh insisted he really needed the det cord, and that he would drive from Arizona to Virginia if Pfaff could get it for him.

Pfaff said he had no intention of getting the det cord for McVeigh, but he told McVeigh that he would try to do so, to keep him on the hook. About a week later, McVeigh called back and asked if Pfaff had been able to get the det cord. Pfaff told McVeigh no, and the call ended shortly thereafter. Pfaff never spoke to McVeigh again.

The calling card records confirmed several calls were made to Pfaff in September, 1994. A final call to Pfaff was made on October 1, 1994, from a payphone in Wamego, Kansas.

Immediately before the call to Pfaff on October 1, McVeigh made another call from the same payphone in Wamego, again using the Bridges calling card. This call was to Michael Fortier's house in Kingman, Arizona. It was placed at 2:08 p.m. and lasted 9 minutes and 48 seconds. Agent Hersley remembered Fortier told agents McVeigh called him in early October a couple of days before McVeigh and Nichols showed up in Kingman with the explosives. McVeigh rented a storage unit on October 4 in Kingman, just days after the rock quarry burglary. Why was McVeigh in Wamego, Kansas?

Glynn Tipton

Glynn Tipton was a salesman and warehouse coordinator for VP Racing Fuels in Manhattan, Kansas. The company's primary business was the sale of racing fuels to the owners and drivers of race cars from its business location in Manhattan and at various racetracks around the country.

On Saturday, October 1, 1994, Tipton was working the Sears Craftsman Nationals races at the Heartland Park Racetrack in Pauline, Kansas, just outside Topeka. He was selling racing fuel from the back of a semi-trailer. Around 1:00 p.m. to 2:00 p.m. that afternoon, a man Tipton had never before seen came to his trailer and asked him if he sold anhydrous hydrazine in 55-gallon drums. At the time, Tipton had never heard of the fuel but later learned it was "rocket fuel." Tipton told the man he would have to check with another company employee on Monday to find out if he could get the fuel. When he asked the man for a phone number, the man said he had no phone because he was in the process of moving from Junction City to Salina, Kansas.

Tipton handed the man a VP Racing Fuels business card. At this point, the man asked Tipton for the price of a 55-gallon drum of nitromethane. Tipton answered $1,200.00, and the man left.

Tipton said that after the man approached him for anhydrous hydrazine and nitromethane on Saturday, he asked Wade Gray, one of his racing fuel suppliers, if he could get anhydrous hydrazine. The answer was no. Wade Gray told Tipton that if anhydrous hydrazine and nitromethane were mixed together, "you would have a bomb."

Tipton said that a few days later he received a call from a man who asked if he had any luck getting the anhydrous hydrazine. Tipton was not certain but believed it to be the same man that had approached him at the Sears Craftsman races. He told the man he could not get that type of fuel. The man hung up, and Tipton never spoke to him again.

Tipton told Agent Hersley and Prosecutor Mendeloff that after he saw news coverage of Tim McVeigh, he was 90 percent certain the man who approached him for anhydrous hydrazine and nitromethane at the racetrack in Pauline, Kansas, was McVeigh. Case Agents Hersley and Tongate noted that the payphone in Wamego, Kansas, where the calls were made from on October 1 to Michael Fortier's house and to Greg Pfaff was only a short distance from the racetrack in Pauline, Kansas. Wamego was less than a two hour drive from Marion, Kansas.

Hundreds of FBI agents followed thousands of leads in the weeks and months after the bombing. Many leads seemed mundane, others produced results. One such lead provided additional verification that McVeigh was in central Kansas during late September, 1994. A Wal-Mart store in Junction City, Kansas, provided agents with a return of merchandise receipt, dated September 26, 1994. The customer's name –Tim McVeigh. McVeigh had written his name on the receipt and also his address, Route 3, Box 83, Marion, Kansas. It was Terry Nichols' address and the same address McVeigh had given to Helen Mitchell when he rented Herington Storage shed #2 under the false name of Shawn Rivers.

On the same day, September 26, 1994, the Bridges calling card was used to make four calls from payphones in Marion and a neighboring town, Lincolnville, Kansas. One call was to the Mid-America Chemical Company in Oklahoma City. Linda Juhl, an employee at Mid-America, told FBI agents she remembered receiving a telephone call during the fall of 1994 from a man who asked about anhydrous hydrazine.

Agents noted that the call to Mid-America Chemical was only five days before McVeigh had approached Glynn Tipton at the Sears Craftsman Nationals races in Pauline, Kansas. What was McVeigh's interest in obtaining anhydrous hydrazine and nitromethane? McVeigh had previously ordered and was shipped the *Homemade C-4* book, which detailed the use of nitromethane and hydrazine to make an ammonium nitrate bomb.

On September 27, 1994, the calling card was used to make ten calls from a payphone at the Coastal Mart in Marion, Kansas. The calls were made in rapid succession to companies listed in the yellow pages under the subtitle "chemicals."

The following day, seven calls were made using the Bridges calling card from a payphone at City Hall in Marion, Kansas. These calls were made within minutes of each other to companies listed in the yellow pages under "chemicals" and "raceways."

There was an eighth call made on September 28 from Terry Nichols' home phone at the rent house provided by Donahue. This call was made to a company in Tonowanda, New York, where McVeigh's childhood friend, David Darlak, worked. Darlak told Agent Hersley and Prosecutor Mendeloff that he remembered receiving a call from McVeigh during the fall of 1994. McVeigh asked Darlak where he could buy racing fuel. Darlak told McVeigh it was sold at racetracks. Darlak had no idea of McVeigh's intended use of the fuel.

On September 29, 1994, six calls were made from Nichols' home phone at Donahue's rented farmhouse. Four of the calls were charged directly against Nichols' home phone bill, and the Bridges calling card was not used. Two of these four calls were made to the Hutchinson Raceway in Hutchinson, Kansas. One of the four calls was made to the Newton Hobby Center in Newton, Kansas. The fourth call was to David Darlak, McVeigh's friend in New York.

Gary Mussatto owned the Hutchinson Raceway. Mussatto had decided to close the raceway and had forwarded the telephone number to his home. He told Agent Hersley and Prosecutor Mendeloff that his wife received a telephone call at their home on Thursday, September 29, from a man who asked about racing fuel. Mussatto said he remembered this date because he and his wife were scheduled to move the next day and he had left to pick up a rental truck for the move. Mussatto said his wife told the man to call back in the afternoon when her husband would be home.

Later that afternoon, the man called again and asked if Mussatto sold nitromethane. When he answered that he did not, the man asked if Mussatto knew where he could get nitromethane. Mussatto told him to go to a drag strip or to a company that sold racing fuel.

Only two days later a man closely resembling McVeigh approached Glynn Tipton for nitromethane and anhydrous hydrazine at the Sears Craftsman races in Pauline, Kansas.

The remaining two calls made from Nichols' home on September 29 were made to companies in the yellow pages listed under "demolition."

C ase Agents Hersley and Tongate orchestrated regular reviews
of the evidence with FBI managers and federal prosecutors.
The investigation produced a mountain of evidence implicating Tim McVeigh and Terry Nichols in the bombing of the Murrah
Building.

On June 9, 1995, Hersley testified for several hours before a federal
grand jury in Oklahoma City, outlining specifics of the government's
growing case against McVeigh and Nichols. Hersley's testimony resulted
in the indictment of McVeigh and Nichols for planning and carrying out
the bombing of the Alfred P. Murrah Federal Building and the deaths of
innocent men, women, and children that resulted.

Listed below is a summary of evidence gathered in the early months of
the investigation.

A 20-foot Ryder truck, used in the bombing, was rented on April 17, 1995, from Elliott's Body Shop by a man using the name Robert "Bob" Kling. Kling's date of birth shown on his drivers license was, April 19, 1970, the anniversary date of the Waco tragedy. The owner of the body shop identified Kling as Tim McVeigh. The address, Social Security number, and drivers license provided by Kling were determined by the FBI to be bogus.

Tim McVeigh was registered at the Dreamland Motel, room 25, from April 14 -18, 1995. McVeigh brought a Ryder truck to the motel two days before the Oklahoma City bombing. A telephone order for Chinese food was placed by a Mr. Kling from room 25.

McVeigh was arrested by Trooper Charlie Hanger on Interstate 35, north of Perry, Oklahoma, at a time and distance consistent with him having been in Oklahoma City at the time of the bombing. Clothing worn by McVeigh at the time of his arrest included the "Tree of Liberty" tee-shirt, complete with blood droplets and the statement, "The Tree of Liberty must be refreshed from time to time with the blood of Patriots and Tyrants." On the front of the tee-shirt was the face of Abraham Lincoln and the Latin phrase, Sic Semper Tyrannis, which means Death unto Tyrants.

PETN residue was found on McVeigh's shirt and pants at the time of his arrest. PETN is a chemical found in Det Cord. EGDN residue was found on a set of earplugs found in McVeigh's pocket at the time of his arrest. EGDN is a chemical found in dynamite.

Anti-government literature was found in McVeigh's car when he was arrested. Among the documents found was this statement, "When the government fears the people, there is liberty. When the people fear the government, there is tyranny." Underneath, in McVeigh's handwriting, were the words, "Maybe now, there will be liberty."

Terry Nichols' admission that he was in Oklahoma City with McVeigh on Easter Sunday, three days before the bombing. Nichols also admitted he drove around the Murrah Building a couple of times looking for McVeigh.

Michael Fortier said McVeigh told him in August or early September, 1994, that he and Nichols had decided to blow up a federal building in response to the government's actions in Waco.

The Mid-Kansas Co-op customer receipt for the purchase of 2,000 pounds of ammonium nitrate, dated September 30, 1994, in the name of Mike Havens, was found in the kitchen cabinet at Nichols' Herington home. McVeigh had rented storage unit #2 in Herington on September 22, 1994, using the false name of Shawn Rivers.

A customer, using the name Mike Havens, purchased a second 2,000 pounds of ammonium nitrate from Mid-Kansas Co-op on October 18, 1994. Nichols rented a storage unit in Council Grove, Kansas, on October 17, 1994, under the false name of Joe Kyle.

Ammonium nitrate fertilizer prills were found on the front porch and sidewalk of Nichols' home during the FBI search on April 22-23, 1995.

The book, *Hunter*, by William Pierce, was found in Nichols' house.

The Daryl Bridges calling card coupon booklet was found in Nichols' house.

McVeigh used the Bridges calling card to contact Greg Pfaff about acquiring det cord.

McVeigh approached Glynn Tipton on October 1, 1994, at the Sears Craftsman races near Topeka, Kansas and asked about anhydrous hydrazine and nitromethane.

A rock quarry ten miles from Nichols' rent house was burglarized during the first weekend of October, 1994. A large quantity of explosives and blasting caps was stolen. A Makita cordless drill and drill bit found in Nichols' house matched the drill bit used to drill a lock during the rock quarry burglary.

Primadet blasting caps, like those stolen from the quarry, were found in Nichols' house. Other explosives of the same type stolen from the quarry were shown to Michael Fortier by McVeigh and Nichols at a storage shed in Kingman, Arizona.

The Evil Plan

ori Fortier told the FBI about a chilling conversation she said took place in the living room of the Fortiers' trailer home while McVeigh was staying with them in early October, 1994. McVeigh told Lori and her husband, Michael, he was going to bomb the federal building in Oklahoma City, using a rental truck to carry the bomb. He diagrammed the box portion of the truck and drew circles, representing barrels, inside the box diagram.

McVeigh told the Fortiers he was going to use ammonium nitrate and anhydrous hydrazine, which he described as a type of racing fuel, in the bomb. These materials would be contained in barrels in the box of the truck. McVeigh said he was also going to use the sausage explosives that he and Nichols had stolen from the rock quarry in Kansas.

McVeigh said he selected the federal building in Oklahoma City because it housed some of the federal agents involved in the Waco incident. He said the high volume of glass on the front side of the building would increase injury to the people inside.

In precise detail, McVeigh told the Fortiers he would run two fuses from inside the cab of the truck to the back. He said the barrels would be situated in the shape of a triangle that would create a shape-charge to cause the most damage to the building. McVeigh said the point of the triangle would face away from the building, and the flat side of the triangle of barrels would face the building, enabling him to get the most impact from the bomb. McVeigh told the Fortiers that Nichols was going to help him build the bomb.

Lori said that on another day, McVeigh further demonstrated to her how he was going to construct the bomb. Michael had gone to work, and Lori and her daughter were alone with McVeigh in the house. McVeigh went to the kitchen cupboard and took out a number of soup cans. He placed the cans in a triangle on the floor to demonstrate for Lori how he was going to arrange the barrels in the back of the bomb truck.

McVeigh also told the Fortiers about a robbery he and Nichols had planned as a fundraiser for their project. McVeigh said they planned to rob a man named Bob, a gun dealer in Arkansas. McVeigh had previously stayed with Bob but had left on bad terms. Bob owned many guns and McVeigh and Nichols planned to steal them. McVeigh said Nichols was probably going to rob Bob alone. McVeigh had considered helping in the robbery but was concerned that Bob might recognize him because of their prior association.

Lori said McVeigh frequently used their telephone. In early October, McVeigh told Lori that he needed to use their phone to make a call regarding the anhydrous hydrazine he had told the Fortiers he planned to use in the bomb. Lori told agents she saw McVeigh make this call, but did not actually hear what was discussed.

Tracking of the Bridges calling card confirmed that McVeigh and Nichols were in Kingman, Arizona, at the time testified to by Michael and Lori Fortier. On October 6, two calls were made from a payphone in Kingman to Lana Padilla's house in Las Vegas. One of the calls was 4 minutes and 26 seconds, and the other call lasted 5 minutes and 27 seconds.

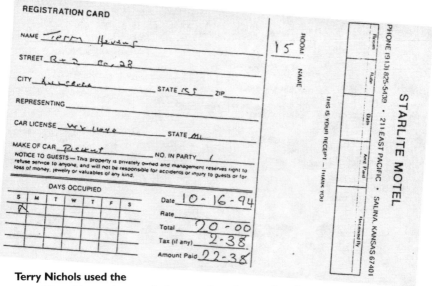

Terry Nichols used the
name Terry Havens in completing a registration card at the
Starlite Motel in Salina, Kansas, two days before purchasing 2,000 pounds of
ammonium nitrate in McPherson, Kansas, using the name Mike Havens.

Lana Padilla had previously told agents that Nichols came to Las Vegas to visit their son in October, 1994. She also told agents that she had never spoken on the phone with McVeigh for more than a minute at a time. Agents believed it was Nichols who made the calls to Padilla's house shortly before traveling there in early October to visit his son.

Jennifer McVeigh told Agent Hersley and Prosecutor Beth Wilkinson that while in New York in November, 1994, McVeigh told her about an occasion when he was traveling with explosives and was nearly involved in an accident. He bragged to his younger sister that he and a buddy were traveling in a caravan and were carrying up to a thousand pounds of explosives. The information provided by Jennifer McVeigh appeared to corroborate similar information provided by the Fortiers.

Michael Fortier told Agent David Brundage and Prosecutor Aitan Goelman that McVeigh and Nichols left Kingman after showing him the explosives and experimenting with them in the desert in early October. To track the two suspects, federal agents were assigned the massive task of checking records of motels along highways between Kingman and Junction City, Kansas. The project became known as the hotel/motel search.

It was a tedious, arduous, time consuming, and often outright boring job. However, at other times it paid huge dividends. While reviewing records at the Starlite Motel in Salina, Kansas, ATF Agent Tony Donaldson located a registration card dated October 16, 1994, in the name of Terry Havens. Salina is just 38 miles north of McPherson, Kansas, where the ammonium nitrate purchases were made by a man using the name Mike Havens. Salina is also about 50 miles west of Junction City, where the Ryder truck used in the bombing had been rented. Terry Havens' address was listed on the motel registration card as Route 2, Box 28, Hillsboro, Kansas. His vehicle was listed as a pickup, Michigan license WX 1640.

Who was Terry Havens? Was this merely a coincidence in names? Could Terry Havens be related to Mid-Kansas Co-op customer Mike Havens. The second 2,000-pound quantity of ammonium nitrate was purchased from the co-op by Mike Havens on October 18, 1994, just two days after guest Terry Havens had registered at the Starlite Motel in Salina. By now, Case Agents Hersley and Tongate were fully aware that Terry Nichols' 1984 GMC pickup had been licensed in the state of Michigan. The license plate on Nichols' pickup read WX 1460, only a slight variation from the tag number given by Terry Havens.

The Starlite Motel registration card was hand carried by FBI Agent Joe Twardowski to the FBI laboratory for fingerprint analysis. Four of Terry Nichols' fingerprints were found on the card. Also compelling was the fact that FBI handwriting experts and Nichols' ex-wife, Lana Padilla, identified the handwriting on the registration card as that of Nichols.

The Bridges calling card provided additional information confirming that Nichols was in central Kansas in mid-October, 1994. On October 17, two calls were made using the Bridges card from payphones in Herington, Kansas. The first call was to Google Trucking, a company identified by Glynn Tipton as a seller of nitromethane at racetracks. The second call was made from the Pizza Hut Restaurant, located diagonally across from the Herington Storage Units. The call from the Pizza Hut payphone was to Lana Padilla in Las Vegas. The duration of the call was 6 minutes and 41 seconds. Agents Hersley and Tongate were certain the caller was Nichols.

Buying Ammonium Nitrate

Mid-Kansas Co-op employees Rick Schlender and Jerry Showalter remembered very little about the sale of ammonium nitrate to customer

Mike Havens on September 30 and October 18, 1994. The last sale was nearly six months before the Murrah Building bombing.

Schlender remembered loading the fertilizer onto a trailer pulled by a pickup. After seeing news coverage of McVeigh after his arrest, Schlender was almost certain the driver of the pickup was not McVeigh. He could not say the same about Nichols. He remembered that Mike Havens told him he was going to use the ammonium nitrate to sow wheat on farmland to the east of McPherson. In the past, it had been common for farmers to use ammonium nitrate prill to sow their wheat—it gave the wheat a boost, which caused it to sprout and pop from the ground.

Even though it was common to sell the fertilizer to wheat farmers, Schlender later struggled over the transactions. He was a decent, honorable, and hard-working family man, the kind of man whose heart and soul America was built upon. Had he sold the ammonium nitrate used in the Oklahoma City bombing to the perpetrators of this awful, horrific crime? Should he have known? No one could have known, but Schlender's anguish made him another victim of the bombing, hundreds of miles from Oklahoma City.

Where was Terry Nichols on October 18, 1994, when Mike Havens bought ammonium nitrate between noon and 1:30 p.m.? Schlender and Showalter knew their customers. They were able to identify the approximate time of the Havens purchase by comparing their numbered receipts with the approximate times of day that known customers came to the store.

The Bridges calling card again provided answers. On October 18, seven calls were made from a payphone at the Coastal Mart in Council Grove, Kansas. Three of the calls were to bottling companies in Hutchinson, Kansas. One call was to the Collingwood Grain Company and another was to Purina Mills. One call was to the Kansas information operator. The last call was to Equity Standard Numismatics, a coin shop in Wichita, Kansas, the same coin shop McVeigh and Marife Nichols had visited on September 14, 1994, just before she left for the Philippines. All the calls were made in a period of 33 minutes, beginning at 3:32 p.m.

Agents had determined that Nichols rented Council Grove storage unit #40 the day before the second fertilizer purchase. They wanted to know if Nichols was in Council Grove on October 18. Had Nichols rented the storage unit in Council Grove to store the ammonium nitrate purchased on that date? McPherson was approximately 80 miles from Council Grove, an approximate 90-minute drive carrying 2,000 pounds of ammonium nitrate.

Agents determined Nichols had ample time to buy the fertilizer, drive to Council Grove, unload the 40 bags of ammonium nitrate with the help of McVeigh, and drive one mile to the Coastal Mart to make the above mentioned calls.

On the morning of October 19, Nichols was the first customer to walk into the Equity Standard Numismatics coin shop. He arrived at 10:07 a.m. and left 10 minutes later, a fact confirmed by a video security camera. If Nichols was involved in the calls from the Coastal Mart payphone, then agents had placed him in Council Grove on the very day the second ammonium nitrate purchase was made at Mid-Kansas Co-op. Also, agents could develop no information that Nichols needed a storage shed on that date for any other reason except in which to store the second ammonium nitrate purchase.

Telephone records confirmed that another series of phone calls was charged to the calling card on October 19. These calls were made to companies listed in the yellow pages under "barrels and drums." Five of the calls were made from a payphone at the Denny's Restaurant in Wichita, Kansas. The restaurant was located diagonally across the street from Equity Standard Numismatics. Nichols had left the coin shop at 10:17 a.m. and the calls made from the restaurant began at 10:24 a.m. Why was Nichols in need of barrels?

On October 20, calling card calls to businesses identified as chemical companies, racetracks, or racing fuel suppliers suddenly stopped. The FBI would soon learn that McVeigh and Nichols possessed all the ingredients to make a killer bomb, but needed containers to mix their deadly ingredients.

The Final Ingredient

Tim Chambers, like Glynn Tipton, sold racing fuel at racetracks across the country. Both worked for VP Racing Fuels. Chambers told Agents Hersley and Floyd Zimms that he remembered selling nitromethane to a man at the Chief Auto Parts races held at the MaryLou Racetrack in Ennis, Texas, during the third weekend of October, 1994.

The cash receipt given Timothy McVeigh for the purchase of three drums of nitromethane at the racetrack at Ennis, Texas, on October 21, 1994. The drums were loaded into a pickup truck similar in description to the truck owned by Terry Nichols.

He remembered the transaction because it was the only time he had sold three 55-gallon barrels of nitromethane at a race. Customers ususally bought the fuel in one to five-gallon amounts. He loaded the three barrels of nitromethane onto a pickup with a faded white camper shell. Chambers remembered the buyer because his facial features resembled that of a possum, with eyes set close together and a long skinny nose pointed downward.

The man told Chambers he and a bunch of his friends got together each year and traveled to the races in Ennis to buy nitromethane to fuel Harley Davidson motorcycles which they raced in the Oklahoma City area. Chambers thought the man's story was odd because of the quantity of fuel sold. He had never sold that much fuel to one customer at a race-track. By reviewing VP Racing Fuels sales records, Chambers was able to identify the date he sold the three barrels of nitromethane at the races in Ennis, Texas, as October 21, 1994. The sales price was $925.00 per barrel, a total of $2,775.00. Chambers also sold the man a used plastic siphon pump for $5.00. The man paid $2,780.00 in cash, another reason Chambers remembered the transaction so vividly.

There was other evidence that McVeigh and Nichols were in Texas to buy the racing fuel. At 9:03 p.m. on October 20, 1994, the night before

The motel registration card of Joe Kyle at the Amish Inn in Pauls Valley, Oklahoma, on October 20, 1994, the night before the purchase of racing fuel in Texas. Pauls Valley was on the normal route from Kansas to the racetrack in Ennis, Texas. The handwriting on the card was identified as that of Terry Nichols.

the purchase at the race-track in Ennis, another phone call had been made, using the Bridges calling card, to the Spotlight Company to check the balance that remained on the account. The call was made from the Amish Inn Motel in Pauls Valley, Oklahoma, a small town located approximately 40 miles south of Oklahoma City on Interstate 35. Agents were dispatched to Pauls Valley immediately where they learned that a man, using the name Joe Kyle, had registered at the Amish Inn on that night. Kyle's address was listed on the motel registration card as Route 2, Box 28, Hillsboro, Kansas, the same address used by Terry Havens at the Starlite Motel in Salina, Kansas, on October 16, 1994.

Joe Kyle's vehicle description was not indicated on the motel registra-tion card, but his license plate number was—Michigan, XW 1640, the same slight variation used by Terry Havens in Salina. WX 1460 was the actual license assigned to the 1984 GMC pickup registered to Terry Nichols.

Lana Padilla and FBI handwriting experts identified the handwriting on the Amish Inn Motel registration card as that of Terry Nichols. FBI Agents knew Pauls Valley was on a direct route from the MaryLou Racetrack in Ennis, Texas, to Herington and Junction City, Kansas.

On October 23, 1994, three calls were made on the calling card from a payphone at the Kede Bo Video Store in Junction City, Kansas. The first call was made at 4:33 p.m. to Michael Fortier's residence in Kingman, Arizona. The call lasted 5 minutes and 45 seconds. The second call was made at 4:41 p.m. to McVeigh's father's house in Pendleton, New York.

This call lasted 10 minutes and 39 seconds. The third call was made at 5:11 p.m. to Lana Padilla's residence in Las Vegas. This call lasted 2 minutes and 9 seconds.

Because of the destination of the calls, agents believed that McVeigh and Nichols were traveling together in central Kansas, close in time to the rental of the Joe Kyle storage unit and the second purchase of ammonium nitrate.

Michael Fortier had told agents that after McVeigh and Nichols left Kingman in early to mid-October, 1994, he received a telephone call from McVeigh's father. McVeigh's grandfather had passed away, and Bill McVeigh wanted to get word of the grandfather's death to his son. Fortier told Bill McVeigh he would pass the information to his son when he next heard from him. Agent Hersley believed it was likely that Fortier told McVeigh of his grandfather's death during the phone call that Fortier

Photographs taken when the FBI searched Herington Storage Unit #2 shortly after the Oklahoma City bombing identified three circular stains on the concrete floor of the storage unit. The diameter and circumference of the circular stains were identical to the diameter and circumference of the 55-gallon barrels of nitromethane Tim Chambers sold to the man at the MaryLou Racetrack on October 21, 1994, the day after Terry Nichols stayed at a motel in Pauls Valley.

received from McVeigh on October 23, 1994. Immediately after McVeigh called Fortier, there was another call from the same payphone to McVeigh's father's house in New York.

The hotel/motel search conducted by agents along Interstate 40 and Interstate 35, routes known to have been traveled by McVeigh and Nichols, produced additional results. On October 25, 1994, a man using the name Joe Havens registered at the Buckaroo Motel in Tucumcari, New Mexico, a small town on Interstate 40 between Amarillo, Texas, and Kingman, Arizona. Lana Padilla and FBI handwriting experts identified the handwriting on the Buckaroo Motel registration card as that of Terry Nichols. Nichols had now used the Havens name at the Starlite and Buckaroo motels around the time that the second purchase of ammonium nitrate was made to Mike Havens. And the receipt for the first ammonium nitrate purchase had been found in Nichols' home. No agent believed it was a mere coincidence.

On another visit to Arizona at the end of October, 1994, Michael Fortier said McVeigh gave more details of his plan to bomb the Murrah Building. McVeigh announced he would carry out the bombing on April 19, the anniversary of the Waco fire.

McVeigh said he wanted to blow up the building at 11:00 a.m. before anyone left for lunch. When Fortier asked his friend what would happen to the people inside the building, McVeigh compared them to storm troopers in the movie Star Wars. He said that while the people in the building might be individually

The registration card from the Buckaroo Motel showing Terry Nichols, using the name Joe Havens, stayed at the motel on October 25, 1994.

Above: Storage space E-10 at Northern Storage in Kingman, Arizona, was used by McVeigh and Nichols to store explosives stolen from the Martin Marietta rock quarry. The storage unit was rented within three or four days of the burglary at the Kansas rock quarry.

Left: Copy of Timothy McVeigh's rental agreement for the storage unit at Northern Storage in Kingman, Arizona, signed on October 4, 1994.

innocent, they were still part of the evil empire, and therefore, guilty by association.

Before leaving Arizona, McVeigh and Nichols invited Michael Fortier to travel into the desert to test explosives. Fortier walked to Nichols' pick-up with McVeigh and saw a plastic milk jug filled with fuel oil and granular material. McVeigh said he was going to ignite the jug of explosives with a blasting cap. McVeigh reached into the bed of the pickup and pulled out one of the Tovex sausage explosives about 12 inches long.

Fortier said that McVeigh and Nichols' excursion into the desert on this occasion sounded like trouble to him. He decided not to go with them. Later the same day, McVeigh returned to Fortier's residence, but Nichols was no longer with him. McVeigh told Fortier that Nichols had gone to Las Vegas to visit his son but that he and Nichols had tested the explosives before Nichols left.

Fortier said he remembered McVeigh waiting and becoming anxious that Nichols had not returned from Las Vegas. Finally, McVeigh decided to leave Kingman by himself. Before he left, McVeigh told Fortier that when Nichols arrived to tell him to "get the things from the storage shed" and meet him in New Mexico at the predetermined location.

Rental records maintained by the Northern Storage facility confirmed that McVeigh was in Kingman, Arizona, in late October, 1994. A $60.00 cash payment was made on McVeigh's storage unit at Northern Storage on October 27, 1994. Rent on the unit was paid through February 4, 1995. Records at the Buckaroo Motel in Tucumcari, New Mexico, had previously confirmed that Terry Nichols, using the name Joe Havens, was at the motel on the evening of October 25, 1994. Again, independent evidence had corroborated information provided by the Fortiers that McVeigh and Nichols had traveled to Kingman in late October, 1994.

Records at the Union 76 Motel in Albuquerque, New Mexico, confirmed that McVeigh was registered at the motel on the evening of October 30, 1994. The next night, October 31, McVeigh was registered at the Catalina Motel in Pratt, Kansas. Jennifer McVeigh identified the handwriting on the registration cards at both the Union 76 Motel and the Catalina Motel as being that of her brother. Agents believed McVeigh and Nichols had left Kingman and returned to central Kansas with a load of explosives and know-how to carry out their plan to build a bomb.

The Fundraiser

G un dealer **Roger Moore** lived part of each year on 10 wooded
acres outside Royal, Arkansas. He had an unusual relationship
with his wife and a woman named Karen Anderson. Moore had
been married to his wife, Carol, since 1955, and spent the winter with her
each year in Florida.

Moore spent the remaining eight months of the year living with Karen
Anderson in Arkansas where they raised horses, ducks, geese, and chick-
ens on their secluded property. Moore and Anderson had a mail order
ammunition business and they sold ammunition at gun shows throughout the country

Moore had learned over the years that being in the gun show business
meant meeting all kinds of people. Some were wonderful—and there
were some whose intentions were not so noble. Moore used the alias, Bob

Miller, on the gun show circuit. Sometimes, customers simply referred to him as "Bob from Arkansas."

Moore had collected guns for many years. By 1994, his gun collection had grown to nearly 90 weapons—shotguns, rifles, and handguns. Moore tried to buy special insurance protection for his gun collection. However, when his agent told him he would be required to list his guns for an insurance rider, Moore thought someone at the home office of the insurance company might wrongly use the information to set him up for a robbery. Thinking that he may be killed in a robbery, Moore decided to forego an insurance rider—loss of his guns was not worth getting killed over. He decided to keep quiet about his collection.

Moore owned a 50-60 piece collection of jade he had discovered while digging on the west coast of Costa Rica in 1974. He also had a collection of Tiki dolls and another of precious stones, which he had acquired in Saudi Arabia and Ceylon. The collection included cut diamonds, sapphires, opals, and emeralds.

Moore stored the jade and precious stones in cigar boxes wrapped in paper towels and toilet paper to hide them. Inside the cigar boxes were keys to two safe deposit boxes he maintained, one in Florida and another in Arkansas.

On November 5, 1994, Karen Anderson left the home in Royal to attend a gun show in Shreveport, Louisiana. Moore was alone. The following morning, he was walking toward the barn to feed his animals when a man shouted, "Lay on the ground!"

As he turned around, Moore saw a man dressed in camouflage with gloves and a black ski mask. The man leveled a pistol grip shotgun to Moore's face. The shotgun was equipped with a garrote wire that dangled from the end of the gun's barrel. The man stood 5'10" - 5'11" and weighed around 165 pounds, but with the barrel of his shotgun in his face, he seemed much larger to Moore.

Again came the shout, "Lay on the ground!" This time, Moore complied. The man moved the barrel of the shotgun to the back of Moore's head and asked, "Is anyone else home?" Moore answered, "No." The man ordered Moore to crawl on his hands and knees back into the house. Once inside, the man told Moore to lie on his stomach on the floor. Moore's hands were secured behind his back and to one of his ankles with police ties. Duct tape was placed over his eyes and a jacket thrown over his head.

As Moore lay frightened on the floor, the robber began going through his home. He could hear and sense the man as he made his way into the bedrooms, down the hallway, and into the bathrooms. The man came back to Moore and asked, "Where is the money?" Moore answered, "It's on the computer desk in the bedroom." The night before, Moore had counted $8,700 in cash and placed it there.

For 30 minutes, Moore heard the robber come and go from the house, obviously carrying stolen goods to a waiting vehicle. Moore told the robber that the ties on his wrists and ankles were cutting off the blood supply. The man cut the ties and wrapped duct tape around Moore's arms, securing them to his body. Moore was frightened and confused. Would he live or die? The man told Moore to be still. He told Moore that he had an accomplice outside with a shotgun, and that they would be back for the rest of the loot.

The robber again moved outside. Moore heard the door of his custom-made van open. The engine started and the van drove away. Moore waited until he was sure the man was gone. He managed to get the duct tape removed from his eyes by catching the end of the tape on a corner of his couch and pulling against it. His arms, legs, and ankles remained secured by the tape. Finally, he managed to knock a penknife off a table onto the floor. The knife was open—Moore had used it the night before to tighten a loose screw in his eyeglasses.

He struggled to reach the knife and began cutting the tape. As he cut, he hoped the robber had indeed left. Finally, he was free. He made it to a phone. The line was dead. It had been cut.

Moore first went to the master bedroom. Everything had been taken. Guns from the master bedroom closet and others that were kept throughout the home had all been stolen. Shoulder weapons, including Rugers, Remingtons, Brownings, Winchesters, Mossbergs, Hopkins, an Uzi prop gun (used in the movies), M-1 carbines, SKS and AK Chinese rifles, Mini-14's, AR-15's, and two .50 caliber rifles.

Silver coins kept in the bottom dresser drawer were gone. So were the cigar boxes with the tiki dolls, jade, and the two safe deposit box keys, the precious stones, and camera and video equipment. The robber had used pillowcases from the beds of Moore and Karen Anderson to carry the loot from his home. Even the comforter from Anderson's bed was gone— most likely used to carry guns and other valuables.

Moore looked inside a closed box next to the lounge chair where he sat to watch television. The robber had missed a .45 caliber stainless steel automatic pistol that Moore kept hidden there. He placed the gun in his waistband before heading outside. He saw Anderson's pickup parked by the barn. She almost always left the keys to the pickup in the ignition. He looked, but the keys were gone. He started down the driveway before deciding to cross the fence and head to his neighbor's house. From there, he called the sheriff and reported the robbery. A deputy found Moore's van abandoned only two miles from his home.

After the robbery, Moore was asked by sheriff's deputies investigating the crime to develop a list of names of people who had visited him at the secluded location and knew about his collection of guns. Moore told the deputy about Tim McVeigh whom Moore had met at a gun show in Florida the previous year. McVeigh had been dressed in military gear and sold ammunition and other items at the gun show. The two had also met at a gun show in Tulsa, Oklahoma, where Moore remembered young McVeigh's strong anti-government rhetoric. After the Tulsa show, McVeigh stayed with Moore and Anderson at their home in Arkansas for about 10 days. McVeigh talked often about Waco during this time. It was before the tragic fire, and McVeigh told Moore he had been to Waco. McVeigh believed the government was infringing on the rights of its citizens by allowing federal agents to surround David Koresh's followers at the Branch Davidian compound at Waco.

McVeigh had become extraordinarily angry at the federal government. He told Moore that he believed the government, without his knowledge or consent, had inserted a tiny glass transistor in his posterior when he was inoculated in Saudi Arabia before Desert Storm.

Moore talked with McVeigh about the lack of security at his Arkansas home. Together, they walked the perimeter of the property. Moore wanted to get McVeigh's ideas on the best kind of perimeter security. He confided to McVeigh that he had no perimeter security or security system at his house.

When McVeigh left Moore's home in Royal, he said he was heading west to Kingman, Arizona. For awhile, McVeigh and Moore exchanged letters. McVeigh wrote that he was very upset at the federal government after the tragic fire at Waco. However, Moore did not see McVeigh again until the Soldier of Fortune Gun Show in Las Vegas, Nevada, in September, 1993. McVeigh had become obsessed with the "New World Order."

Moore saw fire in McVeigh's eyes as he spoke about the Waco fire. McVeigh raised his voice at Moore, and they engaged in a heated argument over McVeigh's expressions of his political philosophy. Moore was concerned that he might be asked to leave the gun show because paperwork handed out by show sponsors specifically stated that political rhetoric was not to be spewed.

McVeigh had asked to stay with Moore and Anderson in their motel room during the gun show. Moore allowed McVeigh to spend the first night with them, but after they argued, Moore told McVeigh he needed to find another place to stay.

Moore next saw McVeigh at the Knob Creek Gun Show held the first week of October each year in West Point, Kentucky. Moore had become concerned about McVeigh's increased level of anger at the federal government. He did not see McVeigh again until April or May, 1994, when McVeigh showed up, unannounced, at Moore's home in Arkansas.

Moore allowed McVeigh to spend the night. McVeigh left the next day telling Moore he was going to scout 300 United Nations vehicles that were located at a military base in Saucier, Mississippi. McVeigh told Moore that he was also going to Avon Park, a military base located in central Florida. McVeigh said he was going to visit his sister while in Florida, and that he would probably work there as an electrical assistant to raise money to continue his travels.

After the robbery of his home, Moore immediately suspected McVeigh. He knew the actual robber, the man who had tied him up, was not McVeigh, but he suspected McVeigh's involvement in planning the robbery. Only three people had visited Moore's home in the two years prior to the robbery, and only McVeigh was not accounted for.

Moore wrote to McVeigh in Arizona, thinking he might be able to persuade McVeigh to visit him. Moore thought he could stare McVeigh down and determine if he knew anything about the robbery. To get McVeigh's attention, he talked about anti-government topics he knew McVeigh would be interested in. Moore concluded the letter by telling McVeigh to watch out for radiation, virus spray, and other types of electron mind-altering devices. He told McVeigh he needed to acquire space blankets to keep him out of the government's satellite eyes. McVeigh had talked a lot about such things when he visited Moore previously.

McVeigh never responded to the letter.

The FBI confirmed that McVeigh was registered at a gun show in Akron, Ohio, the same weekend that Moore was robbed. Several people reported seeing McVeigh who was registered at the Knights Inn in Kent, Ohio. The FBI considered McVeigh's possible involvement in the robbery. Had he planned the robbery as Moore suspected? McVeigh had told Michael Fortier that Terry Nichols was going to rob "Bob in Arkansas" as a fund raiser. Where was Nichols on Saturday, November 5?

The FBI had traced Nichols' activities during the first days of early November, 1994, as he made arrangements for a trip to the Philippines. Nichols had returned to central Kansas. Mesbah Chowdhury, who owned and operated the Sunset Motel, located just outside Junction City, Kansas, confirmed that Nichols stayed at his motel in early November, 1994. Chowdhury had previously met Nichols when he stayed at the motel in March of that same year, shortly before Nichols moved into the Donahue rent house and began working on the Donahue Hayhook Ranch. Chowdhury remembered Nichols because he was always trying to get a lower room rate.

Chowdhury told agents that in early November, Nichols came to the motel and told Chowdhury he wanted to rent a room for a friend that was coming into town. Nichols completed a guest registration card in the name of Joe Kyle. The date on the registration card was November 5, 1994. Nichols paid for the room in cash as he always did. Nichols listed Joe Kyle's address on the Sunset Motel registration card as 1400 Decker, Lum, Michigan.

Joe Kyle was the same name Nichols had used when he registered at the Amish Inn Motel in Pauls Valley, Oklahoma, on October 20, 1994. It was also the same name he used to rent Council Grove storage unit #40 on October 17, 1994. Agents later determined the address of 1400 Decker, Lum, Michigan was a non-existent address. Chowdhury confirmed that Nichols had rented no other rooms at his motel on the evening of November 5. Was Nichols really Joe Kyle?

Agents wondered if Nichols could have robbed Roger Moore in Arkansas on Saturday morning, November 5, and made it back to Junction City in time to check in under the name of Joe Kyle at the Sunset Motel. The distance from Royal, Arkansas, to the Sunset Motel in Junction City was approximately 518 miles.

Agents calculated it would take no more than nine and one half hours to drive this distance even at a very reasonable speed of 55 miles per hour. If Nichols left Moore's house by 11:00 a.m. that morning, he could easily have been in Junction City by 8:30 p.m. A series of telephone calls and other occurrences on November 6 and 7, 1994, led agents to believe that Nichols may well have carried out the robbery.

On November 6, two Bridges card calls were made from a payphone at the Waters TruValue Hardware Store in Manhattan, Kansas, a short drive from Junction City. Both calls were to McVeigh's father's house in Pendleton, New York, and were made at 12:54 p.m. and 3:36 p.m. Each call lasted approximately one minute. Bill McVeigh told agents his son came to visit him in early November, 1994, as a result of his grandfather's death.

A third Bridges card call at 5:24 p.m. on the same day from the same payphone at the hardware store led agents to believe that Terry Nichols had made the Bridges card calls earlier that day to McVeigh's father's house. The third call was a 32-minute call to Esquire Realty, where Lana Padilla worked. If Nichols had used this payphone on November 6 to call Padilla, then it was likely he had also made the calls to Bill McVeigh's house in New York the same day.

The calls to Pendleton, New York, lasted only about one minute each, a fact that caused agents to theorize that Nichols might have been unsuccessful in his efforts to contact McVeigh. McVeigh had attended the gun show in Ohio that weekend and was likely still traveling from Ohio back to his father's house in Pendleton when the calls were made. Also of interest to agents was the fact that when the home of Bill McVeigh was searched after his son's arrest outside Perry, Oklahoma, a small sheet of paper with a telephone number written on it was seized. The number was for the payphone outside the TruValue Hardware Store in Manhattan, Kansas. Jennifer McVeigh told agents the handwriting on this sheet of paper was hers, but claimed she was unable to recall why she had written down the number.

Another Bridges card call was made later on November 6. At 7:41 p.m., a call was made from a payphone near Bill McVeigh's home in Pendleton. This call was made to the telephone number at the payphone outside the TruValue Hardware Store, but the call was not answered.

At 8:23 a.m. on November 7, a telephone call was made from McVeigh's grandfather's house in New York to the same payphone at the Manhattan hardware store. Again, the call was not answered. At 8:46 a.m. that same morning, another Bridges card call was made from a payphone near McVeigh's grandfather's house to the payphone at the TruValue Hardware Store. Again, the call went unanswered. Both Bill and Jennifer McVeigh told agents that Tim McVeigh spent several nights at his late grandfather's house when he returned to upstate New York in early November, 1994.

Another important piece of evidence linking Nichols to the Roger Moore robbery was the rental of storage unit #37 at Council Grove on November 7, two days after the robbery. Sharri Furman told agents that Nichols, using the name Ted Parker, rented the storage unit. She recognized Nichols as Ted Parker after his arrest in connection with the Oklahoma City bombing.

The handwriting on the Parker rental agreement was identified by Lana Padilla as that of Terry Nichols. Also, an FBI fingerprint expert identified Nichols' fingerprints on the agreement. Why did Nichols need a storage unit on November 7, just two days after Moore was robbed and only three weeks after he had rented another storage unit at the same complex?

Registration records at the Travelers Motel in Manhattan, Kansas, indicated a guest had stayed on November 7 under the name Ted Parker. Again, Lana Padilla identified the handwriting on this registration card as that of Terry Nichols. Agents Hersley and Tongate were certain—Terry Nichols was Ted Parker and he was also Joe Kyle.

Agents remembered Nichols had purchased a $100.00 money order payable to the Spotlight Company, in the name of Daryl Bridges, on November 7, 1994. The money order was purchased in Manhattan, Kansas. Another indication that Nichols was in Manhattan, Kansas, on the same day Ted Parker registered at the Travelers Motel.

On the evening of November 7, several calls from Nichols to McVeigh went unanswered. Finally, a Bridges card call made from the Travelers Motel at 7:22 p.m. to Bill McVeigh's house in Pendleton was answered. The call lasted approximately six minutes. Nichols and McVeigh had finally made contact. What was the purpose of these calls? Had Nichols wanted to tell McVeigh about the Roger Moore robbery and the Ted Parker storage rental before he left for the Philippines?

A final Bridges card call made that same evening confirmed that Nichols was at the Travelers Motel in Manhattan, Kansas, on the evening of November 7. At 10:45 p.m., a Bridges card call was made from the motel to Lana Padilla.

Padilla told agents about a call she received from Nichols prior to him leaving for the Philippines. She was having a difficult time with their son Josh and wanted help. But all Nichols talked about was Waco, civil unrest, and how the government was overreaching. He talked about a recent news event in which a man was arrested for shooting at the White House. Nichols said the man was justified in his actions. Padilla said Nichols was obsessed with his cause and predicted there would be civil unrest in the United States.

Michael Fortier confirmed Nichols' involvement in the robbery. He told Agent Brundage and Prosecutor Goelman that McVeigh called him and told him Nichols had robbed "Bob in Arkansas." McVeigh said he was concerned that "Bob" might suspect McVeigh in the robbery and send private investigators to Arizona looking for him. McVeigh cautioned Fortier to watch his backside because the investigators might want to talk to Fortier since he and McVeigh were friends.

While Nichols was robbing Roger Moore, McVeigh spent most of the month of November, 1994, in New York, part of the time at his father's house and several nights at his deceased grandfather's house. It was during this time that McVeigh told his sister, Jennifer, about transporting up to one thousand pounds of explosives cross country.

This comforter, found on Marife Nichols' bed in her home in Herington, Kansas, during FBI searches in the days after the bombing, was stolen in the Roger Moore robbery in Arkansas in November, 1994.

Jennifer McVeigh also told Agent Hersley and Assistant United States Attorney Vicki Behenna about a message Tim McVeigh left on a word processor at her father's house while he stayed there in November and early December, 1994. The message was directed at the ATF. It read:

"ATF",

"All you tyrannical motherf__kers will swing in the wind one day, for your treasonous actions against the Constitution and the United States. Remember the Nuremburg War Trials. But..but..but...I was only following orders!......Die, you spineless, cowardice bastards"!

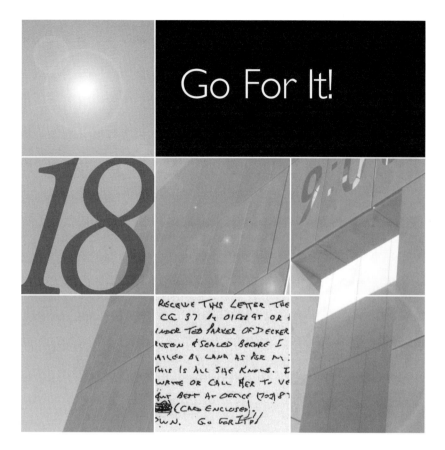

Go For It!

RECEIVE THIS LETTER THE
CC 37 4, 01 et 95 OR +
UNDER TED PARKER OF DECKER
WRITTEN & SEALED BEFORE I
MAILED BY LANA AS PER M:
THIS IS ALL SHE KNOWS. I
WROTE OR CALL HER TO VE
for BEST AT OFFICE (702) 8 1
(CARD ENCLOSED);
OWN. Go For It!/

L ana Padilla told agents her former husband came to visit her and their son in Las Vegas in early to mid-November, 1994, before leaving for the Philippines. Nichols stayed in Las Vegas for about two weeks before Padilla took him to the airport on November 22. While Nichols was in Las Vegas, he rented yet another storage locker, #Q106D, at AAAABCO Storage on Boulder Highway in Las Vegas on November 16. He made a $63.00 cash payment on the locker, which paid the rent through February 16, 1995. He wanted a place to store personal belongings, as well as his 1984 GMC pickup.

En route to the airport, Nichols gave Padilla a package and told her not to open it unless he failed to return. Despite his instructions, Padilla opened the package the following day. Inside, she found two letters. The first was directed to Padilla and provided directions for her to enter

Nichols' storage locker in Las Vegas. The letter also gave the location of another package that Nichols had left in her home. These directions read:

Other storage — located in kitchen behind utensil drawer between the dishwasher and stove. Remove the drawer. There are two small levers — one on each side of drawer on rail — pull drawer out till it stops then flip levers down and pull drawer completely out. Then look all the way back inside. Take and push hard against the back panel. Both sides and bottom are glued, top is not. After it's broke free, remove wood panel, then remove plastic bag.

Padilla said she did not remove the kitchen drawer that day but waited about a month before looking for the package. Finally, Padilla's curiosity got the best of her. Her son, Josh, was away for Christmas vacation when she asked an older son, Barry Osentoski, to help her remove the kitchen drawer. They found a package wrapped in a Wal-Mart bag. Inside the bag was $20,000.00 cash, mostly $100.00 bills.

After discovering the money, Padilla and her son decided to visit Nichols' storage locker in which they found a large quantity of precious metals, gold and silver coins, with a note on top of them indicating the value was $36,000.00 - $38,000.00. They also found a bag containing make-up, pantyhose, a black ski mask, and a wig. Padilla commented to her son, "What is he doing, robbing banks?" Barry opened a cigar box and found it was full of jade.

Padilla said she received a telephone call from McVeigh on December 18, 1994, while Nichols was still in the Philippines. McVeigh wanted to know when Nichols was returning. He asked Padilla if she had any way to reach Nichols in the Philippines, and she told him she had an address in Cebu City. Padilla told agents that McVeigh indicated to her that he was going to write a letter to Nichols but that he would have to write in code because there were snoopy people around.

Also in the package Nichols gave Padilla on the way to the airport on November 22 was a sealed envelope addressed to Jennifer McVeigh, with written instructions from Nichols that the envelope should be mailed on January 28, 1995. Padilla said she never mailed the letter to Jennifer but instead opened the letter herself. Inside the envelope addressed to Jennifer was another envelope addressed to McVeigh. Padilla opened the second envelope and found a note addressed to McVeigh:

Tim:

If you receive this letter then clear everything out of CG37 by February 1, '95, or pay to keep it longer, under Ted Parker of Decker. This letter has been written & sealed before I left (21st of November, '94) & being mailed by Lana as per my instructions to her in writing. This is all she knows. It would be a good idea to write or call her to verify things - (702) 897-6290 home, but best at office (702) 877-2501. Just ask for Lana (card enclosed). Your (sic) on your own. Go for it!! Terry.

Also, liquidate 40.

Have my mail forwarded to Lana but use my name and her address - 7160 Nordic Lights, Las Vegas, NV, 89119.

Mail Boxes Etc.

Cheryl (913) 537-6071. Box #197.

The Parker deal was signed & dated the 7th of November, '94, so you should have till 7th of February, '95, plus 5 days grace, if close or they disagree then should pay another term period.

As far as heat - none that I know, this letter would be for the purpose of my death.

Agents Hersley and Tongate reviewed the documents countless times. Why was Nichols providing instructions to McVeigh in case Nichols did not return from the Philippines? There were specific instructions on how to handle the storage sheds that agents believed held 4,000 pounds of ammonium nitrate, three barrels of racing fuel, Tovex sausage explosives, and blasting caps. Nichols admonition, "Go for it," was nothing more than simply cheerleading for the most grotesque reason fathomable. Nichols seemed to be telling McVeigh to kill innocent men, women, and children in the Murrah Building, whether he was there or not.

Nichols was obviously worried about law enforcement discovering their evil scheme by writing that he knew of no "heat," a common expression used by criminals in referring to law enforcement authorities.

Michael Fortier

Michael Fortier told agents that shortly before his birthday in December, 1994, he received several phone calls from McVeigh. During the first call, McVeigh asked Fortier if he wanted to make some money.

Tim:

If, should you receive this letter then clear everything out of CC 37 by 01Feb95 or pay to keep it longer, under Ted Parker of Decker. This letter has been written & sealed before I left (21 Nov94) & being mailed by Lana as per my instructions to her in writing. This is all she knows. It would be a good idea to write or call her to verify things [702] 897-6390 home, but best at office (702) 877-2501 just ask for Lana ~~████~~ (card enclosed).

Your on your own. Go for it!!

Terry

Also liquidate 40

Have my mail forwarded to Lana but use my name and her address - 7160 Nordic Lights, Las Vegas, NV. 89119 Mail Boxes Etc.
Chery (813) 537-6071   Box #197

The Parker deal was signed & dated 07 Nov94 so you should have till 07Feb95 plus 5 days grace, if close or they disagree then should pay another ~~██~~ term period.

As far as heat - none that I know, this letter would be for the purpse of my death.

A copy of the letter
Terry Nichols left with his ex-wife, Lana Padilla, to be sent to
Timothy McVeigh in the event Nichols did not return from the Philippines.
Nichols told McVeigh, "Your (sic) on your own. Go for it!!"

McVeigh suggested Fortier might be able to make as much as $10,000.00, but did not tell him what he had to do to earn the money. Several days later, McVeigh again called Fortier and told him to arrange about four days off work.

Fortier was still working at the TruValue Hardware Store in Kingman but made up a story and told his employer he needed the days off to drive McVeigh's car back to Arizona from Florida. He told his boss that McVeigh was traveling from the East Coast to the West Coast doing gun shows, and that he needed Fortier to drive his car back to Arizona. The next call Fortier received from McVeigh was from a motel in Kingman. McVeigh asked Fortier to come to his motel room and bring with him Christmas wrapping paper, a couple of boxes, and a pair of scissors.

Once again, phone records confirmed at least part of Fortier's statement to the FBI. On December 13, 1994, at 2:23 p.m., a Bridges card call was made from a payphone in Lincolnville, Kansas, to the TruValue Hardware Store in Kingman, Arizona. Agents knew that Terry Nichols was in the Philippines on December 13, so there was no way he could have made this call. If the call was made by McVeigh, as agents suspected, what was he doing in central Kansas? Lincolnville was only a few miles from Herington.

Agents suspected the phone calls between Nichols and McVeigh on November 6 and 7, 1994, were the result of Nichols' efforts to inform McVeigh that he had pulled off the robbery of Roger Moore without complication. As a result of the Bridges card call from Lincolnville, Kansas, to Fortier at the TruValue Hardware Store, agents now suspected McVeigh was in central Kansas, probably to check on the guns and other loot Nichols had stolen from Moore. Agents Hersley and Tongate suspected that Nichols rented Council Grove storage unit #37 to store the guns stolen in the Moore robbery.

On December 13, 1994, at 10:49 p.m., a second Bridges card call was made from the Yucca Motel in Logan, New Mexico, to Michael Fortier's home in Kingman. Agents identified a registration card at the Buckaroo Motel in Tucumcari, New Mexico, in McVeigh's name for December 13. The Buckaroo was the same motel in Tucumcari where Nichols had registered under the name of Joe Havens on October 25, 1994. Tucumcari and Logan are neighboring communities located only a few miles apart on

Interstate 40 in New Mexico. If McVeigh had made the Bridges card call to Fortier at the Kingman TruValue Store earlier this same day, he would have had ample time to have made the call from the Yucca Motel, in Logan, New Mexico, later that same evening.

Agents in Arizona located a registration card in the name of Tim McVeigh for December 14, 1994, at the Mohave Inn in Kingman. Jennifer McVeigh and FBI handwriting experts confirmed the handwriting on the registration cards from the Buckaroo Motel and the Mohave Inn was that of Tim McVeigh.

Fortier said he and his wife went to McVeigh's motel room in Kingman with the items requested by McVeigh. Inside the room, McVeigh showed the Fortiers a large box of blasting caps. He divided the blasting caps, putting half in each box. McVeigh asked Lori to wrap the two boxes in the wrapping paper. McVeigh told the Fortiers he was going to take the blasting caps to Michigan where he could sell them for $2,500.00 per box. McVeigh wanted the boxes wrapped as Christmas presents in the event he was stopped by police.

In his room at the Mohave Inn, McVeigh told the Fortiers about the specifics of the robbery of "Bob in Arkansas." McVeigh said Nichols parked his pickup on a dirt road near Bob's house and walked through the woods to get to the house. He said Nichols then waited outside the house. When Bob came out to feed the animals, Nichols was waiting for him with a shotgun.

Nichols ordered Bob back inside the house and tied him up. Nichols then loaded the guns into Bob's van and drove to his own pickup to which he transferred the guns before leaving the area.

McVeigh told the Fortiers the guns Nichols had stolen from Bob were now in Kansas. McVeigh asked Fortier to ride with him to Kansas so that Fortier could transport the stolen guns back to Arizona. Fortier decided to rent a car in Kansas rather than drive his own jeep to Kansas and back. It would be better to have a car with a large trunk in which to conceal the stolen weapons. Fortier told agents he agreed to McVeigh's offer even though he knew what he was doing was illegal.

The next day, December 15, was Fortier's birthday. Lori drove him back to the Mohave Inn. McVeigh loaded the blasting caps, contained inside the boxes wrapped with Christmas paper, into his car. McVeigh and Fortier left Kingman and followed Interstate 40 to Amarillo, Texas, where they spent the night of December 15 at a Motel 6, registering under Fortier's name. Motel records confirmed their stay.

As they drove toward Oklahoma City, McVeigh spotted a Ryder truck. He pointed to the truck and said it was the type of truck in which he was going to build the bomb. However, McVeigh told Fortier he wanted a truck that was one size larger.

On December 16, McVeigh and Fortier continued their trip toward Kansas. As they passed through Oklahoma City, McVeigh exited the freeway to show Fortier the building he intended to bomb. He drove into the downtown area and circled the Murrah Building. He pointed to a commercial loading zone on the north side of the building on Northwest Fifth Street. McVeigh asked Fortier if he thought a large truck would fit in that area. Fortier told McVeigh he could probably fit three trucks in this space. Fortier said he noticed as they drove by that the front of the building was mostly glass.

McVeigh also showed Fortier where he intended to park his getaway car in the alley behind the YMCA Building. Fortier said McVeigh told him that he and Nichols were thinking of doing one of two things. Either Nichols would follow McVeigh to Oklahoma City and wait for him on the morning of the bombing or they would drop a car off in this area a couple of days before the bombing. If they dropped the getaway car off ahead of time, McVeigh would drive the bomb truck to Oklahoma City himself. After he set the bomb off, he would run to the car and drive away.

As McVeigh explained to Fortier where he intended to park the getaway car, Fortier asked him why he did not want to have the getaway car closer to the building to aid in his escape. Fortier thought the alleyway just south of the Journal Record Building would be a closer place for McVeigh to park his getaway car. However, McVeigh explained to Fortier that he wanted to have a building between him and the Murrah Building when the truck bomb exploded.

Fortier estimated that he and McVeigh spent about 20 minutes looking at the Murrah Building and the location to park the getaway car in Oklahoma City before heading north toward Kansas on Interstate 35. After crossing the Kansas state line, McVeigh left Interstate 35 and began a zigzag route. McVeigh wanted to avoid freeway toll booths because he believed pictures were taken of people passing through them. Investigation revealed there were no such cameras at the toll booths on the Kansas Turnpike.

McVeigh drove Fortier directly to the storage unit in Herington. While McVeigh checked on items in the storage unit, Fortier stretched his back, which had become stiff from the two days of driving. All he could see when McVeigh opened the door to the storage unit were mattresses stacked in front of the door. Fortier subsequently pointed this storage unit out to Agents Floyd Zimms and Jim Volz. It was storage unit #2, the same unit Helen Mitchell had rented to a man using the name Shawn Rivers on September 22, 1994. Jennifer McVeigh, as well as FBI handwriting experts, had identified McVeigh's handwriting on the rental agreement. Eight of McVeigh's fingerprints were also found on the original agreement.

As McVeigh drove north toward Junction City, he pulled off the highway a few miles south of Junction City and drove around a small lake. Fortier later led FBI agents to this lake. It was Geary Lake, located approximately 16 miles north of Herington and about 8 miles south of Junction City.

Fortier said that before continuing on to Junction City, McVeigh took him to look at another storage unit in Council Grove, Kansas. When they arrived at the storage facility in Council Grove, McVeigh entered one of the storage units and took out a box that contained guns. He placed the box inside his car. Fortier subsequently directed Agents Zimms and Volz to the storage unit in Council Grove, as well. It was storage unit #37, the same storage unit Sharri Furman had rented to Terry Nichols, under the false name of Ted Parker, on November 7, 1994, just two days after the Roger Moore robbery outside Royal, Arkansas. FBI experts and Nichols ex-wife, Lana Padilla, identified the signature of Ted Parker on this rental agreement as that of Terry Nichols.

After leaving the storage unit in Council Grove, McVeigh drove into Junction City and rented a room at the Sunset Motel, the same motel on the Interstate 70 access road where Nichols had previously stayed. Fortier told agents that McVeigh asked him to hide behind the motel while McVeigh rented the room so they could save a few dollars on the room rate. Motel records provided to the FBI by Mesbah Chowdhury confirmed that McVeigh was registered at the Sunset Motel on December 16, 1994. The next morning, McVeigh drove Fortier to the Manhattan, Kansas, airport where Fortier rented a Ford Crown Victoria to transport the guns that Nichols had stolen from Roger Moore back to Kingman.

After renting the car, Fortier followed McVeigh back to the storage facility in Council Grove. McVeigh instructed Fortier to back the Crown Victoria up to storage unit #37, the Ted Parker storage unit. McVeigh stationed Fortier as a lookout as he separated the guns and loaded 20-25 weapons into the rental car. Fortier said McVeigh told him to sell the weapons at gun shows around Arizona, counseling him on what to wear, as well as how to speak and act at the shows.

After the guns were loaded, McVeigh and Fortier had lunch at the Pizza Hut in Council Grove and went their separate ways. Fortier headed to Kingman and McVeigh was on his way to Michigan with the two boxes wrapped in Christmas paper. A day or two after they had separated, McVeigh called Fortier in Arizona and told him that he had wrecked his car in Michigan. McVeigh told Fortier that he was rear-ended and that it had totaled the Chevy Spectrum. McVeigh told his friend that he was fortunate the rear end collision had not caused the blasting caps to explode.

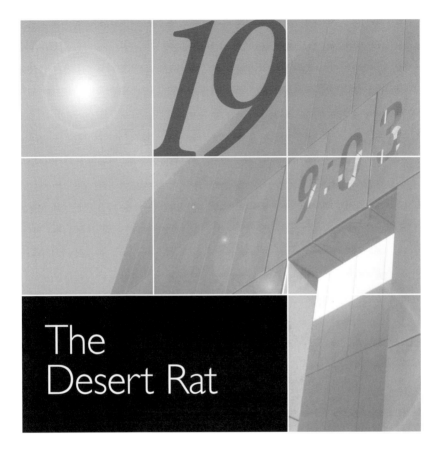

The Desert Rat

Kevin Nicholas worked on the Nichols farm in Decker, Michigan, from 1991 to 1994. It was there that he met Tim McVeigh, who stayed at the Nichols farm at different times. Nicholas was married and lived in Vassar, Michigan, a neighboring community. It was at his home in Vassar that McVeigh stayed on two occasions, the first time in January, 1994.

Nicholas told agents that he accompanied McVeigh to a gun show where McVeigh sold ammunition and several books including *The Turner Diaries*. McVeigh told Nicholas he had obtained the ammunition from a man named Bob in Arkansas and that he and Bob had a falling out over some money that McVeigh had cheated Bob out of. McVeigh talked about how easy it would be to rob Bob because he lived way back in the sticks and was surrounded by woods.

Around December, 1994, Nicholas attended another gun show with McVeigh in Kalamazoo, Michigan. At this gun show, McVeigh identified a man named Paulsen to Nicholas. After the gun show, McVeigh, who was staying at Nicholas' residence, took two short trips with James Nichols. First, they took a trip to collect money for soybeans. The second trip to Chicago was to see the man named Paulsen. Afterwards, McVeigh took a third trip, telling Nicholas he was going out west.

Shortly before Christmas in 1994, Nicholas received a phone call from McVeigh who reported he had been in a car wreck and needed help. When Nicholas arrived, McVeigh already had his personal belongings out of his car, and Nicholas helped him load them into the pickup. As Nicholas reached for one of two boxes wrapped in Christmas paper, McVeigh told him not to touch those two boxes. McVeigh told Nicholas he would handle those boxes himself.

When McVeigh's personal belongings were loaded into the truck, Nicholas helped McVeigh pull the metal fender of his car away from the tire so McVeigh could drive the car to Nicholas' house. Sometime after McVeigh began staying at Nicholas' home on this occasion, he told Nicholas the two boxes wrapped in Christmas paper contained blasting caps.

Nicholas told McVeigh that he could use his home phone while staying with him. However, McVeigh said he had a prepaid calling card that he and Terry Nichols had obtained together. Agents Hersley and Tongate were certain McVeigh was referring to the Bridges calling card since both he and Nichols had made all payments against the card.

From Nicholas, agents learned that McVeigh bought an old Pontiac station wagon from James Nichols to replace the Chevy Spectrum that McVeigh had wrecked. When McVeigh left Nicholas' home around the time of the Super Bowl in January, 1995, he was driving the Pontiac station wagon.

Gwenn Strider, who lived in Caro, Michigan, was an aunt of Kevin Nicholas' wife. She met McVeigh while he was staying with Nicholas in Vassar. In February, 1995, Strider received a letter from McVeigh. She called Nicholas and told him about the letter. She told Nicholas she was concerned about the content of the letter but did not know what to do about it. Nicholas drove to her house in Caro so he could personally read the letter from McVeigh. The letter read:

February 10, 1995
Gwenn

As far as the main context of your letter, I really don't know what to tell you, except write your representatives in Congress - they represent the people and they listen to them - (Yeah right)

No really, let me try to explain - I was in the education/literature dissemination (desert wind is wreaking havoc on my already scratchy writing), field for quite some time. I was preaching and "passing out" before anyone had ever heard the words "patriot" and "militia". (Just got out of the wind)

Onward and upward, I passed on that legacy about a 1/2 year ago. I believe the "new blood" needs to start somewhere; and I have certain other "militant" talents that are short in supply and greatly demanded. So I gave all my informational paperwork to the, "new guys" and no longer have any to give. What I can send you, is my own personal copies; ones that are just getting dust or gathering dust, and a newsletter I recently received.

If you are willing to write letters, I could pass your name on to someone; but let there be no doubt, with the letters I have in mind, the literature that would be forwarded to you for copying; etc., you would probably make a list. (Currently, there are over 300,000 names on the Cray Supercomputer in Brussels, Belgium, of "possible and suspected subversives and terrorists" in the U.S., all ranked in order of threat). Letters would be of an "on notice" nature, like the ones many people (myself included) "wrote to Lon Horiuchi" (the FBI sniper who blew Vicki Weaver's head off), saying in effect "What goes around comes around ...."

Hey, that's just the truth, and if we're scared away from writing the truth because we're afraid of winding up on a list, then we've lost already.
To sin by silence when they should protest makes Cowards of men.
Abe L.

If the founding fathers had been scared of a "list," we'd still be under the tyrannical rule of the crown.

They knew, without a doubt, that by signing the Declaration of Independence, they would be sentenced to death, for high treason against the crown. But they realized something was more important than their soul or collective lives - the cause of liberty.

Hell, you only live once, and I know you know it's better to burn out, than ..... rot away in some nursing home. My philosophy is the same - in only a short 1-2 years, my body will slowly start giving away - first maybe knee pains, or back pains, or whatever, but I won't be "peaked" anymore. Might as well do some good while I can be 100% effective!

Sorry I can't be of more help, but most of the people sent my way these days are of the direct-action type, and my whole mindset has shifted, from intellectual to ..... animal, "(Rip the bastards heads off and shit down their necks)", and I'll show you how with a simple pocket knife ... etc.

So take your time, read all the enclosed paperwork, and maybe pass it on to other interested parties. If you want to go on a propaganda mailing list, let me know>"

"Seeya, The Desert Rat."

Lana Padilla

On the morning of January 16, 1995, between 5:30 and 6:00 a.m., Lana Padilla received a telephone call from McVeigh, who wanted to know if Nichols was coming home that day. She told McVeigh that she was waiting for a phone call from her ex-husband. Later that day, Padilla picked up Nichols at the airport.

Padilla received another phone call from McVeigh early the following morning again asking for Nichols. This time, Nichols was at Padilla's home and spoke with McVeigh. Padilla left for work while Nichols was still on the phone.

He came to her office later that same morning to pick up the package of money she had found behind the cabinet drawer in her kitchen. She took $5,000.00 cash from the package and gave the remaining

$15,000.00 to Nichols at her office. Padilla told agents that Nichols was upset when he realized how much she had taken. They finally agreed on her keeping $3,000. Padilla said Nichols left Las Vegas two or three days after his return from the Philippines, and she did not hear from him again until sometime in March, 1995.

Investigation of telephone records determined six phone calls, using the Bridges calling card, were made between the homes of Lana Padilla and Kevin Nicholas in Michigan from January 16-18, 1995. McVeigh was anxious to talk with Nichols and they met soon thereafter in central Kansas.

Records at the Sunset Motel in Junction City revealed that McVeigh was staying in room 56 from January 19-27, 1995. Agents learned that Nichols was also staying at the motel during the same time McVeigh was there. On January 20, Nichols was issued a vehicle equipment citation by a police officer in Grandview Plaza, Kansas, a municipality adjacent to Junction City, due to a faulty left front headlight on his pickup. Nichols told the officer he was staying at the Sunset Motel, room 56, the same room occupied by McVeigh. The citation indicated Nichols was driving a 1984 GMC pickup, with Michigan license plate WX 1460.

Michael Fortier

Michael Fortier said he did not hear from McVeigh after they departed company in Council Grove, Kansas, in mid-December, 1994, until late January or early February, 1995, when he received another call from McVeigh who was staying at a motel in Kingman. Fortier and his wife went to visit McVeigh at the motel. McVeigh was visibly upset when he learned that Fortier had not attended any gun shows to sell the guns stolen from Roger Moore.

Agents confirmed the information provided by Fortier about McVeigh being in Kingman in late January and early February, 1995. At the Uptown Motel in Kingman, agents located a guest registration card in the name of Tim Johnson for the night of January 30, 1995. Jennifer McVeigh identified the handwriting on this registration card as that of her brother.

Agents found another guest registration card at the Belle Art Motel in Kingman. This card confirmed that McVeigh was registered at the Belle Art from January 31, 1995. until February 8, 1995. McVeigh had registered under his true name at the Belle Art, and again Jennifer McVeigh identified the handwriting on the registration card as that of her brother.

At the Belle Art Motel in Kingman, McVeigh told Fortier he was going to sign them up to attend gun shows in the area. Fortier was no longer working for the TruValue Hardware Store and was free to attend gun shows with McVeigh in Reno, Nevada; St. George, Utah; and Tucson, Arizona. McVeigh told Fortier that Nichols was pressing McVeigh to give him $2,000.00 from the profits that Fortier was to make from selling the guns. Fortier eventually did give this money to McVeigh and presumed McVeigh passed the money on to Nichols.

During February and March, 1995, while they were not at guns shows, McVeigh stayed in Arizona, most of the time at Fortier's house and part of the time at another motel in Kingman. Guest registration cards at the Hilltop Motel in Kingman confirmed McVeigh was registered at this motel from February 12-17, 1995, again under his true name. Jennifer McVeigh identified the handwriting on the guest registration card as that of her brother.

In central Kansas, agents determined that Terry Nichols was registered at the Sunset Motel in Junction City from February 12-16, 1995. Of importance to Agents Hersley and Tongate was the fact that several telephone calls were made from a payphone at the Hilltop Motel to the Sunset Motel during that week. McVeigh and Nichols were staying in touch.

While in Kingman, McVeigh and Fortier talked further about McVeigh's plan to bomb the Murrah Building. McVeigh told Fortier that Nichols no longer wanted to help with the plan to blow up the building. As a result, McVeigh asked Fortier if he would go to Kansas with McVeigh to help mix the bomb. Fortier told McVeigh he would never do anything like that. McVeigh asked Fortier if he would at least help him get from Las Vegas to the desert after the bombing. McVeigh did not tell Fortier how he intended to get from Oklahoma City to Las Vegas, and Fortier did not ask. Again, Fortier said he refused McVeigh's request for assistance.

Michael and Lori Fortier were relieved when McVeigh moved from their home to a motel in Kingman. Their friendship with McVeigh had deteriorated, and McVeigh continued his attempts to pressure Fortier into helping him in some manner either before, during, or after the bombing in Oklahoma City. Fortier and his wife grew more and more concerned about their friend. McVeigh became more desperate to the point that, at times, they were afraid of him. McVeigh had become more volatile and angry.

In late March, 1995, McVeigh moved from the Fortiers' home to the Imperial Motel in Kingman. He stayed at this motel for almost two weeks. Fortier visited McVeigh at the motel several times, mostly out of concern. Each time, McVeigh had another book that he wanted Fortier to read, usually about white supremacists or other related topics. Fortier told agents he was concerned enough about McVeigh's demeanor during these visits that he carried a gun with him. He really did not think McVeigh would try anything, but he wanted to make sure he was armed in case McVeigh did.

Fortier knew McVeigh still wanted him to help in regard to the bombing, but he continued to resist McVeigh's requests for help. He was not interested because he believed McVeigh's plans were too drastic. Finally, McVeigh told Fortier they were heading in separate paths, and as a result could no longer be friends. Fortier left the motel room and did not see McVeigh again. It was the same conclusion McVeigh had reached about another friend, Steve Hodge.

Back in July, 1994, McVeigh had pressed his childhood friend, Steve Hodge, to join him in some type of action against the government. On July 14, 1994, McVeigh wrote one final letter to Hodge, criticizing his friend for not joining in the fight against the government. The content of this letter caused Hodge a great deal of concern about his boyhood friend. Hodge spoke to his mother about McVeigh's letter, but they did not report it to authorities. McVeigh's letter read, in part...

Steve,

I spent 3 days deciding whether to respond or not. The two things I kept tossing around were: 1) He can't be serious, and is only writing this shit to spark me into writing, or 2) He is serious, which, when then realized, means that it is hopeless, at best, to try to reason with him. If you are serious, Steve - you're fried!

The first impression I got, by looking at the overall tone of your letter, exposes to me, the main reason you have not/can not understand history or the material I send you. I cannot figure out how, but it seems that you have no concept of the word 'liberty'.......liberty is not a concept that you can simply look up in the dictionary, it is something you must feel in your heart, in your soul. I tell you Steve, after examining your letter, I began to wonder if you had a soul.

If, somehow, I could explain liberty to you, that would be a start. Maybe this way, have you ever heard of 'Natural Law' or 'God's Law'? That is what you know and feel, in your heart and soul, is right and wrong. No 'religion' has to pump these values into you; no teacher has to make you learn; these basic rights and wrongs should be born into every man. (morals, if you will)

The only other possible explanation, is that you have some sort of learning disability. If anyone reads the Declaration of Independence, it should be plain to them the extreme suffrage those colonists were going through.

Jesus, Steve, don't you understand that??? Your argument that the tyranny could be reconciled: In every stage of these supressions we have petitioned for redress ('Please don't burn us alive anymore in Waco, please punish the agencies who were responsible....'). Our repeated Petitions have been answered only by repeated injury!... Burned 86 men, women, and children alive you say? Murder, Conspiracy to Commit Murder, Negligent Homicide, at least, you say? Not guilty - I say. Because those people deserved it...

No one will listen to us. They turn a deaf ear. And then.....Lexington - the British Army tried to take away our only other option - this is where you really flip me out, Steve. For years, they tried to solve all the above atrocities through political means. Remember they address this! It didn't work - 'answered only w/repeated injury'!!!

The British knew that they (Brits) were ignoring the Colonists, were in fact, pissing all over them, and decided, if they were to continue to impose such tyranny, they must disarm the colonists. The very fact that they tried to disarm the colonists is an admission that they knew they were being oppressive. And then, the shot heard round the world.

There was a pattern to the relationship between McVeigh and his friends. If they agreed with his ravings against the federal government, he took them into his confidence. If they resisted his anti-government rhetoric, he dropped them.

Timothy McVeigh stayed
at the Imperial Motel in Kingman, Arizona, until a week
before the Oklahoma City bombing, evidenced by this registration card.

Records at the Imperial Motel in Kingman confirmed that McVeigh was registered at the motel from March 31 to April 12, 1995. Telephone records determined that during this time, several telephone calls were made using the Bridges calling card from a payphone at the Imperial Motel.

On April 5, 1995, a call was made to Ryder Truck Rentals in Lake Havasu, Arizona. The call was made at 3:43 p.m. and lasted 42 seconds. A representative of Ryder Truck Rentals in Lake Havasu later told Agent Hersley and Federal Prosecutor Beth Wilkinson that she could not positively identify the caller as McVeigh, but did remember a call that day asking for rate quotes on Ryder trucks.

On April 5, another call was made from the Imperial Motel to a telephone number in Elohim City, Oklahoma. This call was made to the residence of David Millar at 3:48 p.m. It lasted 1 minute and 56 seconds. Joan Millar, who was married to David Millar's son, remembered answering the call. She said the caller used a name other than McVeigh, but told her that he was going to be in the area in the next couple of weeks and wanted to know if it was okay to stop by and visit. When Mrs. Millar asked the caller how he had heard about Elohim City, the caller reluctantly told her that he had met some young men from Elohim City at a gun show, and one of the men had given him a card with the phone number on it.

When Mrs. Millar asked specifically who had given him the card, the caller answered he did not know the man's name but that he had a heavy foreign accent. Mrs. Millar said she knew immediately the caller was referring to Andreas Strassmeier, a man of German descent, who had been staying at Elohim City. Mrs. Millar asked the caller if he needed directions to Elohim City, but the man said he would call back when he arrived in the area. Mrs. Millar said she never heard from the caller again.

Elohim City was a small compound of people living about 175 miles east of Oklahoma City near Muldrow, Oklahoma. David Millar or the Reverend Millar, as he preferred to be called, was the founder of Elohim City and its self-professed leader. He taught that the people of Elohim City were the people of Israel. Andreas Strassmeier was a self-appointed security leader at the compound. He had met McVeigh at a gun show in Tulsa, Oklahoma, in April, 1993, but there was no indication they had met or spoken again after that date.

David and Joan Millar both told agents that the people of Elohim City believed the white race was superior and claimed they had never advocated the violent overthrow of the government or even violent acts against it. They also told the FBI they had never met McVeigh and that he had never come to visit.

Joan Millar said that Andreas Strassmeier had been working on a fence for neighbors in the days before the Oklahoma City bombing. Agents confirmed Strassmeier's alibi with the neighbors.

Other calls were made using the Bridges calling card from the Imperial Motel in Kingman, Arizona, during the time that McVeigh was registered there. On April 5 and 6, eight calls were made to an organization known as National Alliance in Fort Mohave, Arizona. National Alliance had been founded by a man named Richard Coffman. The number called by McVeigh in this regard was simply a recorded message containing anti-government rhetoric. Coffman denied ever speaking directly with or meeting McVeigh.

On April 11, two more calls were made from the payphone at the Imperial Motel. Both were to the home of Terry Nichols in Herington, Kansas. The calls were made at 2:49 p.m. and 2:51 p.m., and each lasted only 3 seconds. Later that same day, at 3:36 p.m., another call was made using the Bridges calling card. This call was made from a payphone at Falley's, Inc., a store in Manhattan, Kansas, to Michael Fortier's home in Kingman. The call from Falley's lasted 1 minute and 1 second. Agents believed the caller was Nichols, who was likely returning McVeigh's earlier calls. The next morning, April 12, McVeigh checked out of the Imperial Motel in Kingman. He left Arizona and never returned.

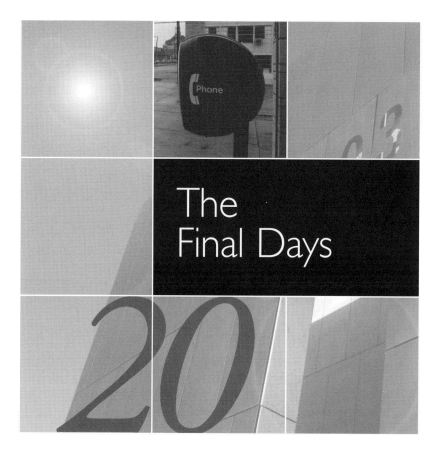

The Final Days

nvestigation by FBI agents in Kansas and surrounding states determined that Terry Nichols spent a good portion of February, March, and early April, 1995, attending gun shows. Similarly, McVeigh and Michael Fortier were attending gun shows in Arizona and Utah. Agents Hersley and Tongate were certain the trio was attempting to sell guns stolen in the Roger Moore robbery to raise additional cash.

Lana Padilla

Lana Padilla said that after Nichols left her home in Las Vegas in mid-January, 1995, she did not talk to him again until March, 1995, in preparation for their son's spring break schedule. Padilla said she initially thought Josh was going to be out of school for two weeks over spring break, and she spoke with Nichols about Josh staying with him the entire two weeks. However, Nichols had other plans. He told Lana that he was going to Michigan to attend a gun show and that Josh could stay with him only one week.

Padilla and Nichols agreed that Josh would fly to Kansas and spend the week beginning April 10 with Nichols in Herington, where Nichols had recently purchased a small home. Josh's return flight to Las Vegas was scheduled to leave from Kansas City on Monday, April 17 at 10:45 p.m.

Terry Nichols

When agents arrested Nichols after the Oklahoma City bombing, Agent Dan Jablonski found a Wal-Mart receipt in his wallet that indicated the purchase of an oil filter and four quarts of oil from the Wal-Mart Store in Arkansas City, Kansas, on April 13, 1995. The time of purchase was imprinted on the receipt as 5:42 p.m. Agents learned that the type of

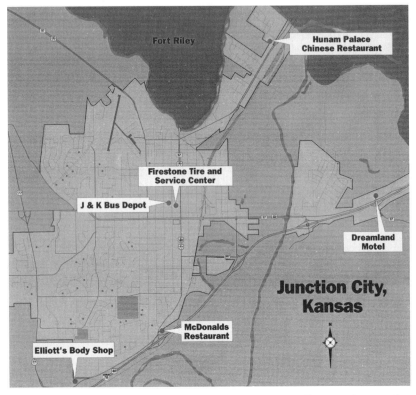

A map of Junction City, Kansas, showing the location of the Firestone Store and the bus depot from which Timothy McVeigh placed a call to Elliott's Body Shop, inquiring about the Ryder truck rental. Other key locations in Junction City are also depicted on the map.

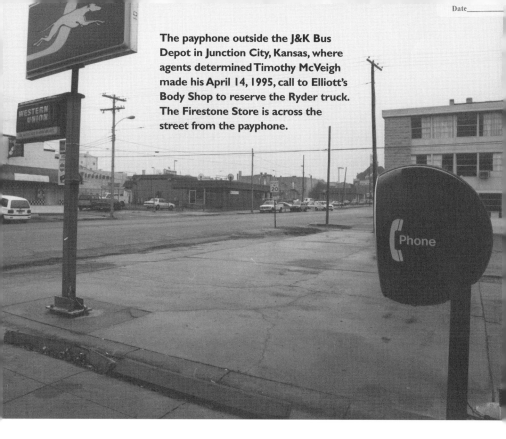

The payphone outside the J&K Bus Depot in Junction City, Kansas, where agents determined Timothy McVeigh made his April 14, 1995, call to Elliott's Body Shop to reserve the Ryder truck. The Firestone Store is across the street from the payphone.

oil filter purchased fit the Pontiac J-2000 McVeigh had purchased from James Nichols. Of even more importance to Agents Hersley and Tongate, the oil filter did not fit Nichols' 1984 GMC pickup.

April 14

McVeigh bought a yellow Mercury at the Firestone Store in Junction City on the morning of April 14. In completing the bill of sale, store owner Tom Manning asked McVeigh for his address. McVeigh told Manning to mail the bill of sale to him at 3616 North Van Dyke, Decker, Michigan, 48426. McVeigh provided Manning with a Michigan telephone number. The address and phone number was that of James Nichols, the same address McVeigh had given Trooper Charlie Hanger and Jailer Marsha Moritz when he was arrested and booked into the Noble County jail, and the same address he used at the Dreamland Motel.

Manning told Agent Hersley and Prosecutor Larry Mackey that before turning the Mercury over to McVeigh, he had one of his mechanics perform some minor service on the vehicle, to include, checking and adding to the car's fluid levels and possibly adding a newer tire. Manning recalled that while this service was being performed, McVeigh left the Firestone Store and returned a short time later. Manning was not sure where McVeigh had gone during this time.

Agents tracing telephone calls determined that a call was made, using the Bridges calling card, from a payphone outside the J&K Bus Depot on Friday morning, April 14, 1995. The bus depot was located diagonally across the street from the Firestone Store.

The 54-second call was made at 9:52 a.m. to the home of Terry Nichols in Herington. Even more important to Case Agents Hersley and Tongate was a call placed from this same payphone at 9:54 a.m., just two minutes after the first call. The second call was made to Elliott's Ryder Truck Rental and lasted 7 minutes and 36 seconds.

There were two telephone lines at Elliott's, one for the body shop itself, and one for the Ryder truck rental business. A trace of incoming calls to these numbers revealed that only one call in excess of two minutes was received on either of the lines on April 14. This was the call that came in at 9:54 a.m.

Vickie Beemer, the officer manager at Elliott's, told agents she remembered receiving a call from a Bob Kling on Friday morning, April 14. She remembered the call came in around 10:00 a.m. It was the only call for a rate quote that Beemer received that day.

Kling wanted to rent a truck for a one way trip to Omaha, Nebraska. When Beemer asked Kling what size truck he needed, the man asked her how many pounds a 15-foot truck would carry. Beemer said it would carry about 3,400 pounds. Kling told Beemer he needed a truck that would carry 5,000 pounds. After reviewing a weight chart, Beemer told Kling he needed a 20-foot truck. Kling told Beemer he was in the military, so she quoted him a price of $280.32, which included a hand truck and a 10% military discount. Kling asked if he could pick the truck up on Monday afternoon around 4:00 p.m. Beemer told the man he would need to come in on Saturday morning and reserve the truck if he wanted to make sure it was available on Monday. She told him that Eldon Elliott would be working on Saturday morning from about 8:00 to 10:00 a.m. Kling said he would be there.

Due to a deficiency in telephone company equipment, the pin number used to make the call to Elliott's Ryder Truck Rentals from the payphone at the J&K Bus Depot on Friday morning was not trapped and recorded. However, phone company records confirmed this call was made using a Spotlight calling card and it was made within a minute of the termination of the previous call to Nichols' home telephone number, a call made using the Bridges calling card. Agents were certain one caller had made both calls. The likelihood of two separate callers, both possessing Spotlight calling cards, making calls from the same payphone this close together in time would be extremely unlikely. And, both calls were made at a time when McVeigh had temporarily left the Firestone Store.

Agents had previously learned that McVeigh checked into the Dreamland Motel on the same day he bought the yellow Mercury from Tom Manning. McVeigh checked in around 3:00 p.m., driving the old, yellow Mercury. He asked the motel owner if he could park a Ryder truck there. She said yes, but restricted where on the property the truck could be parked.

April 15

Eldon Elliott was at work at his body shop and truck rental agency on Saturday morning, April 15, when "Bob Kling" came into the shop alone around 9:00 a.m. Kling told Elliott about the quote he had been given by Vickie Beemer on Friday morning.

The office at Elliott's Body Shop is relatively small, about 13 by 15 feet. There is a counter slightly over waist high that customers walk up to when they come in. On this occasion, Kling leaned over the counter and told Elliott that he wanted to reserve a 20- foot truck for pickup after 4:00 p.m. on Monday. Elliott asked where he was heading with the truck and how long he needed it. Kling answered he was traveling to Omaha, Nebraska.

The rental price was $280.32, which Kling paid in cash. Elliott remembered Kling saying he wanted to make the entire payment while he had the money. Elliott entered the information into the computer as Kling provided it. He entered Kling's address as 428 Maple Dr., Red Field, South Dakota. Elliott told Agent Hersley and Prosecutor Scott Mendeloff that he typed the address into the computer from a driver's license which Kling handed him.

Lori Fortier told the FBI that during the early part of 1995, her husband had ordered a false identification kit for McVeigh from an advertisement in *Soldier of Fortune* Magazine. In February or March, 1995, Lori ironed a plastic laminate covering onto a drivers license for McVeigh. Lori was certain it was a South Dakota license, but she could not remember the name on the license.

When Elliott asked the man if he wanted insurance on the truck, Kling said he did not need it because he had driven two and half ton trucks at Fort Riley and was a good driver. After Elliott completed the paperwork, he placed it on the counter in front of Kling, who was now about 18–24 inches from his face. As Elliott began to explain the paperwork, he looked directly at Kling who signed the reservation form using the name Robert D. Kling and left the office.

Marife Nichols told FBI agents that when she awoke at 10:00 a.m. on April 15, her husband was already gone. She said he returned around 11:00 a.m. That afternoon, Marife, Terry, and Josh Nichols ran errands, stopping at Mailboxes, Etc. in Manhattan, Kansas. Marife said that when Nichols came out of the business he handed her a piece of junk mail and told her it was all that was in the box.

Later, however, Marife saw a one page letter that Nichols had received from McVeigh. She read part of the letter. It seemed to be in code. Marife recalled the letter indicated that Terry needed an excuse for his second half. Marife said she suspected McVeigh and her husband wrote things in code to hide from her what they were writing about. She said that on a previous occasion while they were living in Michigan, she was reading a letter her husband had received from McVeigh. Nichols became upset with her and grabbed the letter from her hand.

Marife told agents that another place they stopped on Saturday afternoon was the Wal-Mart in Manhattan. She said Terry returned an oil filter. Terry failed to collect the money for the refund, and they had to stop at the Wal-Mart Store in Junction City on their way home to get the refund money. Marife said Terry never told her when, where, or how he had obtained the oil filter he was now returning.

FBI Case Agents Hersley and Tongate were very interested in the oil filter that Nichols returned on Saturday afternoon, April 15, 1995. During the interview with Agents Smith and Crabtree on Friday evening, April 21, Nichols told the agents that prior to Easter Sunday, April 16, he had not seen McVeigh since November, 1994. However,

A copy of the original receipt given Tim McVeigh when he bought an oil filter at the Wal-Mart in Arkansas City, Kansas, on April 13, 1995. The receipt shows the date and time, 5:42 p.m., when the sale was made. The FBI determined that fingerprints of both McVeigh and Terry Nichols were present on the receipt.

FBI fingerprint expert Lou Hupp identified the fingerprints of both McVeigh and Nichols on the Wal-Mart receipt for the original purchase of the oil filter. The receipt was found in Nichols' wallet when he was arrested on the material witness warrant. Agents remembered the oil filter purchased on April 13, in Arkansas City, Kansas, fit McVeigh's Pontiac J-2000 and not Nichols' 1984 GMC pickup. If Nichols had not seen McVeigh since November, 1994, then how had he gotten the oil filter receipt that contained the fingerprints of both him and McVeigh before Easter Sunday?

Agents knew Nichols was lying about when he had last seen McVeigh prior to Easter Sunday. Telephone calls made by Nichols from his residence on the afternoon of April 13 made it impossible for him to have been in Arkansas City, Kansas, when the oil filter was purchased. Agents Hersley and Tongate were convinced that McVeigh had passed through Arkansas City on his way from Arizona to Junction City. It was the same route McVeigh and Nichols had taken on their return trip from Oklahoma City on Easter Sunday. If McVeigh had traveled as the Agents suspected, he would have passed right by the Wal-Mart Store on Highway 77 in Arkansas City. And, McVeigh had told the Firestone Store owner that he had problems with his Pontiac. By April 15, the Pontiac had been traded for the yellow Mercury, and McVeigh no longer needed the oil filter. Because of the fingerprints, McVeigh had to have given the receipt and the filter to Nichols before Easter Sunday. Why was Nichols lying?

Easter Sunday, April 16

Marife Nichols awoke at around 9:00 a.m. on Easter Sunday. After attending mass in Junction City with her daughter, Nicole, and Terry Nichols, they returned home and began cooking Easter Sunday dinner. Terry helped her in the kitchen and did not leave the house until after the meal. She said that around 3:00 p.m., Terry received a phone call from McVeigh.

After Terry hung up, he told Marife that McVeigh was having car trouble and needed Terry to pick him up in Omaha. Marife thought this was strange because about a week earlier, Nichols had told her that McVeigh was dropping off the television on his way to New York. She wondered why McVeigh had not called or stopped by as he drove through on his way to Omaha.

Terry left the house about ten minutes after McVeigh called. Josh wanted to go with his father, but Terry refused, telling Josh and Marife that he did not know what kind of trouble McVeigh was in. Terry told Josh there would not be enough room in the pickup for Josh to ride along because McVeigh had their television with him. Marife recalled that Terry returned home very early Monday morning, but he was by himself. Again, she thought it was unusual that McVeigh was not with her husband when they returned. She said Terry told her that McVeigh "stayed there," suggesting he had stayed in Omaha.

Agents continued to identify telephone calls made using the Bridges calling card. At times, the hard work paid huge dividends. On Easter Sunday, a Bridges card call was made from a payphone at Tim's Amoco, a gas station about a quarter mile from Nichols' home in Herington. The call was made at 3:08 p.m. and lasted just over three minutes. The call was to Nichols' home number. Marife was correct. McVeigh called her husband, just as she told agents. What Marife had not realized was that McVeigh was not in Omaha when he made the call—he was at Tim's Amoco in Herington. Why had Nichols lied to his wife? Why did he tell Marife that he was picking McVeigh up in Omaha? To Agents Hersley and Tongate, the answer was clear.

A video camera attached to the Regency Tower Apartments across the street from the Murrah Building had captured an image of a pickup that passed by the front of the apartments twice on Easter Sunday evening.

FBI experts determined that the image of the pickup captured on film was the same size and dimension as Nichols' 1984 GMC pickup. Nichols told agents in his initial interview that he had driven by the Murrah Building a couple of times while looking for McVeigh.

FBI Case Agents Hersley and Tongate did not believe Nichols' statement to Agents Smith and Crabtree that McVeigh had called him from Oklahoma City on Easter Sunday afternoon stating that he had car trouble in Oklahoma City and needed Nichols to come there and pick him up. The call had come from the service station less than a mile from his home.

One thing that was clear to the agents was that Nichols had Omaha on his mind when he spoke with McVeigh on Easter Sunday afternoon. Bob Kling also had Omaha on his mind when he rented the Ryder truck at Elliott's Body Shop and gave Omaha as his destination.

Nichols had told agents that he never saw McVeigh's broken down car in Oklahoma City. Agents wondered why Nichols, who was known for his ability to repair things and working with his hands, did not at least take a look at the "broken down" car.

Agents drew one conclusion—McVeigh and Nichols had parked the yellow Mercury in the area behind the YMCA Building to be used as a getaway car for the horrible crime they planned three days later.

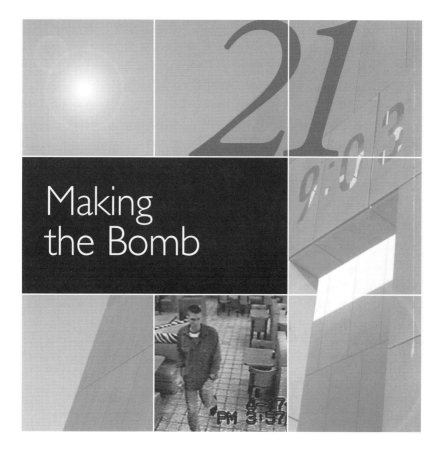

April 17

On *Monday, April 17,* Marife Nichols awoke at about 10:00 a.m. Terry was already up and the television was on in the living room. She did not remember him making or receiving any telephone calls that morning. However, the FBI's exhaustive search of telephone records identified a Bridges card call to Nichols' home that morning at 9:25 a.m. The 57-second call had originated from room 25 at the Dreamland Motel.

Nichols spent all of Monday with his family as his son, Josh, was scheduled to return to his mother's house in Las Vegas that evening. At about 6:00 p.m., Nichols and his family left Herington to take Josh to the airport in Kansas City.

After Josh boarded the airplane, Terry called Lana Padilla from a payphone near the gate to let her know Josh was on his way home. Marife said that while Terry was making this call, she went to the restroom. She said they left the airport in Kansas City before 11:30 p.m. and arrived back home before 4:00 a.m. On the way home, Marife and her husband argued. She was homesick and wanted to return to the Philippines.

Again, the FBI's efforts to trace the actions of McVeigh and Nichols through telephone records provided incriminating information against the pair. Just as Marife had told agents, telephone records proved her husband called Lana Padilla from the airport in Kansas City after putting Josh on the plane. There was a Bridges card call from a payphone in the gate area where Josh boarded the plane to Lana's home in Las Vegas at 10:46 p.m. Josh's flight was scheduled to depart at 10:45 p.m. but the boy boarded his flight several minutes earlier.

Of more interest to Agents Hersley and Tongate was a call made only minutes earlier that same evening from the same payphone. A Bridges card call was made at 10:35 p.m. to the Dreamland Motel. This call lasted 52 seconds. It was clear to the agents that Nichols, after placing his son on the plane to Las Vegas, called McVeigh at the Dreamland Motel. Nichols called McVeigh even before calling his ex-wife.

When Nichols spoke with FBI Agents on April 21, he told them that after dropping McVeigh off at the McDonald's Restaurant in Junction City early Monday morning, April 17, at approximately 1:30 a.m., he did not hear from McVeigh again until Tuesday morning around 6:00 a.m. However, as noted above, telephone records confirmed at least two calls between them on Monday.

At 4:19 p.m. on Monday, Bob Kling returned to Elliott's Body Shop to pick up the Ryder truck he had reserved on Saturday. Kling stood at the counter directly in front of Vickie Beemer as she entered additional information into the Ryder Rentals computer.

She remembered Kling as having dark blonde to light brown hair, worn short in a military-style cut. She was unable to describe the clothing he wore and was fuzzy on his facial features.

Beemer felt certain a second man had come in with Kling on Monday afternoon, but she could not recall anything about him. She was not able to describe the second man in any way and was not sure where he was standing while she completed the rental transaction with Kling. During McVeigh's federal court trial in Denver, Beemer acknowledged that during previous testimony, she had provided a description of a man she believed had accompanied Kling. However, she admitted the description she provided during this testimony was based on what she had seen and heard on television and in the news media, rather than her own independent recollection.

During pretrial interviews, Tom Kessinger, Eldon Elliott's mechanic, told Agent Hersley and Prosecutor Mendeloff that shortly after Vickie Beemer was asked to pull the rental documents for the truck rented by Kling, she came out into the area of the body shop where Kessinger was working. This happened before Agent Crabtree arrived at the body shop. Beemer told Kessinger that it looked as if the truck used in the Oklahoma City bombing had been rented at Elliott's.

She told Kessinger that she could not remember the transaction even though she had completed the rental documents. She asked Kessinger if he recalled the transaction. Kessinger told Beemer about two men he remembered coming in to pick up the truck. He was not certain, but thought he had described the two men to Beemer at this time.

Eldon Elliott completed the "walk around" of the truck before Kling, or McVeigh, drove it from the body shop. Elliott did not pay much attention to Kling but he was certain it was the same man who reserved the truck on Saturday morning.

When Elliott first spoke to Agent Crabtree on Wednesday afternoon, April 19, he said nothing about a second man being with Kling when he came to pick up the truck on Monday. However, when Elliott spoke to Crabtree a second time on Thursday morning, he told the agent that a second man was in the shop when Kling came in. He was not at all certain the second man was with Kling. He glanced at the man for about a half of second as he came around the corner into the office from out in the body shop. He remembered the unusual design on the second man's hat.

There was one thing of which Elliott was certain—the first time he saw McVeigh's photograph on television, he knew Bob Kling was in fact Tim McVeigh.

Several pieces of evidence proved McVeigh was in the vicinity of Elliott's Body Shop near the time when he rented the Ryder truck. At 3:29 p.m., a call from a package store near the Dreamland Motel summoned a taxi. David Ferris, a driver for Bell Taxi, told Agent Hersley and Prosecutor

The security camera at the McDonald's Restaurant in Junction City, Kansas, caught Timothy McVeigh leaving the restaurant at 3:57 p.m. on April 17, 1995, just a short walk away from Elliott's Body Shop where McVeigh picked up the Ryder bomb truck.

Mackey that he picked up McVeigh at the package store and drove him about three miles to the McDonald's Restaurant, located at the corner of Washington and Interstate 70. McVeigh was alone. Hersley and Mackey knew this McDonald's was just over a mile from Elliott's Body Shop. It was the same McDonald's where Nichols claimed to have later departed company with McVeigh on Tuesday afternoon.

A video camera inside the McDonald's Restaurant confirmed David Ferris' statement. The camera captured McVeigh's image on film at 3:57 p.m. McVeigh appeared to be leaving the restaurant.

Agents Hersley and Tongate calculated it would take 15-20 minutes for an average man to walk the distance to Elliott's Body Shop. Was McVeigh headed to Elliott's when he left McDonald's at 3:57 p.m.? If so, how long would it take him to walk from the restaurant to the body shop? In preparation for trial in Denver, Agent Gary Witt of the Kansas City FBI was asked to walk from the McDonald's Restaurant to Elliott's Body Shop at a brisk pace. In making the walk, Agent Witt left the McDonald's at 3:57 p.m., the same time McVeigh was caught on camera leaving the restaurant. The agent arrived at the front door of Elliott's at 4:16 p.m. The rental agreement completed by Vickie Beemer on Monday afternoon, April 17, reflected that Bob Kling picked up the 20-foot Ryder truck used in the Oklahoma City bombing at 4:19 p.m.

April 18

Dreamland Motel owner Lea McGown was certain she last saw McVeigh at the Dreamland Motel during the early morning hours of Tuesday, April 18, one day before the Oklahoma City bombing. At about 4:30 a.m., she looked out from the front window of the office and saw McVeigh sitting in the passenger compartment of the Ryder truck. He had a light on inside the truck and was looking down at something. She recalled thinking McVeigh was probably reading a map. A while later, at about 5:30 a.m., when she looked outside again, McVeigh and the Ryder truck were gone. She saw no one else in the truck with McVeigh on Tuesday morning or at any other time while he was at the motel.

McGown later told Agent Hersley and United States Attorney Pat Ryan that when McVeigh brought the Ryder truck to the motel on Sunday or Monday afternoon, he backed the truck in along side the swimming pool. She was irritated as she had previously told McVeigh to park the truck underneath the sign at the motel. She was concerned it would be in the way of other guests as they arrived and departed. McGown told her son, Eric, to go outside and tell McVeigh he could not park by the swimming pool. After Eric talked to McVeigh, the truck was moved.

Agent Mark Bouton's discovery of the registration card in the name of Tim McVeigh at the Dreamland Motel was huge in the investigation. It proved extremely difficult at trial for McVeigh's team of lawyers to explain why McVeigh was staying at a motel less than five miles from where the Ryder bomb truck had been rented. And McVeigh had checked out of this motel on the morning of April 18, the day before the bombing.

Agent Bouton's discovery also lead to the eventual identification of brothers James and Terry Nichols as close friends and associates of McVeigh. James and Terry Nichols had lived and farmed on land at 3616 North Van Dyke Road, Decker, Michigan, the same address McVeigh used when he registered at the Dreamland Motel.

Herington Storage Units

During the interview of Terry Nichols by Agents Smith and Crabtree on April 21, Nichols talked about the storage unit McVeigh had rented at the Herington Storage facility located just off State Highway 77 in Herington. Agents were immediately dispatched to the storage facility to secure the premises. When they arrived, agents noticed heavy tire tracks directly in front of unit #2. FBI tire track expert Bill Bodziak was asked to measure the tracks to determine if they were consistent with the width and distance between the tires of a 20-foot Ryder truck.

Bodziak measured the width of the tracks, as well as their relative distance from one another. He took three separate measurements of the tracks. The distance from center to center measured 73 1/2 inches. Next, the agent measured the outside to outside distance between the tracks. This distance was 92 3/8 inches. The final distance measured was from inside to inside of the tracks. This distance was 54 3/8 inches.

Two days after the bombing, Terry Nichols told FBI interviewers about the Herington storage unit. Agents were dispatched to the facility and took this photograph showing deep tire tracks outside the unit. The subsequent FBI investigation revealed that the tracks were made by a 20-foot Ryder truck within the previous days. The FBI believed Nichols and Tim McVeigh loaded the fertilizer and explosives into the Ryder truck at this location.

Agent Bodziak compared these distances to the respective distances between the rear tires of a 20-foot Ryder truck. The centermost measurement was exactly the same as the measurement the agent had taken from the tracks in front of storage unit #2. In comparing the inside and outside edges of the tire tracks against the respective distances between the rear tires of a 20-foot Ryder truck, Bodziak noted there was a difference of 5/8 inch between the inner to inner measurement and of 3/8 inch between the outside to outside measurement. He testified at McVeigh's trial in Denver that in his expert opinion these differences were insignificant, and that the tire tracks found in front of Herington storage unit #2 were consistent with the rear tire tracks that a 20-foot Ryder truck would have left.

The depth of the tire track impressions, according to Bodziak, was consistent with those that would have been left by a heavily loaded 20-foot Ryder truck. Other tracks found by the FBI expert at the Herington Industrial Park were not nearly as deep as those found directly in front of storage unit #2.

Where had McVeigh gone after Lea McGown observed him leaving the Dreamland Motel in a Ryder truck in early morning hours of Tuesday, April 18? Agents Hersley and Tongate were certain they had the answer. The double tire tracks in front of Herington storage unit #2 were fresh.

Geary Lake

Sergeant Rick Wahl was in the United States Army, assigned to Fort Riley. On Easter Sunday, he and his 11 year old son, Benjamin, went fishing at Geary Lake located eight miles south of Junction City. They fished from the bank on Sunday but decided they might have more luck if they rented a boat and used a depth finder.

Wahl and his son returned to Geary Lake around 9:00 a.m. on Tuesday morning, April 18. As Wahl exited Highway 77 and drove toward the lake, he saw a Ryder truck parked in the last turnout on the east side of the lake. This concerned Wahl as he thought it unusual that a Ryder truck would be parked there. He slowed his car and studied the Ryder truck carefully. Had it not been for the fact his young son was with him, Wahl said the truck might not have concerned him as much.

Wahl drove closer to the truck but could not see anyone around the vehicle. He continued to keep an eye on the truck and a dark color

Chevrolet or GMC pickup that was parked next to the truck. Both vehicles were backed into the turnout area and were facing southeast. Wahl could see something white sticking up from the back of the pickup but could not make out what it was.

It was a windy day and the Wahl fishing trip was short lived. The wind kept pushing the boat toward shore, prompting Wahl to call it quits. He docked his boat and allowed his son to fish from the dock.

As Wahl backed his car up to the nearby boat launch, he again looked at the Ryder truck and the pickup parked next to it. The pickup had been moved closer to the truck. Wahl and his son loaded the boat and left Geary Lake around noon. The Ryder truck and pickup were parked in the same location when they left.

After hearing and reading about the Oklahoma City bombing and the fact that a Ryder truck was suspected to have been the bomb truck, Wahl contacted the FBI hotline and reported what he had seen at Geary Lake. However, before agents could contact Wahl about the reported sighting, he approached FBI agent Chris Budke in a restaurant in Junction City and told him about seeing the Ryder truck and pickup at Geary Lake.

Agents responded to Wahl's information and began searching the area immediately around the lake. At a turn out near the north end of the lake, agents found what was later identified to be diesel oil spilled on the ground and remaining in the top soil.

During pretrial preparations, Wahl was asked to accompany agents and federal prosecutors to Geary Lake in an attempt to reconstruct the position where the Ryder truck and pickup were parked when Wahl saw them at the lake on Tuesday morning. Wahl was given no instruction except that he should direct the Ryder truck and pickup to be parked in the location he saw them the morning of April 18. After Wahl had completed the placement of the vehicles, photographs were taken to depict the location where Wahl had seen the vehicles on Tuesday morning.

Wahl had not been told nor had it been reported in the news media that agents had found a diesel oil spill in the area. However, Wahl's placement of the Ryder truck and pickup was within several feet of the area where agents found the diesel fuel spill.

Terry Nichols had told Agents Smith and Crabtree that on the morning of April 18 he loaned McVeigh his GMC pickup and that McVeigh dropped him off at the auction at Fort Riley. Nichols said he spent the entire morning looking at surplus property. However, agents were unable to find anyone at the auction who remembered Nichols being there. Bill McDonald, an employee of the Defense Reutilization Management Office (DRMO) said he was present in the auction's small yard the entire morning and never saw Nichols. Registration records showed Nichols had not signed in until 12:50 p.m.

The FBI believed that Nichols needed an alibi and the auction was the only location he could provide. Agents Hersley and Tongate were certain that McVeigh and Nichols were at Geary Lake on the morning of April 18 mixing the bomb components the day before the Murrah Building bombing.

The FBI followed leads of other reported sightings of a Ryder truck at Geary Lake. However, Wahl's story was the most believable. His sighting was reported to the FBI before news coverage about Geary Lake. Wahl described a truck that was similar in size to the truck used in the bombing. He also described a pickup that was generally consistent with Terry Nichols' pickup. The day of Wahl's sighting was also consistent with the time agents believed the bomb was mixed.

Another witness, Bob Nelson, corroborated Sergeant Wahl's story. Nelson worked at Elliott's Body Shop and was very familiar with Ryder trucks. He said he saw a Ryder truck parked next to an older dark-color pickup at Geary Lake on the morning of April 18.

Nelson reported this sighting to Ryder corporate officials in Miami, Florida, prior to any news coverage focusing on Geary Lake. Wahl and Nelson were the only witnesses who reported Ryder truck sightings at Geary Lake before extensive news coverage about the bomb possibly being mixed at the lake.

Marife Nichols

Marife Nichols told agents that on Tuesday, April 18, she received a call from Terry's son, Josh, around 9:00 a.m. Josh asked to speak with his father. However, Terry had already left the house. In earlier statements, Marife said Terry returned home around noon. She said he told her he had been out registering the pickup, and that he was going to a sealed bid auction at Fort Riley. She said Terry left shortly thereafter and did not return until about 2:00 p.m.

In subsequent conversations, Marife changed her statement and told agents that Terry had returned home around 1:30 p.m. on Tuesday and told her that he had already been to the sealed bid auction at Fort Riley. Terry was at home the remainder of the evening. Sometime around 10:00 p.m., Marife remembered, the telephone rang. Terry answered the call and later told her it was his brother, James. Phone records confirmed a 14-minute call from James Nichols' residence to Terry's home at 10:26 p.m. on April 18.

The X marks the spot at Geary Lake where Agents Hersley and Tongate are certain McVeigh and Nichols parked the Ryder truck and Nichols' pickup and mixed the bomb on the mornng of April 18, 1995.

A Summary of the Evidence

The Bomb Site

At **9:02 a.m., Wednesday morning, April 19, 1995,** a large explosion blew away the entire front of the Alfred P. Murrah Federal Building in downtown Oklahoma City. Structurally, the entire building was destroyed. The bomb blast wreaked havoc within a ten-block area, killing 168 men, women, and children and wounding hundreds more both physically and emotionally.

Who could do such a thing? Before noon, law enforcement authorities located the rear axle assembly of a 20-foot Ryder truck. Within hours the FBI traced the axle to a Ryder truck rented two days before by a man who used the name Robert Kling at Elliott's Body Shop in Junction City, Kansas.

Personal identification and telephone and business records proved that Kling was actually Tim McVeigh who registered under his real name and brought a Ryder truck to the Dreamland Motel in the days prior to the bombing. McVeigh and his Ryder truck were last seen leaving the motel before daylight on the morning of April 18.

The FBI soon discovered that a Tim McVeigh had been stopped by the Oklahoma Highway Patrol on Interstate 35 near Perry, Oklahoma, on Wednesday morning, April 19, 1995. Trooper Charlie Hanger arrested McVeigh for carrying a concealed weapon, and McVeigh remained in the Noble County jail until Friday, April 21, when the FBI learned of his arrest.

The correlation between time and distance was telling. McVeigh had been arrested 80 miles from the bombsite at 10:20 a.m., just 78 minutes after the bombing. The correlation was certainly not proof that McVeigh was involved in the bombing. However, it was consistent with McVeigh having been in Oklahoma City at the time of the bombing. And when he was arrested by Trooper Hanger, McVeigh was driving a 1977 Mercury, the exact same year and make of the vehicle driven by the Tim McVeigh who had brought a Ryder truck to the Dreamland Motel in the days before the bombing.

The direction of McVeigh's travel when he was arrested was consistent with his probable return to Herington and/or Junction City, Kansas.

Chemical residue found on McVeigh's clothing at the time of his arrest indicated he had recently handled explosives. PETN residue, found in detonation cord, was identified in McVeigh's pants pockets and on his tee-shirt. EGDN, found in dynamite, was identified on a set of earplugs found in McVeigh's pants pocket. The Tree of Liberty shirt, worn by McVeigh at the time of his arrest, contained the slogan, "Sic Semper Tyrannis" or "Death unto Tyrants." Literature recovered from McVeigh's car pointed toward a deepening hatred of the United States government.

The "Not abandoned, Do Not Tow" sign found in McVeigh's car was consistent with the vehicle having been planted in Oklahoma City to be used by McVeigh to make his getaway after the bombing on April 19. The sign contained the words, "Will move by April 23," McVeigh's birthday.

The Paulsen's business card, found in the back seat floorboard of Trooper Hanger's patrol car, contained the handwritten words, "TNT @

$5/stick—need more—call after 01May, see if I can get some more." These words were in McVeigh's handwriting.

The Bridges Calling Card

Together, McVeigh and Terry Nichols obtained the Daryl Bridges calling card, which was used in September and October, 1994, and in April, 1995, to obtain bomb components. The card was used to inquire about the availability of nitromethane and anhydrous hydrazine, highly explosive racing fuels, and to call Elliott's Body Shop to obtain a quote on the Ryder bomb truck.

The address used to obtain the calling card was 3616 North Van Dyke Road, Decker, Michigan, Terry Nichols' home address. Lana Padilla identified Nichols' handwriting on the application card. Jennifer McVeigh identified the handwriting of McVeigh on the money order used to make the first payment, which accompanied the application card. Padilla identified the handwriting of Nichols on five additional money orders used to make payments against the calling card, and Jennifer McVeigh identified her brother's handwriting on the only remaining money order used to make payment against the card. FBI handwriting experts also identified the handwriting of McVeigh and Nichols on these documents. The payment booklet for the Bridges calling card was found by the FBI in Nichols' house during the search on April 22-23, 1995.

Investigation and analysis of the nearly 700 calls made using the Bridges calling card constituted one of the most intensive telephone record searches in the history of criminal investigation. When and where the calls were made from were determined by agents who also identified the destination telephones, as well as dates, times, and duration of the calls.

Each call was identified as having been placed by and/or for the benefit of McVeigh or Nichols. Tracing the calls proved beneficial to the FBI in tracking the two suspects in the days, weeks, and months leading up to the bombing in Oklahoma City. Even though McVeigh and Nichols acquired the card to conceal their true identity, the Bridges card provided the FBI with a virtual roadmap of their travels.

Acquiring the Bomb Components

The receipt for the purchase of 2,000 pounds of ammonium nitrate fertilizer in the name of Mike Havens, from Mid-Kansas Co-op in

McPherson, Kansas, on September 30, 1994, was found by the FBI in a kitchen cabinet drawer inside Nichols' house in Herington, Kansas. The receipt contained two of McVeigh's fingerprints.

A second 2,000-pound quantity of ammonium nitrate was purchased by customer Mike Havens on October 18, 1994, from the same co-op. McPherson is just 37 miles west of Marion, Kansas, where Nichols lived and worked on the Donahue Ranch.

The exhaustive motel search by federal agents determined that Terry Nichols used the Havens name in registering at the Starlite Motel in Salina, Kansas, on October 16, 1994, just two days before the second ammonium nitrate purchase. Nichols' fingerprints and handwriting were found on the registration card he completed in the name of Terry Havens at the motel. Salina, Kansas, is only 38 miles north of McPherson.

The FBI investigation identified another occasion when Nichols used the Havens name. Nichols used the name Joe Havens when he registered at the Buckaroo Motel in Tucumcari, New Mexico, on October 25, 1994. Two days before and seven days after the second ammonium nitrate purchase from Mid-Kansas Co-op, Nichols used the Havens name to register at separate motels. To Agents Hersley and Tongate, it was clear—Terry Nichols was Mike Havens.

The FBI knew that McVeigh rented a storage unit at the Herington Industrial Park on September 22, 1994, in the false name of Shawn Rivers. That rental was eight days before the first ammonium nitrate purchase. Eight of McVeigh's fingerprints were found on the rental agreement. Again, the evidence was clear—McVeigh was Shawn Rivers.

The FBI learned that Nichols had rented a storage unit in Council Grove, Kansas, on October 17, 1994, using the false name of Joe Kyle, just one day before the second ammonium nitrate purchase at Mid-Kansas Co-op.

The FBI was certain the Tovex and blasting caps used in the Murrah Building bombing were obtained during the robbery of the Martin Marietta Rock Quarry during the first weekend of October, 1994. The quarry was only 10 miles from where Nichols lived at the time.

Jennifer McVeigh admitted to Agent Hersley and Prosecutor Beth Wilkinson that McVeigh had bragged to her about a near accident while transporting up to 1,000 pounds of explosives in October or November of 1994. Michael Fortier told the FBI about a conversation wherein McVeigh confided to him that McVeigh and Nichols had burglarized a rock quarry near Nichols' home and had stolen Tovex and Primadet blasting caps. McVeigh told Fortier that he and Nichols had used a cordless drill to drill the locks from the metal buildings where the explosives were stored. In October, 1994, McVeigh showed the stolen explosives to Fortier in Kingman, Arizona.

During the search of Terry Nichols' home on April 22-23, 1995, the FBI found five rolls of Primadet blasting caps, the exact same time and delay as those stolen in the Martin Marietta burglary. Also found in Nichols' home was a Makita cordless drill and two cases of drill bits. When FBI experts compared the tool markings on one of the drilled locks to drill bit impressions from the drill bits found in Nichols' home, one of the bits was found to leave the exact same tool markings as those left on the drilled lock recovered from the scene of the robbery. The FBI had linked Nichols to the burglary of explosives from Martin Marietta.

On October 21, 1994, Tim Chambers of VP Racing Fuels was working at the races in Ennis, Texas. He told Agents Hersley and Floyd Zimms that he remembered selling three 55-gallon drums of nitromethane, a high-octane racing fuel, to a man whose face he thought resembled that of a possum. According to Chambers, the man's eyes were set close together and his nose was long and pointed downward. Chambers recalled loading the three drums of nitromethane into a dark color pickup with a white camper shell on the back, a description that was consistent with Terry Nichols' pickup.

Motel records proved Terry Nichols rented a room in Pauls Valley, Oklahoma, the night before the purchase of racing fuel in Texas. Pauls Valley is in direct line with the route from central Kansas to Ennis, Texas. In searching McVeigh's storage unit at the Herington Industrial Park, the FBI found three circular stains, the circumference of which matched almost perfectly with the circumference of the barrels of nitromethane sold at the Texas race track. After October 21, the date of the racing fuel purhcase, there were no more Bridges card calls inquiring about the price and availability of racing fuel.

Roger Moore Robbery

Michael Fortier told the FBI that Terry Nichols robbed Roger Moore as a fundraiser. Two days after the robbery, Nichols rented yet another storage unit in Council Grove, Kansas, using the name Ted Parker. Nichols' handwriting was identified on the Parker rental agreement. After the bombing, Fortier pointed out storage unit #37 to Agents Zimms and Jim Volz as the unit from which McVeigh retrieved guns that were later sold at gun shows in Arizona and Utah.

Much of the remaining loot stolen in the Roger Moore robbery was found in Nichols' house during the FBI search on April 22-23, 1995. Guns, cameras, a quilt belonging to Karen Anderson, and the two safe deposit box keys stolen in the robbery were found inside Nichols' home. Pieces of jade stolen in the robbery were observed by Lana Padilla and her son when they searched Nichols' storage unit in Las Vegas, Nevada. The jade was subsequently found in Terry Nichols' house in Herington.

Casing the Building

Michael Fortier told agents and federal prosecutors that on December 16, 1994, McVeigh drove him to Oklahoma City and pointed out the Murrah Building as the building that McVeigh intended to bomb. McVeigh told Fortier he was going to bomb the building because it was an easy target, with a lot of glass on the façade of the building, and because he believed that the ATF issued orders from the building for the operation that ended up in tragedy at the Branch Davidian compound in Waco.

McVeigh and Fortier looked at the building and talked about the best place to park a getaway car. After the bombing, Fortier identified the location behind the YMCA Building where McVeigh had indicated he was going to park the getaway car. The key to the Ryder bomb truck was found in the alleyway behind the YMCA.

Terry Nichols admitted he drove around the Murrah Building twice on Easter Sunday night looking for McVeigh and his supposedly broken down car.

Mixing the Bomb

The deep tire tracks found by the FBI directly in front of and perpendicular to Herington storage unit #2 were a strong indication the Ryder truck had been backed up to the storage unit within the previous several days. The distance between the tracks left in the wet ground in front of the storage unit was almost precisely the exact same distance that separated the rear wheels of a 20-foot Ryder truck.

Rick Wahl, the army seargent, reported seeing a Ryder truck at Geary Lake near Junction City on Tuesday morning, April 18, 1995, from approximately 9:00 a.m. to noon while he and his young son were at the lake fishing. Wahl reported there was a dark color pickup parked next to the Ryder truck this same morning. What Wahl did not know was that the FBI had found a large diesel spill immediately next to where he had seen the Ryder truck and pickup. Nichols lied to FBI agents about his whereabouts on April 18.

The Fortier Statements

Michael and Lori Fortier had known for months that McVeigh and Nichols planned to bomb the federal building in Oklahoma City. The Fortiers were told about the Roger Moore robbery, had seen the loot taken in the crime, and were witnesses to McVeigh's drawings and evil demonstrations using cans of food to demonstrate his proposed placement of deadly barrels of ammonium nitrate bombs in the back of a truck. McVeigh told the Fortiers how he was going to make the bomb and what kind of truck he was going to place it in.

To Agents Hersley and Tongate, cutting a deal with Michael and Lori Fortier was sickening. They believed that one phone call to authorities could have prevented the Oklahoma City bombing. However, as distasteful as it was, the agents agreed with federal prosecutors that it was necessary in a case of this magnitude to have the testimony of an insider. The Fortiers could provide insight about McVeigh and Nichols and their plan that no other person could provide. It was necessary not only to secure the convictions of McVeigh and Nichols, but also to reassure the American public that those responsible for the bombing had been caught.

The Last Call

Agents Hersley and Tongate noticed that the last use of the Bridges calling card was at 10:46 p.m. on April 17. It was the call to Lana Padilla only minutes after a call to the Dreamland Motel in which McVeigh and Nichols agreed to meet the following morning.

They were now in the final stages of their evil plan. Phone calls had served their purpose, but it was now time for action and no phone contact should be made. The card, which irrefutable evidence showed belonged to McVeigh and Nichols, was never used again.

Tracking Terry Nichols after the bombing

Nichols said that when he dropped McVeigh off at McDonald's on Washington Boulevard in Junction City early Tuesday afternoon, April 18, 1995, McVeigh told him he was going back east to visit relatives. Nichols said McVeigh told him that if he did not make it back in time, Nichols should retrieve McVeigh's personal belongings from the storage unit in Herington.

But just two days later, Nichols had apparently decided that McVeigh was not going to make it back in time, because he cleaned out McVeigh's storage unit. How could Nichols have possibly known after only two days that McVeigh was not going to make it back in time to get his things from the storage unit himself? To Agents Hersley and Tongate, the answer was clear. Nichols knew that it would take McVeigh only five to six hours to drive from Oklahoma City to Herington or Junction City, Kansas.

It must have been obvious to Nichols by Thursday morning that McVeigh had run into a problem in Oklahoma City. He clearly could have made it back to Herington after the bombing long before Thursday morning. Nichols was becoming obsessed. Paranoia was setting in. Thursday morning, he cleaned out the storage unit. Thursday afternoon, he purchased three newspapers to read about the bombing in Oklahoma City. Where was his friend? Where was McVeigh? Why had he not returned?

On Friday morning, April 21, Nichols was already up when the cable television serviceman arrived at his house at 9:00 a.m. By the time Chad Albin switched the television to CNN and told Nichols he would now be able to watch news coverage of the bombing, FBI explosives experts had described the bomb used in Oklahoma City as an ammonium nitrate/fuel oil mixture. It was also being announced that the FBI had traced the bomb truck to Elliott's Body Shop in Junction City, only 25 miles north of Nichols' house in Herington.

Nichols knew he had used the Havens name to register at motels in Salina, Kansas, and Tucumcari, New Mexico. The ammonium nitrate had been purchased using the Havens name at Mid-Kansas Co-op, only

37 miles west of where Nichols lived in Marion, Kansas. Nichols still had ammonium nitrate in his house. In a state of panic, he began throwing the fertilizer prills onto his front yard. He had not realized that Gladys Wendt, while visiting a relative, was watching. She told Agent Tongate and Prosecutor Beth Wilkinson it looked as if it was snowing in Nichols' front yard.

When asked by Agents Smith and Crabtree why he had thrown the ammonium nitrate out in such a rush, he answered, "I thought it might make me look guilty to a jury." Certainly, Nichols did not realize the September 30, 1994 receipt for the purchase of 2,000 pounds of ammonium nitrate in the Havens name was still in the kitchen cabinet drawer of his home.

A rescue worker hands an injured baby to a woman who was also badly injured in the Murrah Building bombing on April 19, 1995. *Courtesy Oklahoma Publishing Company.*

Emergency workers search through debris after the ammonium nitrate/racing fuel bomb destroyed the Murrah Building. *Courtesy Oklahoma Publishing Company.*

There was no doubt McVeigh and Nichols had the technical know-how to build an ammonium nitrate/fuel oil bomb. *Hunter* and *The Turner Diaries*, books authored by William Pierce, described in detail how an ammonium nitrate bomb could be used to blow up a federal building. *Hunter* was found in Nichols' home by the FBI. McVeigh had given *The Turner Diaries* to many of his friends. It was a book he fantasized about. These books, along with the book, *Homemade C-4*, which McVeigh ordered by mail in 1993, provided specific details about where to buy the components of an ammonium nitrate bomb and how to build such a bomb using ammonium nitrate, Tovex, and nitromethane.

Tim McVeigh and Terry Nichols had the motive—their hatred of the federal government—the knowledge to build a massive deadly bomb, and the opportunity to waste the lives of innocent victims in Oklahoma City on a spring morning in 1995.

The FBI knew they had their men.

Was Anyone Else Involved?

N o other aspect of the Oklahoma City bombing investigation received more attention from the media and the public than the search for John Doe #2.

The origin of John Doe #2 was at Elliott's Body Shop in Junction City. Witnesses at Elliott's told the FBI they remembered two men picking up the Ryder truck on Monday afternoon, April 17, 1995. When Eldon Elliott, Vickie Beemer, and Tom Kessinger were interviewed by Agent Scott Crabtree, it was Kessinger who was able to provide the best description of these men. FBI artist Ray Rozycki worked with Kessinger to prepare composite drawings of the two men.

After FBI management decided to release the drawings of John Doe #1 and John Doe #2, a nationwide manhunt followed. Most agreed that John Doe #1 was Timothy McVeigh—the likeness was startling. When the owner of the Dreamland Motel saw the drawing of John Doe #1, she immediately concluded it was McVeigh.

However, the existence or non-existence of John Doe #2 caused the FBI much heartache and resulted in thousands of man hours of investigation looking for another unidentified suspect.

An FBI hotline was publicized and more than 18,000 callers reported having seen either or both of the men depicted in the drawings. The sightings were in many parts of the United States. Many callers reported seeing the men in Oklahoma City on the morning of the bombing, as well as in the days, weeks, and months before and after the bombing.

Each call was analyzed separately, as well as conjointly, by the FBI. Agents across the country began tracking down callers for further interview to determine the validity of their reports. Many callers were women who claimed the men depicted in the drawings were former husbands or boyfriends. Many others reported having seen the men in restaurants, nightclubs, stores, and almost everywhere imaginable. Callers described men they either knew or had seen and said the men they were calling about looked just like the men in the drawings.

Each call was analyzed for validity and, where practical, leads were set out for further investigation. Calls continued to come in on the hotline for months after the bombing. Agents continued to run them to ground. However, none of the calls produced positive information. Many times, callers provided information that was in direct conflict with information reported by other callers. One caller would report having seen the men at a specific location at a certain date and time, while another caller was just as certain he or she had seen the men at a completely different location at the same time.

The bombing in Oklahoma City was a horrifying experience and most of the callers simply wanted to help. Memories were stretched. Other times, reported sightings of the men were completely false, made up by people who wanted to enjoy a few fleeting moments of fame that news coverage might bring them. Some callers probably hoped to collect some of the reward money that was being offered for information leading to the identification, arrest, and conviction of those responsible for this senseless act.

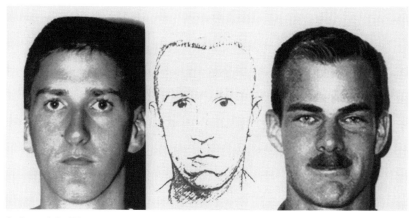

Left to right, Timothy McVeigh, the artist's sketch of John Doe #1, and Michael Hertig, the soldier who rented a truck at Elliott's Body Shop in Junction City, Kansas, the day after McVeigh rented the truck used in the Oklahoma City bombing.

With daily news reports about the search for John Doe #2, the FBI's investigative machine kept churning. In late May, 1995, Eldon Elliott and Vickie Beemer, the owner and employee of Elliott's Body Shop, were asked by the FBI to provide rental agreements for all Ryder trucks rented by Elliott's in the days leading up to the bombing. The FBI hoped the additional rental agreements might shed some light on the identity of John Doe #2.

The FBI methodically identified and interviewed each person who rented a Ryder truck at Elliott's, hoping to sort out the dilemma involving John Doe #2. Finally, in early June, Michael Hertig was located and interviewed. Hertig had rented a Ryder truck from Elliott's Body Shop on Tuesday afternoon, April 18, 1995, one day after McVeigh picked up the truck used in the bombing.

Hertig was in the army and assigned to nearby Fort Riley. He received transfer orders and rented a Ryder truck from Elliott's to move his personal belongings to his new assignment location. Hertig's physical description generally matched that provided by Eldon Elliott and Tom Kessinger of John Doe #1. However, McVeigh looked more like the man depicted in the composite drawing than Hertig did. Both Elliott and Kessinger were certain McVeigh was John Doe #1. McVeigh was Robert Kling. Case Agents Hersley and Tongate were also confident that McVeigh was John Doe #1, but who was John Doe #2?

Hertig told agents that when he went to pick up the Ryder truck at Elliott's Body Shop, another man was with him. He said a friend, Todd Bunting, had driven him to Elliott's. When they arrived at Elliott's, both men went inside. Hertig said that when he saw the composite drawing of John Doe #2, he had to admit the man in the drawing looked a lot like his friend, Todd Bunting.

Tom Kessinger, the only witness at Elliott's that could provide a description of John Doe #2, told agents the man was a white male, 5'10", 200 pounds, muscular build, dark brown hair, brown eyes, clean shaven, with an olive or tan complexion. Hertig told agents this description fit Bunting almost perfectly. Kessinger and Eldon Elliott told agents the man they had described as John Doe #2 wore a baseball cap that was white in color with blue scallops or lightning strikes on the sides of the cap. Kessinger said the second man wore a black, short sleeve tee-shirt, and that he could see what appeared to be the jagged edge of a tattoo sticking out from under the man's left shirtsleeve.

When agents finally located Todd Bunting, he confirmed he had driven Hertig to Elliott's to pick up the Ryder truck on April 18. Bunting said he was wearing jeans, a black tee-shirt, and a Carolina Panthers cap when he walked inside Elliott's. Bunting also showed agents a tattoo on his left arm. It was a playboy bunny. Bunting was asked to put on the black tee-shirt he wore to Elliott's. He was photographed wearing the tee-shirt and a Carolina Panthers cap. Protruding just below the shirtsleeve of his left arm was what appeared to be the jagged edge of a tattoo. It was the edge of the playboy bunny tattoo.

Agent Hersley and Federal Prosecutor Scott Mendeloff observed that the photographs taken of Bunting bore similarities to the composite drawing of John Doe #2. Even Bunting commented that the photographs looked a lot like the man depicted in the composite drawing of John Doe #2. When Tom Kessinger was presented with the photographs taken of Bunting, he told Agent Hersley and Prosecutor Mendeloff that he was absolutely certain the man he described for FBI artist Ray Rozycki as depicted in the composite drawing of John Doe #2 was Todd Bunting. Kessinger said the mental image of Bunting that remained in his mind was what he had attempted to recreate with artist Rozycki in the composite drawing of Joe Doe #2.

Todd Bunting accompanied Michael Hertig to Elliott's Body Shop the day after
Timothy McVeigh rented the Ryder truck used in the Oklahoma City bombing. It
was Bunting's description that resulted in the artist's drawing of John Doe #2.
Tom Kessinger, who gave the description for the artist's sketch, later agreed that
he was absolutely sure that John Doe #2 was Bunting, who had no association
with the Oklahoma City bombing.

Agents Hersley and Tongate and federal prosecutors were confident the men depicted in the composite drawings of John Doe #1 and John Doe #2 had been identified. They were Tim McVeigh and Todd Bunting. Kessinger had taken the mental image of Bunting from his observations of Hertig and Bunting in the body shop on Tuesday afternoon and crossed this image over in his mind to the image he had of McVeigh coming into the body shop on Monday afternoon, just one day earlier. In his mind, Kessinger had mistakenly believed that Bunting came to Elliott's with McVeigh rather than Hertig. In law enforcement circles, the misassociation of suspects from one sighting to another is a not so uncommon occurrence.

Of particular importance to the FBI was the fact that when Agent Scott Crabtree first interviewed Eldon Elliott about his memory of the man or men who came into the body shop and picked up the truck rented to Robert Kling on April 17, 1995, Elliott talked about only one man. His description of the man fit McVeigh. Elliott said nothing about a second man being with Mr. Kling. The theory of a second man was born in the mind of Tom Kessinger, who had taken his mental image of Todd Bunting and mistakenly linked it to McVeigh.

There was no other credible evidence of a John Doe #2. McVeigh was alone when he was at the Dreamland Motel, when he purchased the yellow Mercury from the Firestone Store, and at the McDonald's just before he picked up the Ryder Truck.

Middle Easterners and the Brown Pickup

The involvement of Middle Easterners and a brown pickup in the bombing originated with the reported sighting by M.A. who was present in downtown Oklahoma City looking for temporary work on the morning of the bombing. M.A. reported seeing two males, both of whom he said were Middle Eastern in appearance, hurry away from the Murrah Building and enter a dark brown pickup with smoked windows and a smoke color front bug guard.

The reported sighting of these two Middle Easterners and the dark brown pickup, coupled with the release of the composite drawings of John Doe #1 and John Doe #2, lead the news media and many Americans to believe others besides McVeigh and Terry Nichols were involved in the bombing. It was a natural reaction to want to reject the idea that two clean-shaven, short-haired American army veterans could inflict such destruction upon their own people.

An investigation by KFOR-TV news reporter Jayna Davis focused on the involvement of Middle Easterners in the bombing and served to throw fuel on the fire that others were involved. The FBI, determined to identify and catch those involved and prevent another bombing, unwittingly increased the publics' attention on the possibility of others being involved. The release of the composite drawings, based on erroneous information from witnesses at Elliott's Body Shop, caused a nationwide manhunt for John Doe #2.

M.A., who reportedly saw the men of Middle Eastern appearance hurry away from the Murrah building on the morning of the bombing, was inconsistent in later statements he made to the FBI about what he had seen. During the initial interview, M.A. reported the two men had entered a dark brown pickup, which then turned west on Northwest Fifth Street before turning north on Hudson, a one-way street to the south. The next time he was interviewed, M.A. told agents the pickup turned south on Hudson, the opposite direction from what he had earlier stated.

As investigators, Agents Hersley and Tongate questioned why M.A. had been able to provide such a detailed description of not only the pickup allegedly driven by the men, but also of the clothing they wore. He described both men as wearing white shirts, jeans, black boots, and black hats. The agents considered whether or not it was reasonable for M.A. to have focused so sharply on the clothing worn by the two men, as well as the vehicle they were driving and their direction of travel, all before the bomb blast. There was no reason to focus on the men before the explosion. Why had he focused so closely on them? Why could he not keep his story straight?

In spite of the inconsistencies in M.A.'s story, an all-points-bulletin was put out for the two men and the dark brown pickup. Of paramount importance to the FBI at this crucial time was to prevent another bombing. The suspects must be caught before they had a chance to strike again. By Wednesday afternoon, the news media had flooded the airways with reports of the alleged sighting of the brown pickup, the Middle Eastern men, and their possible involvement in the bombing. The seed

04-19-95 WED
08:57:15 24

The security camera at the Regency Tower Apartments showed a Ryder truck headed in the direction of the nearby Murrah Building just five minutes before the bombing at 9:02 a.m. on April 19, 1995.

was planted that more than one suspect was involved in the placement of the bomb truck in front of the Murrah Building.

As the investigation developed, Agents Hersley and Tongate became convinced that McVeigh had delivered the bomb truck to the Murrah building on the morning of the bombing. The image of the Ryder truck was captured on video camera in front of the Regency Tower Apartments only minutes before the blast. The ignition key to the Ryder bomb truck was found in the alleyway behind the YMCA building, in the exact pathway of escape that Michael Fortier had described to agents. When McVeigh was arrested, his clothing and a pair of earplugs found in his pocket contained chemical residues consistent with that found in det cord and dynamite.

There was no doubt in the agents' minds that McVeigh had personally delivered the bomb truck to the Murrah Building. In the naivety of his own mind, McVeigh was a soldier on a mission, albeit a cowardly mission. There was no stopping him. It was personal. He was not about to allow anyone else to deliver the bomb truck. He wanted that satisfaction for himself.

If McVeigh had, in fact, delivered the bomb truck to the Murrah Building, as the agents were convinced he had, there was no reason or need for anyone else to have been hurrying away from the building on the morning of the bombing as M.A. had suggested. Except for the alleged sighting by this man, and the alleged sighting of Middle Eastern men with McVeigh at an Oklahoma City motel on the morning of the bombing, which sighting was later retracted, there were no other believable sightings of Middle Eastern men with McVeigh or as having been involved in the bombing. Other than in the minds of certain local news reporters, there was absolutely no credible evidence suggesting the involvement of Middle Easterners in the Oklahoma City bombing.

The key to the Ryder truck used in the Murrah Building bombing was found in the alleyway behind the YMCA Building, where Timothy McVeigh told Michael Fortier he would leave his getaway car.

As with the alleged sightings of John Doe #1 and John Doe #2, there were numerous calls to the FBI hotline by callers who claimed to have seen a dark brown pickup. Many of the callers reported sightings that were inconsistent with those reported by other callers. A brown pickup had been sighted all over Oklahoma City and other parts of the state, often at the same time at different locations.

One caller reported seeing a dark brown pickup stopped alongside the roadway in front of the location where Trooper Hanger arrested McVeigh. Hanger said he was certain there was no pickup in the area and a review of the videotape in Hanger's highway patrol unit confirmed the absence of a pickup.

There were other theories of the involvement of Middle Easterners. The McVeigh defense team conducted numerous interviews in the Philippines regarding Terry Nichols. One member of the team insisted to the media that Nichols had links to Ramzi Yousef, convicted for the first bombing of the World Trade Center in New York City.

The FBI conducted an extensive investigation in the Philippines and found no credible link between Nichols and Yousef or any terrorist organization operating there. In spite of all the rhetoric and allegations, no testimony or evidence was presented at either the McVeigh or Nichols federal trials linking either of them to Middle Eastern terrorists.

The X marks the spot where FBI agents found the Ryder truck key in the alleyway adjacent to the YMCA building.

Elohim City

The community's residents live on an approximate 400-acre parcel of land near the side of a small mountain in far eastern Oklahoma near the town of Muldrow. Elohim City's residents come from many different religious backgrounds. However, the common belief of the group is that the white race is superior. Followers of the late Reverend Millar believe that Scripture teaches that the white race comes from the lost tribes of Israel who migrated through Europe and Britain to settle in America. They believe they are part of this chosen white race. They are opposed to interracial marriages and will not allow certain races of people to live with them. People of the black race or the Jewish faith are not welcome at Elohim City.

Prior to the incidents at Waco and Ruby Ridge, Idaho, Elohim City followers were perceived by law enforcement officers in Oklahoma to be more vocal than physical in their expressions against the federal government. While they had engaged in anti-government rhetoric, they had not as a community taken violent physical action against the government.

After Waco and Ruby Ridge, the men of Elohim City believed they must arm themselves and organize security patrols to protect themselves against similar raids or infiltration by the ATF or other agencies of the federal government.

A German national, Andreas Strassmeier, who came to Elohim City around 1992, headed up the effort to organize security patrols. Millar and others at Elohim City believed Strassmeier was best equipped for this task as he had been trained in weaponry while serving in the German army. He was also familiar with first aid and fire prevention procedures.

Some members of the news media suspected the involvement of residents of Elohim City in the Oklahoma City bombing after it was revealed that McVeigh had called Elohim City and spoken to the daughter-in-law of Reverend Millar on April 5, 1995, just two weeks before the bombing.

However, the FBI discovered that McVeigh had met Strassmeier at a gun show in 1993 and had written down the telephone number at Elohim City. McVeigh did not remember Strassmeier's name but told Joan Millar that he wanted to talk to a resident with a thick foreign accent. Strassmeier was the only resident of Elohim City with such an accent. McVeigh said he might visit Elohim City but would call for directions if he did. Millar said McVeigh never came to Elohim City and never called again.

Millar testified at the federal court trial of Terry Nichols in Denver that Andreas Strassmeier was at Elohim City in the days before the Oklahoma City bombing and could not possibly have been with McVeigh or anyone else in Junction City, Kansas. She said that Strassmeier was working on a fence for some neighbors on the morning of the bombing, a fact that was verified when the neighbors were contacted by the FBI. Millar testified that the leadership at Elohim City did not advocate the use of violence, and the Reverend Millar never preached or advocated violence against the government. She said that if any resident spoke of or advocated violence in this regard, the person(s) would not have been allowed to remain in Elohim City.

In the fall of 1994, a young woman named Carol Howe was spending a good amount of her time at Elohim City. Howe believed she had been the victim of a racial incident involving African Americans. In response to this incident, Howe called a "racist hot line" and listened to a recorded message. Subsequently, she followed up this call by writing a letter and mailing it to an address provided in the message. Howe wanted to meet people who believed in white supremacy as she did.

Through these contacts, Howe met and began seeing, on a social basis, a man named Dennis Mahon. She said Mahon lived in Tulsa, Oklahoma, and that he was associated with a white supremacist group known as the White Aryan Resistance. Through Mahon, she was exposed to Elohim City and began visiting the compound on an irregular basis, many times with Mahon.

Howe testified at the federal trial of Terry Nichols in Denver that she heard Mahon and others at Elohim City, including the Reverend Millar, espouse physical violence against the federal government. During this time, Howe became even more caught up in the white supremacist movement that she said was part of the Elohim City ideology. She dressed and looked the part of a white supremacist, complete with the tattoo of a swastika on one of her shoulders.

On April 21, 1995, after the composite drawings of John Doe #1 and John Doe #2 had been released to the news media, Howe reported to ATF agents that she believed she knew the identities of the men depicted in the drawings. She told the ATF she thought the Ward brothers, who lived at Elohim City, might be the men depicted in the drawings. She told the ATF that she did not believe the photographs she had seen of Tim McVeigh looked anything like either one of the composite drawings.

Howe said nothing to the ATF in April, 1995, about possibly having seen McVeigh at the compound during the previous year. However, when she testified at the federal trial of Nichols, she said she believed she had seen McVeigh at Elohim City in July, 1994. She testified that McVeigh was walking across the lawn near the church building inside the compound, a distance from her of about 70 feet, and that he was with Strassmeier and Peter Ward.

Under cross examination by Assistant United States Attorney Beth Wilkinson, Howe acknowledged that she was shown photographs of McVeigh, as well as the composite drawings of John Doe #1 and John Doe #2, when she met with ATF agents on April 21, 1995. She acknowledged under cross examination that she told the ATF she thought the Ward brothers looked like the men depicted in the composite drawings and that McVeigh did not. Howe admitted that when she met with the ATF initially, she did not tell the agents that she had seen McVeigh at Elohim City in July, 1994.

Howe admitted she knew this was important to investigators, but she did not tell them she had seen McVeigh at the compound even though she knew he had been arrested in connection with the bombing. As a defense witness for Nichols, Howe's testimony at trial about having seen McVeigh at Elohim City in July, 1994, was a significant variation from what she had told ATF Agents in the days, weeks, and months after the bombing.

What was Howe's motivation for the change in her testimony? Of importance to Agents Hersley and Tongate was the fact that in 1997, Howe was tried and acquitted of federal explosives charges in Tulsa, Oklahoma. Afterwards, she did not meet with agents or federal prosecutors to discuss her potential testimony as a defense witness in the Nichols' trial.

For years, federal agents had been aware of the strong anti-government rhetoric coming from the late Reverend Millar and other Elohim City residents. However, even though Millar allowed criminal elements to stay at his compound from time to time, there was no credible evidence the residents themselves had engaged in violent acts against the government.

A Concocted Story

David Paul Hammer, who was serving time for various convictions including kidnapping and robbery, was transferred to federal prison from the Oklahoma prison system for his own safety. While in federal prison, Hammer murdered a fellow inmate and was sentenced to death. He was housed on the same death row at Terre Haute, Indiana, where Tim McVeigh was awaiting execution.

Hammer, who had a reputation as a con man and user of intimidation against other inmates, witnesses, and law enforcement officials, claimed that McVeigh confided in him that other people, including a gang of bank robbers, were involved in the Oklahoma City bombing.

McVeigh wrote a letter from his death row cell indicating he did not trust Hammer and "there is no telling what he will say."

The FBI determined that Hammer's concocted fantasy was not corroborated by anyone or any piece of evidence uncovered in the largest criminal investigation in history. Hammer was a death row inmate looking for another opportunity to manipulate the judicial system and spend his moment in the spotlight. Victims of the Oklahoma City bombing saw Hammer's statements as a cruel prank and a desperate attempt to remove the spotlight from the guilt of McVeigh and Nichols.

Aryan Republican Army

Peter Kevin Langan, also known as "Commander Pedro," was the leader of the Aryan Republican Army, a small white-supremacist group that robbed a bank wearing Richard Nixon and Ronald Reagan masks in Springdale, Ohio, in June, 1994. Later, Langan was convicted for two bank robberies and an assault on federal officers and sentenced to life in prison without possibility of parole.

Langan used David Paul Hammer's allegation that McVeigh said a group of white supremacist bank robbers helped him bomb the Murrah Building to gain additional notoriety while locked up for the rest of his life in prison. However, there is no evidence to support Langan's claim that he knew or had ever met McVeigh.

Langan was arrested during the time of the Murrah Building bombing investigation. The FBI found no phone calls from McVeigh or Nichols to Langan or any of his associates. Long distance telephone records and millions of motel records failed to show any link between McVeigh and Nichols and Langan's group.

The Hammer and Langan statements are examples of unfounded conspiracy theories that will in all likelihood continue in the future. Unfortunately, the tragic significance of the Murrah Building bombing will indefinitely give rise to those who for selfish purposes and attention-grabbing try to create doubt as to the perpetrators of this enormous tragedy.

Bob Jacques

A retired Sergeant Major from the United States Army reported to authorities that McVeigh, Terry Nichols, and a man named Bob Jacques came into his real estate office in Cassville, Missouri, on November 2, 1994, wanting to buy property in a secluded area. The man described the car McVeigh was driving. The description was eerily similar to the yellow Mercury that McVeigh was driving at the time of his arrest.

Agents Hersley and Tongate were suspicious of the information from the retired Sergeant Major because of inconsistencies in his story. The man said Nichols introduced himself as "Terry Nichols from Herington, Kansas." However, Nichols did not move to Herington until March, 1995, so it was unlikely he would have introduced himself as Terry Nichols from Herington, Kansas, several months before he lived there.

Also, McVeigh did not purchase the yellow Mercury from Tom Manning until April 14, 1995, almost six months after the alleged sighting by the Sergeant Major. Still, hundreds and thousands of agent man hours were expended attempting to confirm or refute the Sergeant Major's story.

Ironically, the reported sighting of Bob Jacques with McVeigh and Nichols originated as a result of previous investigation by the FBI. During motel searches carried out by agents in the aftermath of the bombing, it was determined that two men, Bob Jacques and Gary Land, had rented a motel room across the street from the Noble County jail where McVeigh was being held after his arrest by Trooper Hanger. The men indicated on the registration card they were from Arizona. Agents knew McVeigh had been living in Arizona immediately before traveling to central Kansas in the days before the bombing.

This unrelated coincidence received immediate investigative attention and an all points bulletin was put out for Jacques and Land. The FBI wanted to know more about them. Why were they registered in a motel located not only in the same town but across the street from the jail where McVeigh was being held? When the FBI finally caught up with the men near Joplin, Missouri, it was determined they were merely drifters. It was only happenstance they had rented a motel room across the street from the Noble County jail. The men had nothing to do with McVeigh or the Oklahoma City bombing.

However, it was important to the news media that the men were being sought for questioning by the FBI regarding their stay at this motel. The incident received heavy television and news coverage. It was only after the extensive news coverage in which the names of Jacques and Land were released that the Sergeant Major reported that McVeigh, Nichols, and Bob Jacques had come into his office. The Sergeant Major wanted to help. He was an honest man, but the information he provided was simply not accurate.

The FBI was able to substantiate that one day after the alleged sighting of McVeigh in Missouri, he was in Pendleton, New York, at his father's home, a fact proven by McVeigh's use of the Bridges calling card.

The Bridges calling card

McVeigh's and Nichols' use of the prepaid Bridges calling card provided a virtual roadmap of their whereabouts and activities in the days, weeks, and months before the bombing. In the nearly 700 calls traced, the FBI was able to determine with whom McVeigh and Nichols communicated. McVeigh used the card to contact Michael Fortier in Arizona, his family in New York, and friends in Michigan. McVeigh and Nichols used the card to call legitimate businesses and gun show dealers. They even used the card to contact each other.

Of more importance to the FBI, McVeigh and Nichols used the card during the fall of 1994 to inquire about and obtain bomb components, including ammonium nitrate, nitromethane, and barrels to contain the explosives. On April 14, 1995, McVeigh used the card to obtain a quote for a 20-foot Ryder truck from Elliott's Body Shop in Junction City,

Kansas. On April 16, 1995, Easter Sunday, McVeigh used the card to call Nichols at his residence in Herington, Kansas, to tell Nichols it was time to leave for Oklahoma City to plant the getaway car there.

In tracing the calls made against the Bridges calling card, the FBI learned that all of the calls were made by or for the benefit of either McVeigh or Nichols or both of them. Of paramount importance to the FBI was the fact that no one other than McVeigh, Nichols, and possibly Nichols' wife had used the card. Certainly, McVeigh and Nichols were comfortable and confident in using the calling card to inquire about bomb components. Agents Hersley and Tongate were confident that McVeigh and Nichols would have used the calling card to contact other conspirators if any had been involved in the planning or execution of the Oklahoma City bombing.

The FBI determined that McVeigh and Nichols used James Nichols' home address of 3616 North Van Dyke Road, Decker, Michigan, on many documents, including the Bridges calling card application. Much investigative time was spent concerning James Nichols and the Decker, Michigan, address. Detroit FBI agents arrested James Nichols on a material witness warrant issued in Oklahoma City on April 21, 1995. Several court-authorized searches were conducted at the Nichols farm and many neighbors, relatives, and acquaintances were interviewed. James Nichols remained in custody until May 23, 1995, when he was released due to insufficient evidence to charge him with knowledge of or participation in the Oklahoma City bombing.

How many people would it take?

The evidence gathered during the investigation of the Oklahoma City bombing proved the bomb components were obtained by McVeigh and Nichols. Evidence was overwhelming that McVeigh rented the Ryder truck, and that both he and Nichols planted the getaway car in Oklahoma City on Easter Sunday. The evidence also showed that McVeigh and Nichols mixed the bomb at Geary Lake on Tuesday, April 18, 1995, one day before the bombing.

There has been much speculation about how many people it would have taken to mix the bomb. In reality, all that was needed was one or two able bodied men capable of lifting eighty 50-pound bags of ammonium nitrate and dumping them into 55-gallon barrels, pouring in the nitromethane, slicing the Tovex so that Primadet blasting caps could be inserted, and coordinating the explosion with the use of det cord. A time fuse was necessary, but that was one of the easiest components to obtain.

As tragic as the story ends, only McVeigh and Nichols were needed to carry out the most destructive act of domestic terrorism in American history.

Epilogue

T**he FBI concluded that two men,** Timothy McVeigh and Terry Nichols, planned and carried out the making of the bomb, and McVeigh delivered it to its destination outside the Alfred P. Murrah Federal Building on the morning of April 19, 1995.

Many people have wondered if anyone else accompanied McVeigh to pick up the bomb truck at Elliott's and to deliver the truck in front of the Murrah Building on the morning of the bombing. The answer might lie in this simple fact—no one else was needed. McVeigh had ample time to walk from the McDonald's Restaurant in Junction City to Elliott's Body Shop when he picked up the truck on April 17, 1995.

McVeigh told Michael Fortier that Terry Nichols was either going to accompany him to Oklahoma City on the morning of the bombing or would help McVeigh plant the getaway car in Oklahoma City beforehand. Nichols chose the latter. He helped McVeigh plant the getaway car in Oklahoma City on Easter Sunday, three days before the bombing. As a result, McVeigh did not need anyone to go with him to Oklahoma City. He needed only to drive the truck to its fateful place in front of the Murrah building, ignite the fuse, exit the vehicle, run to his getaway car, and drive away.

All other theories proved implausible. The story of the witness who said McVeigh stopped by his business to ask for directions to the Murrah Building on the morning of the bombing is not believable. It would have been totally out of character for McVeigh not to have been intimately familiar with his target. In fact, he had personally pointed out the target to both Michael Fortier and Terry Nichols previously.

Another witness reported seeing McVeigh in an alleyway near the Murrah building 20-25 minutes after the bombing. However, Trooper Hanger arrested McVeigh 80 miles from the Murrah Building only 78 minutes after the bombing. It would not have been possible for McVeigh to have driven 80 miles from the bomb site by 10:20 a.m., the time he was stopped by Trooper Hanger, if he had lingered near the bomb site for even 20 minutes after the explosion.

With a crime as horrific as the Oklahoma City bombing, it is natural to assume that many suspects had to have been involved. However, the reality is that one man alone could have carried out the crime. Two men were more than enough. Other than uncorroborated and unsubstantiated eyewitness testimony, no credible evidence existed that anyone other than McVeigh and Nichols were involved.

The actions of Michael and Lori Fortier were disgusting, outrageous, and unforgivable. Either of them could have prevented the bombing with a single telephone call. Their identities could have remained anonymous. Was 12 years an adequate sentence for Michael Fortier and immunity from prosecution appropriate for Lori Fortier? The FBI says, "No." Many agents believe an eternity behind bars might not be long enough for the despicable and cowardly actions of Michael and Lori Fortier. However, practical necessities under our system of justice and our laws prevented such a sentence.

One positive result of the investigation was a change in federal law. Diane Leonard, whose Secret Service Agent husband died in the bombing, led the fight to increase the punishment for a person committing a terrorist act in the United States. Section 1114 of the federal criminal code, known as the "assaulting a federal officer statute," allowed prosecution for assaulting federal law enforcement officers, but not employees of the government. Most of those killed and injured in the Murrah Building bombing were not law enforcement officers but employees of many federal government agencies. Federal law allowed McVeigh and Nichols to be indicted only for the deaths of the officers, a distinction that did not please families of others killed in the bombing.

Leonard testified before Congress to gain passage of a new Section 1114 that now begins with the phrase, "Whoever kills or attempts to kill any officer or employee of the United States Government." The change was a positive addendum to a tragic chapter in American history.

After Timothy McVeigh and Terry Nichols were indicted by a federal grand jury in Oklahoma City on charges of conspiring to blow up the Murrah Building and kill the occupants inside, their very public trials were held in Denver, Colorado, far away from a potentially prejudiced jury pool in Oklahoma.

United States District Judge Richard Matsch presided over the separate trials that dominated news coverage. After months of testimony, a jury of 12 men and women found McVeigh guilty and recommended the death sentence on June 19, 1997. On September 8, 1998, the United States Court of Appeals for the Tenth Circuit upheld the verdict and sentence. McVeigh was put to death by lethal injection on June 11, 2001, at the Federal Penitentiary in Terre Haute, Indiana.

Terry Nichols was later tried in the same Denver court room with a different jury. However, the result was the same—GUILTY. When the jury was unable to agree on the appropriate sentence for Nichols, Judge Matsch pronounced the sentence of life without parole. That verdict and sentence were also upheld by the United States Court of Appeals for the Tenth Circuit.

During the FBI investigation, the State of Oklahoma accepted responsibility for pressing state charges against McVeigh and Nichols for the worst criminal act in state history. The Oklahoma County district attorney's office planned state criminal charges to follow the federal prosecution of the accused men.

In 1999, Terry Nichols was charged under Oklahoma state law with the murder of 160 victims and the unborn child of victim, Robin Huff. The crime against these victims had never been tried because the federal indictments had involved only the murders of federal agents in the Murrah Building.

On March 22, 2004, under the watchful eye of respected Pittsburg County District Judge Steven Taylor, Oklahoma County Prosecutors Sandra Elliott, Lou Keel, and Suzanne Lister, assisted by Detective Mark Easley of the Oklahoma City Police Department, began the presentaion of the state's case to a jury in McAlester, Oklahoma.

On May 26, 2004, the jury found Nichols guily of 161 counts of first-degree murder. He was later sentenced on the state charges to life in prison.

McVeigh and Nichols, through the literature they possessed and conversations between themselves and with Michael Fortier, as well as others, tried to project themselves as patriots and heroes. They were neither.

They attempted to compare themselves with the likes of Thomas Jefferson and Patrick Henry, men of honor. McVeigh and Nichols were neither. To Agents Hersley and Tongate, the comparison was offensive.

Jefferson and Henry were willing to die for the cause of freedom. They were total heroes for both their time and our time. They signed the Declaration of Independence, a very public notice of their intention to pursue freedom for their countrymen.

But what about McVeigh and Nichols? Did they stand up and shout for the world to hear what they had done and why they had done it? Did they take any responsibility for and were they accountable to anyone for their actions?

We know Patrick Henry, by his words, "Give me liberty or give me death!" was sincere about his willingness to die for freedom. He had never killed innocent men, women, and children, and never would. Such an act would have been unthinkable for any of our forefathers, men of strength and honor.

Who could do such a thing? Not even on the eve of his execution did McVeigh stand up and publicly state why he committed this horrific act. Not to this day has Nichols taken responsibility for this senseless act.

It is true that Thomas Jefferson said, "The Tree of Liberty must be refreshed from time to time with the blood of patriots and tyrants." But in no way did Jefferson mean to imply that any citizen of the United States has the right to impose his own selfish will against the rights and liberties of others.

The actions of McVeigh and Nichols speak for themselves. McVeigh planted the Ryder truck bomb in front of the Murrah Building and ran away like a coward. Nichols helped McVeigh plant the getaway car in Oklahoma City on Easter Sunday so he could hide behind his wife in the comfort of their home in Kansas on the morning of the bombing.

Their actions are the actions of cowards. Hopefully, our great country and the world will remember them as such.

When all is considered, the simple truth is that Timothy James McVeigh and Terry Lynn Nichols tried to satisfy their hatred for the United States government by killing innocent men, women, and children in the heartland of America. May their dastardly and cowardly deed never be repeated—nor forgotten.

Terry Nichols being led into the Pittsburg County courthouse in McAlester, Oklahoma, during his state murder trial.

Index